Contents

Mae West is the eldest surviving daughter of Fred and Rose West. This is her story.

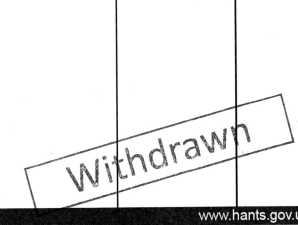

Love as
Always, Mum
xxx

Love as Always, Mum xxx

The true and terrible story of surviving
a childhood with Fred and Rose West

MAE WEST
with NEIL McKAY

SEVEN DIALS

First published in Great Britain in 2018 by Seven Dials
An imprint of Orion Publishing Group Ltd
Carmelite House, 50 Victoria Embankment,
London, EC4Y 0DZ

An Hachette UK Company

1 3 5 7 9 10 8 6 4 2

Text © Mae West with Neil McKay 2018

The right of Mae West and Neil McKay to be identified as
the authors of this work has been asserted in accordance with
the Copyright, Designs and Patents Act 1988.

A CIP catalogue record for this book
is available from the British Library.

Hardback ISBN: 9781409144960
Trade paperback ISBN: 9781409139645
Ebook ISBN: 9781409144977

Typeset by Input Data Services Ltd, Somerset

Printed and bound in Great Britain by Clays Ltd, Elcograf S.p.A.

MIX
Paper from
responsible sources
FSC
www.fsc.org   FSC® C104740

www.orionbooks.co.uk

Prologue

Stigma

I want you to feel that you can talk to me about anything. You must feel awful sometimes and I know you feel very isolated at times. I know I miss you so much sometimes that I feel angry. It must be really rotten for you when you need a family member to talk to or you need mum to sound off to ... I love you and I want to do anything I can do to help you get over things and to be as happy as possible!!!

Love as always,

Mum

It was January 1996. I was nearly nine months' pregnant. All I knew for sure, having been told at my twenty-week scan, was that I was having a girl. Everything else was uncertain. I expect most women get nervous as the birth of their first child approaches. I certainly was. All kinds of worries enter your mind. Will the baby arrive on its due date, or be early or late? How painful will it be? Will there be complications? What will I feel when I see my baby for the first time? Will I feel love straight away or does that take time? And, as the years pass, will I be a good mum? Will my child love me? I imagine it's a

1

time when many women turn to their mothers for advice and support. Perhaps sometimes even asking them to be there at the birth.

But I knew that for me that was not going to be possible, because my mother was Rose West.

Only two months earlier, in November 1995, she'd been convicted of the murder of nine young women and a little girl at one of the most notorious criminal trials in history. One of those young women was my sister, Heather. My mother had been sentenced to life imprisonment and told by the judge that she should never be released.

In the eyes of many, she was the most evil woman that had ever lived.

After my mother's conviction I decided to make a clean break from Gloucester, the city where I had grown up and where, at 25 Cromwell Street, the crimes of both my mother and father, Fred West, had come to light. I needed to start a new life for my baby and myself in a new town, far away from my own terrifying childhood memories and where I hoped the Fred and Rose West legacy would not follow and haunt us. For many reasons, which I'll come to later, there wasn't much time to plan or think through how or where to do this. But I knew I had to try. I ended up renting a three-bedroomed house twenty-five miles away with my half-sister Tara and her toddler son, Nathan. Tara was nineteen and I was twenty-three. We didn't know anyone and couldn't risk anyone finding out who we were, so we kept our heads down. Tara and I could only depend on each other. When she went out I felt very anxious, the unfamiliar creaks from the pipes or sudden sounds from next door would make my heart race, and I'd have one eye trained on our front door the whole time waiting for her to come back through it. On the rare occasions when we went out together, just to a café for a cup of tea, I'd do my best to sit where I couldn't be seen and yet always make sure I knew where the door was so I could get out in a hurry if we were recognised. Tara and I were totally alone in that town but at least it meant we had a chance of escaping the media attention.

As my due date drew near, the baby stopped moving as much as she had been and I became very worried. I had no clue if this was normal or not. It was one of the many things I might have asked Mum's advice about if she had been there; after all, she'd had eight children of her own. But of course I couldn't, and, although Tara had a baby, she was only a young mum with little experience. So I rang the hospital – Cheltenham General – and they told me to come in so they could monitor me.

The hospital was a grim, depressing place with a grey stone façade and huge windows which made it look like an asylum, but at least it was clean and the best thing about it was that it wasn't Gloucester. I didn't want my baby to be born with Gloucester on her birth certificate.

After a day or so of being monitored, the doctors said everything was fine and before long I went into labour naturally. Tara came in to be with me; growing up, us kids had to stick together as best we could to survive Dad's advances and Mum's rage, so having her there was a familiar comfort. I had also been with her when she gave birth to Nathan, so it was nice to have her support in return. But I was still frightened. Mum had always made childbirth sound so easy. She used to speak about it in such a matter-of-fact way, as if it was like shelling peas. She never mentioned pain or complications.

I remember the midwife who gave me my initial examination did nothing to make me feel better. 'We'll not be taking you to the labour ward yet,' she said dismissively, as if I had been wasting her time.

'Why not?' I asked.

'You're only two centimetres dilated. You need to be at least five before we take you down.'

Her manner was cold and unsympathetic, or perhaps because I was so on edge – and for so many reasons – it came across that way to me. Thank goodness I at least had Tara for support. We waited together as my labour continued and eventually I got to five centimetres and the midwife agreed we could go down to the labour ward. The pain was unbearable, but then they gave me an epidural and after that I just lay there, in the tiny room, talking to Tara. Waiting. But after thirty hours of labour there was still no sign of the baby being born. I was so tired. I wondered how Mum could have done this eight times over. I worried I was doing something wrong. And when there were pauses in mine and Tara's conversation, I found myself wishing Heather had been with me too.

Eventually the doctor and midwife said I was fully dilated and needed to start pushing. I did as I was told. I tried and tried until I thought I must be blue in the face and the blood vessels in my eyes were going to burst. Still there was no sign of my baby. Eventually they said I was going to have to have a Caesarean. I began to get really upset. I was fighting back tears. I told them I didn't want that, I wanted to have a normal birth. I couldn't tell them the reason – that so much in my life had been abnormal, that I lacked confidence about becoming a mum and it felt so important that I could bring my baby into this world as most other babies arrive.

They didn't seem to be paying attention in any case. A mid-wife gave me some tablets which she said I needed to take before having the Caesarean. But then a young doctor, seeing how

4

upset I was, said they'd give it one more go using the ventouse
– a kind of vacuum device that they put onto the head to help
draw the baby out. I was given another top-up of the epidural
and then they took part of the bed away. I could hear a machine
start up and the doctor got to work, and then – after all that pain
and panic – within seconds she was born. Ruddy-faced, chubby-
armed, beautiful and mine. They laid her on my stomach; she
felt so small and yet so heavy at the same time.

I looked at her and thought, *At last she's here. My baby, to care
for and love.* Tara was crying. 'She's the most beautiful baby I've
ever seen,' she said. I was utterly exhausted and there were so
many monitors beeping and tubes coming out of my arm, but it
was worth it. She was here. My daughter, Amy.

One of the midwives weighed her. She was 7lb 6oz, ten fin-
gers, ten toes, completely healthy and normal except for her
cone-shaped head caused by the ventouse, which they said
would go down in a few days. I was cleaned up and we were
both moved to a ward with other mums and newborns. It was
mid-afternoon and Tara seemed almost as exhausted as I was.
She'd been a tower of strength for me throughout. I told her to
go home and get some rest.

My legs were still numb from the epidural and at some point
in the night I tried to get out of bed but fell on the floor and
hurt my back. It was just like me – thinking I could carry on as
normal with things instead of resting. I sat on the cold lino floor
and looked around me at the unfamiliar surroundings: at the
bright strip lighting out in the corridor and at the other beds
with the sleeping mums in; girls like me with newborn babies –
but who weren't like me at all. I sat back on the bed and, with
Tara gone, emotions which I'd managed to hold back suddenly
began to well up inside me; my throat and chest felt tight and
for a second I thought I was going to cry.

Then I looked into the clear plastic cot next to me – Amy was asleep. She looked so tiny and vulnerable. I lay back down and just stared at her, watching her tiny chest rise and fall, and, gradually, because she seemed so content and settled, became calmer myself. I kept thinking, *She's mine – someone in my life to give love to and get love back from.* It was something magical to hold onto. But, despite everything, I couldn't stop myself from thinking, *I wish Mum was here to see her.* Eventually I fell asleep.

The following day was hard. All the other mums seemed to have lots of visitors with balloons, flowers and cards. I was so relieved when Tara came back to visit me. I felt really ill, sore and tired. I'd started to get fluid retention from the epidural, my legs had swollen and I couldn't move very well, but I wanted to show the midwives that I could do whatever was necessary to look after Amy. Unlike now, when maternity wards discharge you as soon as they can, you weren't allowed to leave before then. One of the things you had to be able to do was make up a bottle correctly.

'Have you ever done this before?' the midwife asked me.

'Plenty of times,' I told her.

'But this is your first baby, isn't it?'

'I come from a big family. I had to do it for my younger brothers and sisters.' I felt myself go red – suddenly wondering if I'd given something away, if she'd start asking me questions about them.

But she didn't notice. 'Show me,' she said.

She stood and watched as I made up a bottle of formula milk, before saying she was satisfied that I knew how to do it.

But because of the fluid retention they weren't ready to discharge me, so I went back to the ward. Another midwife came to ask if I wanted a magazine to read while Amy was asleep. I was grateful and a few minutes later she returned with a copy of *Cosmopolitan* magazine. I began to browse through it: post-Christmas diets, hair tips and then – to my horror – I turned the page to see an article about women who kill. One of the women featured was my mum. I tried to tear my eyes away but I couldn't: as I scanned the article I found myself reading about all the crimes my mum had been convicted of, her life with my dad, the discovery of the bodies of nine young women who had been sexually assaulted, dismembered and buried at the so-called 'House of Horrors' – 25 Cromwell Street where I'd grown up – and my dad's suicide a year before.

I felt sick. The realisation that I would never be able to truly escape what had happened began to close in on me, making me feel crushed and helpless. Then I started to wonder if the midwife had deliberately given me the magazine. Perhaps she'd realised who I was? It seemed perfectly plausible to me because although my maternity notes were in my new name, the staff might have access to my old GP's records and have worked out that I was the daughter of Fred and Rosemary West. Had they given me the magazine as some kind of cruel joke?

I knew deep down that that was so unlikely, but I couldn't completely shake off the suspicion. I kept trying to tell myself it was sheer coincidence, but I felt as if the staff were watching me. One of the midwives had told me to keep Amy lying flat because there was mucus on her chest. But when Tara came to visit that evening she wanted to have a quick cuddle with Amy. She picked Amy up out of the cot, but the midwife saw her and came over.

'I told you to keep her lying down,' she snapped, and snatched Amy from Tara.

'I only wanted to hold her for a minute!' said Tara, upset.

'She's my sister, please let her,' I said.

The midwife was having none of it. 'I don't care who she

is. You're the mother, you should be doing what's best for the baby!'

That midwife couldn't have known how much saying a thing like that would affect me, but it was horrible and humiliating and threatened to destroy what little confidence I had in myself to be a good mum to Amy. The hospital had felt cold to me from the start but now it seemed as if everyone was against me. All I wanted to do was pick Amy up and run away out of there.

Eventually, on the Sunday, I was discharged. I wasn't in a relationship with Amy's dad by that point, but he drove all the way down from Essex to see her and brought a new baby seat for her so we could take her home.

So there I was, finally, in my new home with my new baby, hoping against hope I could make a new life for us, but afraid too that my old life would always keep following me, that I would never escape the stigma of being the daughter of Fred and Rose West. Even if I could escape it, even if I could succeed in blocking out the memory of Dad and keeping Mum out of sight, I knew there would always be something missing; a feeling that something was gone, an absence where Heather should have been. And deep inside me was the echo of a question I will never be able to answer: why had I survived – why had I been the one lucky enough to have a beautiful child of my own – when she hadn't?

Chapter One

Into the Nightmare

It's Wednesday and another letter from Mum has arrived. She wants to make things easier for us both, and has asked me to write to her with the things I need answers to most. I don't know where to start. How much did you know? How much did you do? I want the truth but I don't know where to begin, or even if I can trust that's what she'll give me. I feel completely alone, and she knows that . . .

<u>HM PRISON DURHAM</u>

There must be a thousand things all rattling around inside your head so please remember my beautiful daughter. I'm HERE FOR YOU!!!
    Love, as always,
    Mum xxx

From the moment police officers arrived, on 24 February 1994, with a warrant to search our home for the body of my sister Heather, it was as if I'd walked into a nightmare. As my father Fred West was arrested, our house dismantled, our garden excavated and the remains of the victims began to be unearthed, my mum and I (and, to begin with, my brother Steve too) were placed in a series of 'safe houses' by the police. To say that I was in shock doesn't even begin to describe my state of mind. Despite a strange and deeply abusive upbringing, I'd known nothing of my dad's – and later, as I have come to accept, my mum's – murderous crimes. Nothing can possibly prepare you for such an experience. I felt numb, as though it was all happening to someone else, and yet I knew it wasn't. I knew this was my life and nothing would ever be the same again.

We'd always been a very private family. 'What happens in this house is our business and nobody else's!' Mum would say. We'd hardly ever have anyone but family round and it was up to Mum and Dad who came over the threshold. And yet suddenly our home was at the centre of the entire country's attention. It was literally being taken apart, every shelf, cupboard and wardrobe searched and dismantled, every floorboard lifted, all our memories now evidence. And all the while I was trying desperately to cling onto some sense of reality, to get my head round at least some of what was happening.

In the following days, as the body of my sister Heather and those of the other young women were discovered, I had little trouble accepting that Dad was responsible for what had happened to them. It's hard to get across the two sides of Dad's character; he wasn't violent like Mum was – he'd even defend us sometimes when she was going at us hell for leather. But he was a strange man, who we knew had dark and horrible interests, and all of us kids eventually became suspicious about what he might be capable of. Not that it wasn't still the most terrible shock – serial murder, on that scale, carried out in that way, was beyond anything we could have imagined. Yet, as the details of the murders began to emerge – the sexual abuse of those young women before they'd died, the dismembering of their bodies, their burial inside and behind the house we'd played and grown up in – there was never a moment when I believed Dad to be innocent of them. Looking back, that was one thing at least which helped me to keep some sort of grip on my sanity.

With Mum it was different. Though the police treated her as a suspect from the beginning, it was some time before she was formally arrested and questioned. When that did eventually happen – and even when she later stood trial – there was no direct forensic or witness evidence against her. Mum's guilt or innocence has always been more a matter of opinion and judgement of her character – of what she was considered capable of doing – rather than about concrete proof. From the very beginning she denied all knowledge of the murders and blamed everything on Dad, something she still does to this day.

'That fucking man, Mae, the trouble he's caused me over the years! And now this! Can you believe it?'

She'd always had a sharp tongue and she was relentless in her anger towards him. She never for a moment seemed to doubt that I believed her. She had this powerful emotional grip on me and she knew it. When I was young she often flew off the handle and would hit me and my brothers and sisters or take out her anger on whatever was around her. Yet as I grew older, reaching my later teens and twenties, she used to confide in me more and more: about her troubled childhood, her difficult family and her turbulent relationship with Dad. She seemed glad of my support and, looking back now, all these years later, I can see that she used that sense of obligation I felt towards her. She knew exactly how to make me feel sorry for her, and because of that she could always rely on me to take her side. So, when the murders came to light and she denied all knowledge of them, I believed her. Despite the turmoil I was in, it was something positive I could hold onto: that I was supporting my mother.

'Thank God I've got you, Mae,' she kept telling me in the

safe house. 'I don't know how I'd be getting through any of this without you!'

I truly couldn't imagine she was capable of such crimes. Especially the murder of Heather – her first baby, who I knew that, more than twenty years earlier, Mum's parents had tried to force her to abort. She'd refused, absolutely determined to bring that baby into the world. Heather's birth, she'd often told me, had given her such joy and fulfilment. So my loyalty to her never wavered, not even when the police finally came to arrest her on suspicion of murder. It didn't occur to me to doubt her. I never questioned that standing by her was the right thing to do. Steve had moved out of the safe house to live with his girlfriend by then so it was just Mum and me when they arrived to take her away. She was absolutely livid as they led her to the car, pushing, shoving and yelling at them: 'You've no fucking right whatsoever to treat me like this! Fuck you, fuck the lot of you!'

I wished she hadn't been so abusive towards them. I knew it wouldn't help matters. But I also knew that it was her nature: she hated the police, hated everyone in authority in fact, and had done so since her childhood. Things had happened to her in her early life that gave her very good reason not to trust anyone in a position of power.

As the police bundled Mum into a car an officer told me I'd have to leave the safe house. My heart thumped in my chest. 'Leave? When?'

The officer looked around the only four walls I was safe within, 'We can give you till the end of the day but that's all.'

For a second I had no words. Then I managed to stutter, 'Where am I supposed to go?'

'Not back to Cromwell Street, that's for sure. We've pretty well taken it to pieces. Besides it's a crime scene.'

'So what am I supposed to do?'

'Sorry, love, can't help you with that. I'm afraid you're no longer our responsibility.'

I was stunned. I didn't understand what they thought had changed that day for me to no longer need protection from the press. Afterwards, when they admitted to us that the house had been bugged, I realised it was because they had what they needed: I'd been interviewing Mum for them and now my job was over, I wasn't needed any longer.

The police officer I spoke to walked out to the police car and I watched them drive Mum away. It's strange now to think that was the last time I ever saw her in the 'real' world and not within a jail or a prison. But at that point in time, all I could focus on was that I had nowhere to go. The panic began to rise through me until I felt sick with it. I technically had a house in Gloucester, but I had rented it out a couple of years earlier when I moved back home after my younger siblings had been taken into care – again to support Mum. Besides, I'd been told the press were now camped outside there, trying to find me.

Where else was there? I didn't have friends or relatives that I thought would stand by me through something like this; it already felt as if I'd been tainted by what my parents had done. So I asked the police to make contact with Steve for me. He was staying with his girlfriend at her mother's house and asked if she would put me up too. She agreed that I could stay that night, sleeping on the sofa, but it was made clear she didn't want me there longer than that.

The following day, I sat on a patch of grass outside the house with Steve, trying to work out what to do. I'd had to quit my job immediately after Dad's arrest earlier that month because of moving into the safe house away from the world's press, so I also had no income or money saved. I couldn't think of a place that would let me hide from them and live my life at the same time.

Then Steve told me that the people at the *News of the World* – who, much to Mum's anger, he'd signed a contract with to tell our story – wanted the two of us to do a book. I was adamantly against it, but he said they couldn't do it without me, that it was a chance for us to put our side of the story across and would protect us from other press attention; that I'd never be able to get a job now and this was the only way I was going to get any money to live. I was twenty-one and naive, so I said yes.

It was all beyond surreal. I moved into a place on my own, I was visiting Mum, giving her moral support, even doing her laundry, and still having regular visits from the police who must have believed I might give them – accidentally or otherwise – evidence which would help to convict her. For months on end I just lived from day to day. Then, out of the blue, as the long wait for my parents' trial continued, came the news that my dad had committed suicide while on remand. I can't say I felt sorrow, but he was still my dad – he'd been such a huge part of my life. I was in total shock. Things seemed to be spinning more and more out of control and it seemed that life could not get any worse. I found myself literally praying that I would wake up and find it really all had been a dream. I felt totally paralysed.

For a time I felt that I would be stuck in that state of mind, unable to make sense of any of it, forever. The idea of ever having any kind of future, let alone one worth living, was un-imaginable. But time passed and events moved on and I had to get through them as best I could, and hope eventually to make some kind of life for myself.

Over twenty years have now passed, and this book is an at-tempt to tell the story I couldn't have told then, because of the emotional turmoil I was in and because there was so much I could not possibly understand, not least how what had hap-pened would affect my entire future life.

At the heart of it all is my changing relationship with my mother. The hardest part for me – and something that has taken me years to be able to admit to myself, let alone to anyone else – has not been coming to terms with the reality that she didn't love and protect any of us as children, especially when we were young and at our most vulnerable. I think I always knew that part deep down, even though I find myself clinging to the hope that I'm wrong even now. No. The hardest part of all has been accepting that, despite her countless denials, she did play a part in the crimes she was accused of.

People may wonder how it's possible to understand any of what happened. The crimes my parents committed are almost beyond comprehension, and among the most terrible and infamous in history. Only the crimes of Ian Brady and Myra Hindley, and separately Peter Sutcliffe, the 'Yorkshire Ripper' and Harold Shipman, have been comparable. Journalists have filled countless column inches about them, writers have written books, criminologists and psychologists have studied them. The wider public – understandably – has remained both repelled and fascinated by them, struggling to make sense of them even with the advantage of looking at the story from the perspective of outsiders. Both myself and my brothers and sisters have had to wait a long time for a sense of perspective to arrive. From the day we were born, we were unknowingly caught up inside the story.

But my feeling is that only by looking at the story from the inside can any of it properly be understood. For us, Fred and Rose West were real people; 25 Cromwell Street, Gloucester, was our home – a *real* home – not, as it has since become in the minds of many, a 'House of Horrors' as it was dubbed by the press. Although we all directly experienced terrible things at my parents' hands – from physical to emotional and sexual abuse

– none of us knew the worst they were capable of until the rest of the world found out.

What may be very hard for people to get their heads round is that, although nothing in our household was ever what other people might regard as 'normal', in many ways throughout my childhood we got on with our lives in the same way that other families do. We did ordinary things. We ate meals and watched TV together, celebrated birthdays and Christmas, and went on family holidays. Yes, there was abuse, misery, violence and distress, but it wasn't constant – and it certainly wasn't the whole picture.

There was also laughter, tenderness and affection in the house. People may find that extraordinary, but it's true. I don't mean between my parents, although they did sometimes laugh and joke with one another and there were occasional flashes of what seemed like real affection towards us, their children. But the bonds between myself and my brothers and sisters were strong. We played and laughed, fell out and made up as siblings do in any normal family. Astonishing as it may seem, our family mattered deeply to us – as much as it does to any child – and the focal point of our lives was our home.

Later on, after the remains of the victims were found and our house became the 'House of Horrors', it was obviously impossible for us to see the place in the same way. Yet even now for me, though 25 Cromwell Street was long ago demolished and I can't detach it from the dreadful things that happened there, it remains, in my mind, a home. One with terrible memories and associations, but a home nonetheless. Being able to think and accept both those things at the same time is something that doesn't seem logical, but that's the honest truth.

When the police finally came to the safe house to arrest Mum, the two of us were given a few moments alone together to gather up some of her things before they took her away.

'My wedding ring, Mae,' she whispered. 'It's in the pocket of my big coat in the wardrobe. Look after it, will you? I'm not taking it to the police station, those bloody idiots'll only lose it.'

I frowned at her, confused. 'But when he was arrested you said you were never going to wear it again?'

Her eyes flashed. 'Just do as I bloody say, Mae! Look after it!'

I didn't dare challenge her again. Didn't dare ask why the ring mattered to her when she'd already sworn she'd never put it on again. But it was clear that in spite of the situation she was in, and the fury she felt towards Dad, it still meant something. And if the ring was still important to her then I could only think that meant the marriage was too.

After she'd gone, when I was packing up my few things, I looked in the coat and found the ring in a zipped inner pocket. I still have it. It's a constant reminder to me that, however badly they fell out, Mum and Dad's marriage never stopped mattering to them even to the end, that their relationship was a reality not a dream, and that like it or not I am a child of that union.

It's a reality I know I can never escape and so, even though that knowledge has caused me so much pain and confusion, I've wanted, as time has passed, to try to understand my parents and what has happened in my life. The alternative – trying to live as if none of it had really happened – would have been impossible and probably have driven me mad.

But trying to understand leads to questions. Countless questions.

Why did my dad commit the murders? How could he have carried some of them out in the same house where his infant children were being raised? How could he possibly, evil man though he was, have brought himself to murder his own children? How much did my mum know about his crimes? How closely involved was she in carrying them out? How could she have committed such cruelties while continuing – in some ways at least – to display such a strong maternal instinct towards us, her children?

The only two people capable of fully answering these questions were my mum and dad. But Dad committed suicide. He never stood trial, never went before an open court to answer for his actions and perhaps help give me, and the families and loved ones of those poor young women, some kind of understanding at least. Most of his crimes may have come to light, but the police suspected there may have been other murders which he had not confessed to – whether that was true or not there was no doubt he took secrets to the grave.

My mum, though, is alive to this day. She did stand trial. But her trial was more about establishing her guilt, of finding out what happened, rather than why it happened. Her main intention, when she stood in the dock, was not to tell the truth but to be acquitted of the murder charges – which meant making excuses, denying everything, and trying to ensure that all the blame was put onto Dad.

And over the many years which followed my mum's conviction, years during which – for reasons I'll come to later – I stayed in close touch with her, exchanging letters, speaking to her on the telephone, visiting her regularly in prison, providing her with emotional support, she continued to avoid telling me the truth.

Her letters from prison became a big part of my life. Some contained advice, others described her life inside, many contained lists of clothing or other items she wanted me to buy and send to her. Often it was a combination of all these. Her letters were sometimes full of self-justification and self-pity, at others they were chatty, full of jokes and prison gossip. When I picked each one up from the doormat, heart thumping in my throat, I never knew what to expect. All I knew was that they would reconnect me with her and that I wouldn't be able to read them and throw them away because that would have felt like a betrayal. So, over the years, they accumulated – a record of our relationship while she was in prison, and a growing burden too.

Despite the fact she has given me no real help, no honest answers, I have kept on searching for the truth about my mother. She's my mum, it's ingrained in me to trust her; coming to terms with the fact that I can't has been more painful than I can put into words. This book is in part my account of that search and the painful journey towards accepting that she has lied to me over and over, time and again.

Beyond that, I have another reason for writing it. I want to describe my experience – shared by my siblings – of being connected biologically and emotionally to two people who are regarded by people as evil, and of living in the shadow of their terrible actions. None of us chooses our parents. I can't wish away the connection I have to mine. I can't undo what they did. I can't escape the past and never will. These are all facts which myself, my brothers and sisters have had to learn to live with and still do so on a daily basis.

I would never want to regard myself as a victim in the way that those who were murdered (including my sister, Heather) were victims. Nothing can compare with their suffering and the way their lives were brutally ended, and the devastating effect on their families and loved ones. Yet, for me and my siblings, the consequences of what happened have been enormous. Our family was shattered, our trust in almost everything and everyone destroyed. Although we had no knowledge of, or responsibility for, the crimes, we have still felt guilt and shame through our association to them – and we have all acquired a stigma that has threatened to follow us for the rest of our lives.

Yet we have all had to soldier on with those lives as best we could. So much of what has happened to me since my parents' crimes were revealed has been immensely difficult. But slowly, and with many mistakes and setbacks along the way, I have tried to build a new life for both myself and for those I love. I want to describe something of that journey, to show that however terrible the past may be, it doesn't necessarily have to claim you forever and there can be a future worth living for. I want people to know that, however dark parts of my story have been, there has been light too, and if there has been evil there has also been love. I make no special claims at all for myself, in terms of possessing strength, courage, insight, or self-belief, but somehow I have pulled through, have a life worth living and a future I look forward to – and for that I am hugely grateful.

In telling my story I have needed to tell the story of my parents too. To understand my own past I have needed to understand theirs. To some people they were simply monsters. Even my mum, later in her life, encouraged by psychologists and others who had befriended her, expressed just such an opinion of my dad.

But, whatever his crimes and hers, to me this can never be true. I – like my brothers and sisters – experienced them as human beings. To put them in a separate compartment, outside the rest of humanity, seems dishonest and wrong. Whatever was abnormal about them can only be understood by recognising what was normal (or at least human) about them too – or there is nothing at all to be learned. I have never really been a practising Christian as such, but I know that the Bible teaches that all of us – even the worst examples of humanity – were made in God's image. If people go on to commit evil acts it doesn't help to regard them as creatures from another planet. Apart from anything else it excuses them of responsibility for their actions.

Like most people, I found out about my parents' past gradually as I grew up and then through my adult life. Their life stories came to me in fragments, which I pieced together slowly over the years into something like a complete picture. Some of the detail they told to me themselves, or came from other relatives. In the case of my dad, I discovered some of what I know from family visits to Much Marcle, the Herefordshire village twenty miles or so from Gloucester where he grew up. Other parts of the story came from comparing notes with my brothers and sisters, or later on from what I learned from the police, social workers, journalists and other sources.

In some ways it took longer to build up a picture of Mum's past. While Dad had his secrets, he would sometimes speak quite freely about his early life, including cheery, sometimes strange and gruesome anecdotes about growing up at the farm cottage. Mum came from further afield – Devon – and I never saw the places where she grew up or had much contact with her relatives. When I reached my teens I sensed that, while her past also contained secrets, they were of a different kind to my dad's. There were shadows there – pain and damage. Things she wanted to conceal because they made her feel vulnerable. Which is not to make excuses for her – although some people, including criminologists and psychologists, have done just that – but understanding her has involved trying to understand what those shadows were.

And trying to understand my mum and dad can never be done entirely by looking at their lives separately. As individuals they were unusual, and, in their different ways, frightening, but as a couple, locked in a strange intense relationship, they seemed to turn into something else. It was as if the marriage unlocked something in both of them and they became another entity. Fred and Rose. And – despite the bitterness and recriminations – they remained, in Dad's view if not hers, lovers until the end. As he wrote in his suicide note:

'We will always be in love. The most wonderful thing in my life is when I met you . . . our love is special to us. So, love, keep your promises to me. You know what they are . . . When you are ready come to me. I will be waiting for you.'[1]

Chapter Two

Early Days

Another letter from Durham. Mum's thinking about Dad again and I think she likes slagging him off to me. When I read her handwritten words, it's hard for me to believe she wasn't Dad's victim too. But was she? She says she lived in fear of him and he took over her totally and utterly. She asked for help, she writes she cried out for it but that he got stronger every day. He crushed her hope and dished out punishments . . . is it true?

HM PRISON DURHAM

I was barely surviving – I was systematically being mentally, sexually and physically tortured and abused. I existed from one moment to the next not daring to contemplate just 'what' might happen in the next half hour!! . . .

My dad, though there was often some truth in what he said, was a liar. And although at times Mum could be more honest and open than him, she too mostly only gave you the version of events she wanted you to hear. So finding out about their relationship before I was born and during the early years of my life has been a long process. In some ways it's one that's never really ended. It's been like peeling the layers of an onion and has involved separating fact from a lot of fiction. But by the time I reached my early teens I'd built up some sort of picture, even if there was a lot – including the most shocking and terrible stuff – still to discover.

I was due to be born at the end of May 1972, but was several weeks late, eventually arriving on 1 June at Gloucester Royal Hospital. It had been Mum's plan to call me May after the month, but when I was born in June she gave me that as a middle name. So I became May June West.

I think she found it funny, but I could never see the joke and I was teased about it when I got to school. So much so that eventually, when I was fifteen, I made a decision to change the spelling of my name. I'd read up about the actress Mae West and I thought that a more interesting spelling, so I became Mae West and dropped the June altogether.

I was Mum's second child and the biggest of her babies, but she had no problems giving birth to me – she told us she found having all her children very easy. She used to say she could have them standing up. Emotionally, she said, it was a different matter; she told me she suffered from depression in the final months of her pregnancy with me and that Dad had no sympathy.

Her time in hospital was miserable. She was kept in for several days and her family, who disapproved of her relationship with Dad, didn't visit her once. Dad, who showed little interest in my arrival, wasn't even at the hospital, let alone present at the birth. When Mum was eventually allowed to go home he didn't even bother to come to collect her in his van. She had no choice but to gather me up in her arms along with all the baby things, carry me out of the hospital and catch a bus home.

Later, when my younger brothers and sisters were born, Dad

24

took more interest, going to see them in hospital and fetching them and my mum back when they were ready to come home. Why he was so uninterested in my birth it's hard to be sure, but it was probably because he already had two daughters and was hoping to have a son. My arrival was a disappointment to him whereas their next child was a boy – my brother Stephen – who he had a much closer relationship with, even though it was very complicated.

Mum, on the other hand, was happy, despite her depression. She always said she didn't mind what sex her children were. She just loved babies. When they got beyond the toddler stage – independent and their personalities starting to show – it was a very different matter; she lost patience with them easily. But while they were tiny and compliant and vulnerable she was absolutely in her element.

How she was with me as a mother in the first weeks and months of my life I can only guess at, but I think she would have looked after me much as I saw her look after my younger siblings when they were babies. She'd have put me in the crude wooden rocking crib with a canopy that Dad had knocked together for Heather. I reckon she'd have been a pretty attentive mother in those first few months and would have picked me up and cuddled me when I cried. I was bottle- rather than breast-fed because she needed to get back to work as soon as possible. The nature of that 'work' I didn't get to understand for many years.

Home then wasn't Cromwell Street but a rented ground-floor flat at 25 Midland Road. Midland Road was another scruffy residential street of run-down houses in Gloucester, mostly split into flats and bedsits, where my parents were already bringing up two children, Anne Marie, Dad's daughter by his first marriage to Rena Costello, and Heather, Mum and Dad's first child who had been born the year before me. The flat was no palace;

it was cold, damp and badly in need of renovation, but it was an improvement on the cramped bedsit in Cheltenham and the dilapidated caravan out in the Gloucestershire countryside that they'd shared before that.

From time to time as I grew up both Mum and Dad would talk about how they first got together and their life before I was born. Their two versions merged together in my mind to form one story – although it turned out to be far from the full picture.

Mum had been working as a waitress in a tea room in Cheltenham when Dad first saw her. It was 1969 and she was fifteen. He was twenty-eight and working as a driver for a bakery which made deliveries there. She'd hardly even registered him but something about her looks and manner had taken his fancy.

One night soon afterwards, as she waited for the bus home, he came up to her and started to chat her up. She wasn't sure what to make of this curly-haired, scruffy man at first, but he had a sense of humour and a kind of fairground charm and made it obvious he fancied her. She was flattered – she liked the attention of older men. He asked her where she was going. 'Bishop's Cleeve.'

'That's where I live!' he said. 'We can get the same bus then.'

In the beginning, their relationship was in some ways very run of the mill. Dad doing the chasing; Mum being interested in him but wary and playing hard to get. Dad persisting, determined to win her over.

Though people might be surprised to hear it, he could be a proper charmer. It was a charm he used on many people – including the girls he'd successfully chatted up and seduced as a youth in Ledbury, the little Herefordshire town near the village of Much Marcle where he'd grown up. He even used it on the police after they arrested him and began digging up the garden at 25 Cromwell Street. The transcripts of all those hours

26

of interviews, with all their descriptions of horror, are peppered with banter shared with the officers who were questioning him. He could make almost anyone laugh. There's a photograph taken as he was led away from Gloucester magistrates' court, having just been charged with eleven murders, where he's smiling broadly, as if he's sharing a joke with his escorting officers.

Mum said he used plenty of that charm on her on that first bus journey. He told her all manner of stories – some true, some which turned out to be sheer fantasy, but she found them all entertaining. They laughed together, especially when they discovered they both had mothers called Daisy. But she was no pushover. She thought he was an oddball and didn't like his unkempt appearance. 'Like a bloody tramp, he was,' she used to say.

Soon afterwards he asked her out. The invitation came in a typically eccentric way. One day a woman came into the tea room. She was a total stranger but she had a present for Mum – a plastic necklace or some other worthless trinket of the kind Dad often gave to her over the years – and said that a man had asked her to give it to her. Mum accepted the gift, intrigued. Shortly afterwards, Dad came into the shop and called out to her: 'The Swallow – eight o'clock!' He grinned and left before she could answer.

Despite her reservations, Mum decided to go along to The Swallow – a pub in Bishop's Cleeve – and meet him, even if it was only to return the present. They sat talking and drinking, though Dad hardly touched alcohol in general, and he told her more about his own personal situation.

He said that he was a single parent whose wife, Rena, had abandoned him, leaving him with two young girls to bring up. It would have been difficult for him to avoid mentioning Rena since he had her name tattooed on his arm, but he never tried to make a secret of his relationship with her, either when he first met Mum or to us children later on when he spoke about his life before then.

He explained that Rena had gone back to Glasgow where she was originally from and they weren't in contact. Mum felt sorry for him. Though she was only in her mid-teens herself, hearing Dad talk about the girls – six-year-old Charmaine and five-year-old Anne Marie – stirred a maternal instinct in her, she said. She had younger brothers who, for reasons I only came to understand much later, she'd come to feel the same instinct towards.

Dad used her sympathy for his situation as a single parent and her interest in the girls as a kind of bait. And once he'd got her hooked, his charm became all the more effective. He could make her laugh at will – and he'd already realised there hadn't been much laughter in her life. For her part, she sensed he was something of a rebel and a bad boy, just as, in her family's eyes, she had a wild side and was out of control – it seemed to her like they were two of a kind. She started visiting him at his scruffy caravan on the nearby Lakeside site. She always told me she was very taken with Charmaine and Anne Marie from the moment she met them, and that she was drawn to Dad's lifestyle – living on the fringes of respectable society. He played her his records – such as his favourite Charley Pride, the black American country music star. And while neither Mum nor Dad ever said so explicitly, I've never doubted that their relationship became an adult one almost immediately, even though she was only fifteen and he was more than ten years her senior.

Early on in their relationship, Mum discovered Dad had had other girls in the caravan. When I asked her how she knew this she told me it was because she'd found some of their underwear

28

under the bed, something she was furious about. She challenged Dad about it and he claimed the girls had only been there to look after the children, but she didn't believe him – why would they leave their pants? Now the two of them were together, she made it clear she wasn't going to share him with any other woman. She knew about Rena, of course, but as far as she was aware she was hundreds of miles away in Scotland and they were no longer in contact.

The caravan became a second home to her. Mum was always a bit of a homemaker; she soon had it clean and shipshape and began to skip work at the tea rooms to act as a part-time nanny to the girls. Dad was thrilled. For Mum it was a welcome escape from the miserable atmosphere at home. Her father, Bill Letts, was an electrician from Devon who'd been in the navy, was made to leave and, after a long period of unemployment, was forced to move the family to the Midlands. There he took on various kinds of menial work that he thought was beneath him, before he found a job with Smiths Aerospace in Bishop's Cleeve. Mum described him as a short, bitter, angry man – I later heard he'd been diagnosed as a schizophrenic – who was often violent to his wife Daisy, and to Mum and her six brothers and sisters.

Daisy, Mum's mum, was apparently a neurotic woman who – not surprisingly considering the man she was married to – was worn out from the demands of raising so many children and coping with Bill's violent temper, and she often suffered with depression. She'd left him more than once during the course of their marriage, though always ended up going back to him.

Dad was keen to meet Bill and Daisy, so Mum agreed to take him home one day. It was a disaster. He lied to them, boasting about various properties he owned and claiming he ran a fleet of ice-cream vans but, according to Mum, they saw through him immediately. They thought he was a horrible man and hated the idea of their fifteen-year-old daughter being involved with him. They sent him packing.

They ordered her to write a letter to him breaking off the relationship. Reluctantly she did so. 'Go back to your wife and make a go of it,' she wrote. Dad ignored the letter. He was no stranger to criticism from respectable people, and he knew that Mum's feelings for him wouldn't have really changed just because her parents disapproved. And he was proved right. She carried on seeing him in secret. Bill reported Mum to social services for her wild and promiscuous behaviour which, in those days, was enough for her to be taken into care and placed in a home for troubled teenagers. But as soon as she turned sixteen she escaped to be with Dad again, and soon afterwards she became pregnant. Her parents found out and gave her an ultimatum – she either had to give Dad up and abort the baby or they'd disown her for ever. She refused and went to live with him in the rented flat at Midland Road which belonged to a man Dad had done some odd jobs for.

Mum had burnt her bridges with her parents and had no choice then but to make a go of her life with Dad. But it wasn't easy. They didn't have much money. Dad was scraping a living as a tyre-fitter and odd-job man, supplementing his income with bits of petty thieving. They had two children – Charmaine and Anne Marie – to look after, not to mention a baby of their own on the way. It was a lot of responsibility for Mum, who wasn't much more than a child herself. When she spoke about it she didn't make any secret of how hard she found that period of her life.

'I hadn't the faintest idea what I was letting myself in for,' she would say.

'What do you mean?' I'd ask.

'It was worse than you can possibly imagine, Mae. Much worse.'

'Worse in what way?'

She'd become angry with me then and refuse to say any more.

Both Mum and Dad tended to be evasive about this period in their lives if you asked too much about it. They'd mention it occasionally but I always felt the picture they gave us was the tip of the iceberg, and that something much bigger and darker existed below.

Then Heather was born. Though Mum never said so, it must have been a momentous experience for her. Not least because she was a child Mum's parents had put huge pressure on her to abort. But she was also only sixteen herself, learning to be a mother for the first time with no one to ask for support and advice. I know a little of what that was like and it's really tough. She had Dad, but he was useless with babies and out and about earning whatever he could – doing odd jobs and getting up to who knows what – so he was hardly at home. Once they'd brought Heather back to the flat, she had to cope alone not just with her own baby but the other two little girls as well.

And things rapidly got much worse. Dad was caught stealing tyres from work. He not only lost his job but, as it was far from a first offence, he was sent to prison. Now it was Mum who was the single parent.

Mum and Dad never really spoke at all about the time Dad was in prison, except for one thing. They said that one day Rena turned up out of the blue at the flat and took Charmaine away with her.

'Best thing, really,' Dad told us. 'Your mum had enough on her plate with Anne Marie and Heather.'

It was the last they ever saw of Charmaine, they said.

'Didn't you miss her?' I asked Mum.

'Couldn't be helped,' she said. 'Your dad was away. And when all's said and done she was Rena's child and not mine. What else could I do but let her go?'

From time to time Dad would claim he'd tried to keep in contact with Rena by writing to her but received no reply.

'They must have moved,' he'd say. 'They could be anywhere. They could be in Australia for all I know. I'm not sure we'll ever see Charmaine again. Pity, she's a lovely little girl, but there you go. I'm sure she's happy wherever she is.'

Looking back now, I can't believe they said all that; I can't believe how easily it spilled out of their mouths. They said it with such conviction, as if they really believed every word. It was a long time before I discovered what a monstrous lie it all was. It wasn't until Dad was arrested that I finally heard Charmaine had been murdered and buried at 25 Midland Road when she was just a child, while Rena had met a horrific death at Dad's hands – I read that he dismembered her body before burying the pieces in separate plastic bags at a place near Much Marcle.

They were much more forthcoming about the period of time after that. Mum rarely said anything nice about her relationship with Dad, but things must have still been good between them after he came out of prison as Mum decided she wanted them to get married and Dad agreed.

The wedding took place at Gloucester register office in January 1972. Dad was late getting home. He'd spent the morning lying under a car at a garage and was filthy and covered in oil. Mum had to hurry him to get himself cleaned up and dressed so they could get there in time. There were only two guests, Dad's brother John and a friend of his called Mick. Mum often spoke about that day. 'Absolute shambles it was from start to finish,' she would say, though the memory of it seemed to amuse as much as annoy her.

After the brief ceremony she wanted to go for a drink to celebrate. Dad was keen to get back to work; his van had broken down and he needed to get it fixed, but he agreed. At the pub she asked for a gin and tonic but she said he irritably told her, 'You can have a bloody shandy and like it!' Soon afterwards he went back to fix the van. It was far from being a romantic occasion but it was typical of the way they did things as a couple.

And while Mum would often complain about being unhappy with Dad, it was still obviously very important to them that they'd got married. She kept hold of their marriage certificate which passed to me; I keep it with Mum's wedding ring and the collection of family photographs the police let me have after they stripped 25 Cromwell Street. On it Dad is described as a 'bachelor', even though he'd been married before. Clearly he didn't mention his previous marriage to the registrar. It was yet another act of dishonesty on his part.

They went on a brief honeymoon to Northam, Devon, the village where Mum had grown up, then returned to their life in the Midland Road house. A little while later, I was born.

With the family growing, they decided to try to find a bigger home. Dad asked their landlord if he owned anything else which was suitable and they were shown a property which he thought might be ideal – a large three-storey terraced house on Cromwell Street, close to the city centre. It was a dilapidated place, on a run-down street of similar houses – mostly converted into flats and bedsits for students and other temporary residents in the city. But there was plenty of room, it had a garage and a decent-sized garden. Next door, there was a Seventh-Day Adventist church, but the landlord assured Mum and Dad they kept themselves to themselves.

Dad, especially, was over the moon with the new house, and they ended up buying it rather than renting. He felt it was the perfect opportunity to put his skills as a jobbing builder to use. What's more, because it was so big, Mum and Dad reckoned on renting out some of the rooms, which would cover the necessary mortgage payments.

And so, in September 1972, when I was just three months old, we moved into 25 Cromwell Street, Gloucester.

Chapter Three

Basement

Reading Mum's letter today brought back memories of Anne Marie. I knew their relationship was complicated before but she makes it sound different to how I remember it growing up. She writes that she was close with Anne Marie, but that Dad put a stop to that and made her abuse Anne Marie herself. She says she agreed so he wouldn't touch us, the rest of the children – that Dad would have killed her and Anne Marie both if they hadn't gone along with it. It makes no sense to me – Mum was always so strong; how could Dad have made her do it? And how could she do it? To a child she claims she loved? Why didn't she take us and run? Why did she keep having children to put in his path? She says she tried to get help but she takes no blame, she says she told Dad she would do anything – cut her to pieces, beat her, torture her – to stop him going at us. Is it true? Is that true mother's love?

HM PRISON DURHAM

Little did I know that I might as well have tried to bargain with the Devil himself. It meant NOTHING to him and he carried on doing what he liked whilst I was out of the way believing that I was doing what was needed to keep you children safe . . .

Love as always,

Mum

My earliest memory of 25 Cromwell Street is Mum putting me to bed in the basement where I slept along with Heather and my brother Steve, who was born the year after we went to live there. I was four years old. You couldn't get to the basement from the main house back then; you had to go out the front and round to the side. We'd put our slippers on and run; sometimes it would be raining and we'd have to huddle under the make-shift corrugated-plastic porch Dad had made until the door was open. The basement was always cold and damp, and there was just one small thin window that had a view to the street at pave-ment level. It was too small to climb out of or bring in any light. We weren't allowed back in the house in the night to go to the toilet so there was always a bucket in the corner. In that first memory of mine, Mum tucked the three of us in really tight, as she always did – she'd take the sheet off and place it back over you, then fold it under the mattress in the hospital-corner way so that the covers were rigid and you could hardly move. There'd be no bedtime story or goodnight kiss – there never was.

I remember watching her reach up and unscrew the light bulb from the bare bracket in the ceiling.

'Why are you doing that, Mum?'

'Never you mind, Mae!' she snapped.

She always did that when she put us to bed and I eventually worked out why: she did it so that when she went back up the steps and shut and locked the basement door on us for the night, we wouldn't switch the light back on and make any mischief.

But even though it was pitch-black that's exactly what we used to do. We'd wriggle out of the sheets, get out of our beds and lark about, playing childish games in the darkness until we were absolutely exhausted and fell asleep. Sometimes we'd be so noisy Mum or Dad would hear us from the house and come thump on the basement door.

'Shut that bloody row up and get to sleep!'

It didn't frighten us. Fear was for upstairs when we were with them. Once we'd been shut in for the night they never came down. They were busy doing their own thing. Though it was dark we had each other for company and I felt a kind of safety during those night-time hours.

We hadn't been made to sleep in the basement when we first moved into the house. As I've said, Mum liked babies and tiny children and seemed genuinely quite maternal around them, so when we were that age she let us sleep upstairs where she could look after us. This meant that in those early years of living at 25 Cromwell Street, the basement was always free for the both of them to do whatever they wanted with it. It also meant that by the time they made us use it as a bedroom, it was a graveyard. Our beds, which sat on Dad's recently laid concrete floors, had unimaginable secrets beneath them.

When we were little, the basement wasn't plastered and done out as it was in later years; Dad was still in the fairly early stages of the massive series of alterations he carried out to the house over the course of two decades. The walls were just bare brick and the ceiling open-beamed. Stray cats used to gather outside the one window, and I have a very vivid memory of putting my hand out of it, up through a metal grill, to try to feed them. Even now I love cats. I think I associated them with freedom. Mum didn't like me playing with them: 'That's bloody silly, Mae. Don't come to me for sympathy when they scratch you,' she said, but I never was. At some point the cats stopped appearing. I asked Mum why.

'The council had them all killed,' she said.

'Why?'

'Cos they're a bloody nuisance that's why.'

I don't know whether that was true or not, but at the time I believed her and it made me so sad. Mum must have known it would, but that wasn't something she cared about – upsetting or disappointing us. She seemed to want to toughen me up.

I was looking at the cats through the window one evening when it was still light when I slipped and fell down onto the pointed bedpost of my bed and it went through my chin. I knew it was bleeding but I couldn't tell how to stop it. The pillow was getting soaked and I can still remember the searing-hot pain where it had broken my skin. Heather tried to have a look but it was too dark to see properly. I panicked. I fumbled my way up the steps to the basement door and banged on it. No one came. It was so frightening – I was only little and I was terrified I was going to bleed to death. I screamed and screamed to try to get Mum and Dad's attention but either I couldn't make them hear or they were purposely ignoring me. Heather and Steve banged and shouted too but it made no difference. Eventually a neighbour who was passing on the street heard my cries coming through the window and knocked on our front door to tell Mum. I had to go to hospital and have stitches.

It makes me feel cold thinking back on it now – that Mum, especially, had no qualms at all about locking us in down there. It was so dangerous; if one of us had been taken seriously ill and our shouts for help had gone unheard, who knows what could have happened? But we were too young and innocent to question it. All we thought was that Mum found us hard work and wanted us out of the way at night so her and Dad – and Anne Marie, who had a bedroom in the house – could have quiet time away from us.

It didn't occur to us then that Mum and Dad wanted to keep us down there so that we wouldn't see what it was they were doing. Or even that they sometimes went off out together, leaving us all by ourselves in the house, which later on I learned they sometimes did. One night, as I was walking round to the basement, I saw them putting a mattress into Dad's van. It didn't cross my mind to question why, or that the two of them were planning on going out in it once they'd put us down below for the night.

In the mornings Mum would open the basement door and come down to get us. She'd be impatient and hurry us into getting dressed and either Heather, Steve or I would have to carry the bucket upstairs to the toilet and empty it. Then she'd give us breakfast in the kitchen just above the basement. It was a room where we spent a lot of time. Dad had done it up in his usual crude way with fake pine panelling and cheap units he'd knocked off from somewhere. Anne Marie, who was in her early teens by then, would come down and join us and Dad too would sometimes be there, although often he'd already left for work. He used to work very long hours and was often away from the house.

Breakfast, like every family meal, was a tense affair. The slightest irritation – spilt milk, a dropped knife or cereal bowl, too much noise and chattering – could trigger yelling and violence from Mum. She'd pick up anything that was to hand – a spatula or wooden spoon – and whack us with it. Sometimes we didn't have to do anything at all to provoke her. Simply being unable to find something would trigger her rage. Frequently it was a tea towel.

'Where is it? Where's the fucking tea towel? Come on, which one of you brats has had it?' she'd scream, her neck straining, her eyes bulging behind her glasses.

More often than not it would be lying over her shoulder where she'd thrown it, but such was her fury she'd never give us a chance to point it out – and we probably wouldn't have dared to anyway. Sometimes us kids would see the funny side about those moments when we were on our own, but mostly her anger just made us terrified and miserable.

It wasn't much of a childhood. From a young age she gave us jobs to do round the house: washing up, mopping the kitchen floor, cleaning the toilet, vacuuming, loading the washing machine. She'd show us how to do them properly and if we didn't follow her instructions to a tee she'd lay into us.

'That's far too much washing powder, Mae! You're wasting it! Do you think I'm made of fucking money?'

'Sorry, Mum,' I'd flinch, knowing what was coming.

'I'll give you fucking sorry, girl!'

The slaps and cuffs would rain down.

'Fucking useless you are! Go on, get out! Go and help Heather clean the bathroom!'

More blows would fall as she chased me from the room.

Sometimes you could half-understand what had provoked her, but on other occasions she seemed to be cruel just for its own sake. Once, when Steve was making cakes, he threw away some raw egg while Mum's back was turned because he'd got shell in it. A few minutes later, I saw her coming towards him, angrily.

She stood with her hand on her hip, her eyes flashing. 'Did you put them egg yolks in the bin, Steve?'

He swallowed and mumbled, 'I got shell in it, Mum.'

She dragged him to the bin, lifted the lid and pointed at the yolks, which were covered in other rubbish.

'Now bloody well eat it. Go on, eat it!'

My stomach turned watching, I was so scared of what she was about to do. Steve did exactly as he was told: he took the yolks out of the rubbish, put them in his mouth and swallowed them.

'That'll teach you to waste food!'

Mealtimes could be bad for the same reason. If there was

something we didn't like, we'd hide it in our pockets: if we left anything on our plates Mum would poke us hard in the back or hit us round the head.

If Dad was around he took little notice of such behaviour, although he never encouraged her to hit us or join in. He might stop whatever he was doing for a moment and watch, and very occasionally if he thought she was going too far – and often she went way beyond what any parent would regard as a reasonable telling-off – he'd intervene.

'Steady on, Rose. That's enough, isn't it?'

But it was only ever a mild reproach and she wouldn't listen. He never physically tried to stop her. It was as if he thought it was just Mum being Mum. I don't recall Dad ever hitting us himself which, considering the savagery of the crimes he later admitted to, might surprise people. But most of the time he had little interest in our behaviour, whether it was good or bad – and no care whatsoever for our safety or wellbeing. He had other things on his mind, and although it was usually hard if not impossible to know what, it was likely to involve sex. He had absolutely no boundaries in talking about that in front of us and there'd be a steady stream of crude and disgusting jokes which no decent parent would think of making in front of young children.

At that age, the house seemed absolutely enormous to us younger kids. Most of it, apart from the basement, the kitchen, bathroom and ground-floor sitting-room was out of bounds to us. We hardly ever went to the first and second floors and only – in those very early years at least – with Mum's permission. When we did go up it seemed like a maze, another world, and was often cluttered with Dad's tools and strewn with building materials from the endless ongoing house alterations.

We were dimly aware that other people were living upstairs. 'The bloody lodgers,' Mum and Dad called them, as if they were just an inconvenience and not paying rent – or, as it turned out, having relationships with them that went far beyond landlord and tenant.

Dad had made a separate entrance for the lodgers so we seldom ever saw them apart from occasionally bumping into them in a corridor or outside the front of the house when we were going out or coming home. We never really knew how many of them there were at any one time. They just seemed to appear in the house, stay for a while and then move on.

Most, but not all, the lodgers were young women. Some of them, we learned when we were older, had acted as babysitters or even temporarily as nannies to us, but I have no memory of that. I remember none of them individually except for one, Shirley Robinson, who I thought of at the time as a grown-up though she was actually only seventeen. The memories I have of her are hardly more than fragments. In my mind she's pretty and fat – it was only much later that I realised what made her seem so was the fact she was pregnant and that Dad was the father.

I have few memories of Anne Marie at that early stage of my life although, along with Heather and Steve, I came to realise that her position in the family was different to ours. One clue was that she sometimes referred to my mother as Mum and some-times she'd call her Rose. Whether it was this that first made me realise we didn't share the same mother, or whether Mum, Dad or even Anne Marie herself just told me, I can't remember.

Anne Marie seemed to be treated differently to us. It wasn't that I ever saw either Mum or Dad deal with her more harshly than us – although I had no idea what went on upstairs when the three of them were alone together. Yet she always seemed to have a relationship with them that was private and that only the three of them understood. Above all, Anne Marie always gave me the impression of being troubled, lonely and very unhappy.

When Mum and Dad did talk about Anne Marie being a child from Dad's previous marriage to Rena, Charmaine was also sometimes mentioned. I had a sense there'd been a strong sisterly bond between Anne Marie and Charmaine and wondered if the fact Anne Marie was so sad and withdrawn was because she was no longer in contact with Charmaine or her biological mother. It was a long time before I learned there were much more terrible reasons for her misery, and a longer time still before I understood the awful truth about Mum's part in making her like that. Thinking about it now makes me feel both desperately sad and angry.

In those days, and for years afterwards, I assumed Anne Marie and Charmaine were full sisters. It wasn't until I reached my early teens that I found out this wasn't so. Mum had a photo album with a picture of Charmaine in it. One day when I was looking at it with her she referred to 'Charmaine's dad'.

'I thought Dad was Charmaine's dad,' I said.

'No, he was a fellow from Glasgow. Indian or Pakistani, according to your dad. That's why Charmaine's skin was dark, see.'

I'd never thought about it until then, but when I looked at the photograph again, I could see what she meant about her skin colouring.

'Will you ever see Charmaine again?' I asked her.

'I doubt it. Your dad never hears anything from her mother these days. He says she's probably in Glasgow, but for all we know she's in Timbuktu.'

As the years went by, Dad would embellish the details about where Rena went according to his mood. He'd say he'd heard rumours she was working as a prostitute, or had become a drug addict. He'd claim he couldn't go back to Scotland to find out because she knew people who would kill him for her. Or he'd change his tune and say he had no idea where she was. Although he spoke about them in the present tense he made it very clear she and Charmaine were part of his past. A family that was now lost to him. And that must have been tough for Anne Marie, because he made it clear she was neither part of that family nor the new one he had made with Mum.

Apart from the lodgers who were kept away from us, few others came to the house at that time. One of them was Mum's father, Bill Letts. As a young child I hadn't yet learned how horrible, controlling and abusive he'd been towards Mum when she was growing up, or how he'd done everything possible to destroy her relationship with Dad, who he'd hated from the moment they first met. If I had known, I would have thought it very strange that he came to the house at all, and even stranger that Dad seemed to welcome his visits which were quite regular. The two of them gave the impression of sharing a friendship of kinds, and although I never saw anything that resembled affection between Bill and Mum, she didn't seem to mind him coming round either.

Bill showed no interest at all in us children. I don't recall him ever acting as you might hope a grandparent would towards their grandchildren. There was no laughter or joking or any warmth in his manner when he spoke to us. Like Dad, it was as if he had other things on his mind and, when he came to visit, the two of them would usually be together in the parts of the house where we weren't allowed.

Looking back, the one positive thing to have come out of my

44

childhood was my friendship with Heather. Those early years locked down in the basement together at night, chattering, playing games, wondering what was happening in the rest of the house – all those times when we had suffered Mum's beatings, and consoled one another afterwards – had bonded us together. We were close to Steve too, at that age, for the same reasons, and the three of us often played together. But as a boy he was given different chores to do by Mum and he had his own interests – and was, in some ways at least, close to Dad, which we certainly weren't.

Despite it being a long way from typical childhood, we made our own fun. Heather and I were real tomboys back then. We didn't bother with dolls or other girly things. We had very few toys so we invented most of our own games. In the basement we played a game where we put cushions on the floor and had to jump from one cushion to the next, imagining that the floor was a sea of sharks or crocodiles which might eat us. It is strange and chilling to think about that game now – now that I know there really were horrors under that floor.

Mum taught us to crochet at a very early age and we loved making babies' blankets. We'd also play cat's cradle with coloured string, and often we just sat and drew pictures together. On rare occasions when we did escape into the parts of the house where we weren't supposed to go, we loved sliding down the bannisters or playing hide-and-seek – sometimes hiding inside the old fireplaces, looking for birds. When Mum was out of the way we used to sneak into the kitchen and play around with different foodstuffs. Heather liked to make butter. She'd steal milk from the fridge, put it in a jam jar with salt and shake it from side to side until it churned into something solid.

Sometimes, when Mum wanted us out of the way, she'd lock us out in the garden. We loved it – almost as much as we loved the park where, when we were older, we were occasionally allowed to play. We had a swing and a climbing frame, and an old bike without tyres which we used to ride round and round on. We made perfume from blossom or rose petals by soaking them in water and then bottling it. Sometimes we'd dig red clay from the garden and make pots, cups, bowls and plates – and leave them to dry in the sun. The problem with memories like that is they mean something different to me now. This clay was from the same ground as the graves of unknown faces buried beneath our feet.

As we got older, Heather, Steve and I grew braver. Sometimes we'd climb the fence into the garden which backed onto ours and play with the Staffie dog that lived there. Or we'd climb the wall of the Seventh-Day Adventist church next door and look down, curious and giggling, through the skylights at the congregation as they sat through their traditional Saturday service. We loved doing daredevil things, thrilled by the risk that Mum and Dad might catch us. We never had more fun than when we'd put on Michael Jackson records and dance wildly about the house knowing they might come in and find us at any moment.

Although being scared was such a big part of my early life, it was mainly the fear of Mum's violence: of her smashing up the breakfast table and sending us to school hungry; or smacking us so much we'd have bruises to show for it. But by trying to avoid annoying her as much as possible or simply staying out of her way, you could keep that to a minimum. Dad was a different matter when we were older, but at that age he wasn't a threat. So, although the house was far from being a happy place, I did feel some sense of security when I was little. The 'House of Horrors' was just our home and I didn't sense anything worse waiting to happen. How could any of us have known what lay below us in the basement, or what was really happening above us on the upper floors of the house? How could any of us have known there were much more terrifying things in store?

Chapter Four

Uncle John

Mum's letter was a painful read today. She wrote about him. Uncle John and the pain I've tried to bury. She said sorry about it and what happened to us. I think that might be the first time she's properly admitted some fault. And about Louise too. She says she knew it would all come to a head one day and that the children would have to be taken away from her. I don't know what to think! Can I believe her? I have craved for any signs of love from her all of my life. And she knows what I want and need to hear . . .

HM PRISON DURHAM

Mae, I'm so sorry about Uncle John and all that happened to you and the others, Louise and everything!! . . . I truly did care for all of you, I still do. I did what I thought was the best thing at the time, but I realise now just how inadequate I was!!!

Apart from Mum's dad, the other regular visitor to the house when I was young was Dad's brother, Uncle John. He was only a year younger than Dad and they'd been close since they were little boys.

He had a job as a bin man, working in Gloucester. He used to come round to our house with toys or old video tapes that had been thrown away and he'd salvaged. Sometimes he brought electrical appliances or other junk – televisions, toasters, VCRs, rusting tools – that he'd rescued from the tip to give to Dad.

I remember always thinking he was a disgusting man. He smoked a pipe constantly and always stank of stale, bitter tobacco, and he was big, with a huge belly. Once, when I was quite young, he took his top off and made me look at a scar which ran down his entire chest and his bulging stomach, tracing it with his finger – he said it was from a heart operation. It made me feel sick to look at it. Everything about him made me feel ill and he had a personality to match. He used to tell us children stories of how if cats came into his garden he would break their necks and throw them over the fence. I loved cats so those stories would break my heart and he knew it.

Uncle John continued to live and work in Gloucester and occasionally he'd bring his wife Anita, a small quiet lady who was a nurse, and their son to visit us at Cromwell Street, and Mum and Dad would sit and talk with them. He didn't swear or speak in a vulgar way about sex like Dad, especially when his wife was there. He wasn't scruffy like him either. When he wasn't in his work clothes he used to dress quite smartly and he and his wife lived in a neat modern bungalow and drove a decent car – not like Dad's terrible old bangers. But there was something seedy about him, something far more troubling than just his crooked smile and terrible body odour. Simply being near him made me feel very uneasy in a way I could not understand.

Throughout my childhood Dad would often cheerfully tell stories about his early life in Much Marcle and John featured in lots of them. They'd played together, done jobs on the farm where

Dad's father worked, wandered the fields and woods looking for rabbits and squirrels to shoot with an air rifle. It sounded like they'd been inseparable.

Dad's memories of his early days were always vivid – knowing what I do now, some of it was exaggerated and other, darker parts left out, but I believed then (and still do believe) much of it. The country life he described sounded remote and strange – almost like something from Victorian times, not the 1950s. Sometimes he took us kids back to Much Marcle with him to visit his family and I was struck by how in the middle of no-where it felt: fields and gentle hills as far as the eye could see, broken only by trees and hedgerows. Even the accent sounded much more countrified than Gloucester – and that can be broad enough. There were dialect words and phrases I didn't under-stand. He would talk about 'eyebrowns' instead of eyebrows, use words like fires instead of radiators, and phrases like 'get the baccy tin out, Mae, don't roll me a prisoner!' when he wanted a generous roll-up – that was the language he'd grown up with.

He was born in 1943, at Bickerton Cottage, to Walter, a farm labourer, and Daisy, his second wife who was – according to Dad – a strict and domineering woman. I was always told he was their first child, although I later discovered that they had previously had a daughter called Violet who had lived for only a few hours. But he was their oldest surviving child, and was soon followed by John and another brother David, who died at a month old. Later they moved to another house in the village, Moorcourt Cottage, which was attached to a farm, and Dad's parents had more children – young Daisy, Douglas, Kitty and Gwendoline.

Eight children, two of them not even surviving infancy. My grandma must have been tough as nails. You can see it in a photograph I have of my two grandparents together: she looks stern, straight-backed. Dad said she would sometimes beat him and his brothers and sisters with a thick leather belt – though he also gave me the impression he was his mum's favourite.

But it was his dad that he hero-worshipped, learning all about farming from him, especially livestock: how to tend sheep, pigs and cows. It sounded like a harsh life: for lunch (so he would tell us when we moaned about our own school packed lunches) he'd be given a raw turnip or parsnip. But he made some of it sound like fun – there was hop-picking, apple-picking, hay-making. Dad seemed to love being close to nature and knew every field, hedgerow and wood around Much Marcle like the back of his hand. They were his stomping ground. And, living so close to the land, he was also used to slaughtering animals and it sounded as if it never fazed him. I remember him telling us how his mum made him kill the family pet pig for food.

'I hadn't got a clue how to do it. Chased the fuckin' animal all the way round the yard and into the barn. Eventually I cornered it, managed to grab hold of its head and slit its throat. But it wouldn't die. Kept running round, squealing and squealing till eventually it dropped down dead. Proper bloodbath it was. We hung it up in the kitchen after and let the blood drip out of it for hours.' Why he thought we wanted to hear stories like that escapes me, but he always seemed to get a perverse kick out of saying things to shock us.

He also knew how to kill chickens and rabbits. Once, when I was four or five, on one our trips back to the cottage, he went shooting for rabbits. He gave some of them to his mum but we brought one home to Gloucester with us. I remember it lying on the kitchen table, its eyes black and lifeless, and my chest going tight looking at the poor thing. 'That'll be dinner tomorrow, Mae. Rabbit stew. Delicious,' he grinned maliciously at me.

None of us, including Mum, could bear the thought of eating

it, but he carried on skinning it anyway on the kitchen table. He said he wanted us to watch him pull the skin off. Heather, Steve and I covered our faces with our hands so we didn't have to. 'What's the matter with you all?' he said, annoyed now. 'It's only nature.'

'It's horrible, Dad!'

'You're all weaklings, that's what you are.'

Once he'd skinned and gutted it, he chucked it into a pot for mum to cook.

'It stinks, Fred,' Mum said.

'Does it heck, Rose. That's proper fresh, that is.'

But she wouldn't have it in the house and put it outside the back door. In the morning we found the cats had got to it, so Mum had an excuse to throw it away before Dad could force us to eat it.

Aside from the skills he was so proud of, Dad had a fascination with the way animals' bodies were put together – especially how they bred and their reproductive systems. He would tell us gleefully about how he used to help with lambing and that sometimes the ewe would push its womb (he'd call it the 'lamb bed') out along with the baby lamb – a prolapsed uterus. The job of the shepherd would be to put the uterus back carefully or the ewe would die, but Dad said they just used to push everything back inside in any order. I suppose that should have been a clue about what I later found out he was capable of. But no one thinks their dad can kill a person simply because they can kill an animal; we just put it down to him being weird. It was just Dad being Dad.

John had been such an important part of that strange and harsh world Dad grew up in. They'd even slept in the same bed as little boys – something Dad would remind us about if we ever complained about our sleeping arrangements down in the basement. 'At least you lot have beds of your own. I had John farting and elbowing me in the back!' Their relationship often seemed innocent and funny the way he described it. Yet there were also hints of something else, something which seemed secret and sinister.

'Oh John could tell some tales about me, when I was young. And I could tell 'em about him,' he'd say. We'd take the bait and ask him what sort of tales, but he'd just reply, 'Oh you know, things we got up to.'

'But what kind of things?'

'Never you mind. A man never tells on his brother.' I'm glad he didn't tell us, to be honest. I later read about the charges that had been brought against Dad when he was younger, that he'd abused his sister, and rumours of him doing unthinkable things with animals. I found none of it surprised me, but I think hearing it then, when we were young and impressionable, would have been confusing.

Outside the family, Dad seemed to find it hard to fit into village life. He hated school. He'd arrive each day in big hobnail boots, stinking of the farm, and was a poor pupil, barely able to read or write even by the time he left school. He was often in trouble with his teachers and would sometimes get teased by other kids for his odd appearance and manner. If it came to blows he would fight back and John was always there to make sure he won.Though he was younger, Uncle John soon became the bigger of the two boys, and Dad knew he could rely on John to protect him. Where Dad had the gift of the gab, John was quieter, but you wouldn't cross him lightly. And their mother Daisy, no matter what Dad did wrong at school, always stuck up for him. She was strict with her children at home, for sure, but she would take their side against anyone outside the family. No teacher was going to push her son around.

In his teens, Dad became keen on motorbikes and saved up the money to buy one. He loved to tinker with it and show it off. He'd grown in confidence as he got older and would drive into Ledbury and pose on it – especially for the girls. According to him, it worked like a charm. 'Queuing up for a ride, they were,' he'd brag. He was never short of female attention or – he used to hint – sexual conquests. John would often join him on those trips. 'Ended up chasing after the same girls, sometimes we did!'

Whatever Dad had, it seemed that John wanted too.

Dad also loved the freedom the bike gave him. 'Ride for an hour and you could be in another world,' he'd say. 'Worcester, Hereford, Cheltenham, Gloucester. I knew I didn't want to be stuck in that village for ever.'

The story from their teens which both of them told most often was about Dad's motorbike accident when he was sixteen. There were several versions of this and the one Dad used to tell when I was a child was that he'd been riding home one night and simply 'slid on some cow shit', come off the road and smashed into a wall. He lay in a ditch for hours, so he claimed, and was as good as dead when he was eventually found. He was taken to hospital where his heart stopped beating and a doctor pronounced him dead. Then, to the astonishment of everyone present, he came round on the mortuary slab and was resuscitated.

I learned later that the truth was probably less dramatic and more complicated than that. But whatever actually happened that night, Uncle John said it changed Dad for good. He said that for months afterwards Dad would sit at home, staring at the walls, refusing to look at people.

'Fly off the handle if you so much as said a word to him,' he said. 'Shout and yell and go nuts at you, he would. Never the same again he was.'

I still don't know if that was true – if the effects of that accident on Dad's personality really had been that serious. There was another story the two brothers told in different ways at different times, about Dad being kicked in the head at a youth club dance for flirting with another lad's girlfriend. Uncle John suggested that too may have affected Dad, but it also may just have been him making excuses for his brother – something that, so it turned out, he had very good reason to do. Whatever the truth of it, the impression I had from an early age was that Uncle John looked up to Dad. He was the follower and Dad was the leader.

Dad was always completely open about sex. His father had told him, so he said, that it was a father's 'right and duty to break his daughter in'. I don't remember when he first said this in front of us, and as a small child I didn't understand. Even when I did come to realise it meant he felt he had some right over our bodies, I didn't feel threatened to begin with. As a child, you have little understanding or concern about the future, do you? It was something that would happen when I was grown-up, I thought, which felt so far away. And so, although Dad was a strange man, he was often cheerful and full of jokes and could make me laugh – I didn't feel fear when I was around him.

Uncle John was different. There was nothing to like, no warmth in him at all. Once I'd heard it I could never get the story of him killing cats out of my head.

The first time something happened was when I was five. Mum and Dad went out – I can't remember them telling me where – and left Uncle John to look after me, Heather and Steve. It wasn't something I can recall them doing before. At some point, Uncle John came into the room where we were playing and asked me to come into the bathroom. He said he wanted me to help him with something. I remember very clearly not wanting to go in with him and that I felt scared. But I was only little, and so I had no choice but to do as I was told.

Dad had built Mum a wooden nappy-changing area over the bath and he lifted me onto it, shut the door and locked it. At that age, I had no idea what sex was, so I didn't know what was coming next, I thought we were just playing a game. But I do remember my feeling of fear getting thicker, feeling panicked about being alone with him, being frightened of what he was going to do. Without saying anything he took my underwear off, unzipped himself and got on top of me. I felt the weight of him, pressing down, crushing me. I tried to get out from under him, wriggling against him, but he got angry, ordering me to stay still. He pressed down harder on me, lifting his his revolting fat stomach out of the way as he pinned me down and carried on. The smell of stale tobacco and sweat on his clothes was overwhelming and made me want to be sick – even to this day when I smell tobacco I feel sick and am reminded of that night. But I kept moving and wriggling to get out from under him and just willed it to be over. It didn't last long. I know it must have hurt, probably hurt a lot, but I have blocked the memory of the pain out. I'm sure I must have bled although I can't remember that either.

Afterwards, he zipped himself up and lifted me down off the board, and told me to go back and play with Heather and Steve. Then, almost as an afterthought, he dug a coin out of his pocket, threw it to me and told me not to tell anyone what had happened.

In the years afterwards I tried to shut the memory out of my mind as best I could, almost as if, by not thinking about it, I could make it into something that hadn't ever happened. I didn't even mention it to Heather who would have been the natural person for me to share it with. It's hard to explain, but when something happens to you that you can feel in yourself is bad, but no one's ever told you what it is, or given it a name, or said that it's bad and that it's not your fault – it's hard then to know how to tell anyone about it, or even if you're allowed to. It's as if you just haven't been given the vocabulary to say what the problem is. Only as I grew older did I understand that there was a term for it, and that what had happened was rape. Even then, it was just one incident in a long line of being touched in inappropriate places by Dad's friends who came to the house: all I could ever do was wait for it to be over so that I could run back outside and play.

I didn't tell anyone until years later, when I was in my early teens and went swimming with Anne Marie. This was after she'd left home. After we got out of the pool and were changing back into our clothes, she started to talk about Mum and Dad. Out of nowhere, as if she suddenly felt an overwhelming need to un-burden herself, she told me she'd been sexually abused by both of them. I was horrified. I'd had no idea, and it made me view her life upstairs in the house while we were shut away down in the basement quite differently. She said it had gone on for years, though she didn't go into great detail or tell me how serious it was. She warned me that they might try to do the same to me. I told her that Dad had already tried to grope me on a few occasions but I'd managed to distract him, and that although Mum knew he'd tried it on with me, she hadn't assisted in any way. Although I didn't think for a minute that Anne Marie was lying about Mum helping Dad to abuse her, I was so shocked by the idea I just couldn't take it in. And then she mentioned that Uncle John had also abused her and warned me to watch out for him too. So I blurted out about what he had done to me. She didn't seem at all surprised and began to ask me about it, but I didn't want to talk about it in detail. I clammed up. I just wanted to shut the memory away. It was never mentioned between us again.

Then, two years after the murders at Cromwell Street had been discovered, I received a letter saying I was being called to give evidence against Uncle John, who was facing rape and assault charges. Anne Marie had given a full statement against him and she had told the police that it had happened to me too.

I didn't want to face Uncle John and have to relive in detail what had happened, certainly not in a courtroom full of people. I had a solicitor write a letter saying I didn't want to give evidence, but I was told I had no choice – they would just come and get me when they wanted me in court. I kept hoping it wasn't true or that the trial wouldn't go ahead.

I was living with Tara at the time. She'd just had her second son. He was only a day old and we'd just got back from the hospital on the day the trial was due to start. I prayed the authorities had changed their minds and weren't going to call me as a witness. I didn't want to leave Tara on her own with a newborn baby, as well as her other son who was two, and my daughter, who was nine months old. I thought it would be too much for her and we still didn't know anyone there who we could rely on to help her out.

But the police came to the door and said I had to go with them. They drove me to the court. I remember hanging around in the witness room feeling incredibly nervous. When I was eventually called I went into the witness box and stared straight ahead of me. I was aware that Uncle John was in the defendant's stand to the side of me, but I was desperate not to make eye contact with him.

I was sworn in and gave my evidence, which I found incredibly hard. They asked me to explain what John had done to me.

58

I tried to just say he abused me but they wanted me to go into anatomical detail. I had to use the correct terminology. 'He put his penis inside me', and so on. I felt violated all over again and just wanted to get out of there.

When the defence barrister started to cross-examine me, he was horrible to me.

'The defendant says you've made this story up,' he said in a loud posh voice, holding onto his black robes.

'I haven't,' I swallowed, still staring straight ahead.

'He claims he caught you smoking and told you he was going to inform your mother and father so you invented the story to get back at him.'

To not be believed when you say something like that – a private memory that haunts you and that you didn't want to share in the first place – is indescribably gut-wrenching and humiliating. I couldn't believe Uncle John was trying to wriggle out of responsibility for it by pushing the blame on me, even more so because how could I – at five years old – have known how to make that particular story up? 'I don't smoke,' I quivered, 'I've never smoked. I hate the habit.'

And so it went on. The defence claiming I was a liar, that I'd tried to blackmail Uncle John into keeping quiet to avoid getting into trouble with Mum and Dad. They didn't believe my denials. By the time I left the witness stand I felt that I was the one in the wrong, the one who was on trial. Anne Marie then went in to give her evidence against Uncle John, which was incredibly damning. I went home and tried to put it out of my head.

A day later, I received a phone call from the *News of the World* asking me if I'd heard that Uncle John had been found dead. He'd hanged himself in his garage. I was totally shocked, and however much I hated him and what he'd done to me – raping me as a five-year-old and trying to make out in court that I was a liar – I really felt for his wife and son. What happened was no fault of theirs. I hadn't for a moment imagined he would ever do anything like that. I felt somehow responsible for his death.

Looking back on it now, I still find myself clutching for answers. When Mum and Dad went out and left Uncle John to look after me, did they know he couldn't be trusted? Did they suspect he might do what he did? Might Dad and he have even planned it? Did Uncle John do it partly because he was jealous of Dad – after all, he had a son but no daughters to 'break in'?

Whenever I discussed it with Mum she never said anything other than that she was sorry about what John did to me. For all Mum's faults I'd always wanted to believe her regret was genuine. After all, I was so small and vulnerable and totally defenceless. What mother wouldn't be outraged? But since she hasn't been honest about so many other things, how can I be sure?

She once brought it up in a letter to me from prison, a throwaway remark sandwiched between things she clearly cared more about than me – her shellsuit bottoms and her budgie, Oliver:

HM PRISON DURHAM

Hello Sweetheart,

Blimey Mae, you didn't waste time sending me some money did you? It arrived the day after I asked you for it! Thank you very much. Funny but I have just received your Christmas card. It's lovely darling, I shall keep this one. I was ironing my shell-suit bottoms the other day and my mind wandered (as it does quite often) on to the matters of John West. Guess what I did? When I looked down I had burnt them!!! I was so angry with myself, my friend had given them to me yonks ago and I had to wait until I could lose weight to wear them. I only managed to wear them 3 times! Curse that bloody family!!

I've got Oliver fluttering around my ears, he's learnt how to go in and out of his cage now by himself . . .

Love as always,

Mum xxx

There is another answer I will never find: the question of whether Uncle John was involved in the murders. Some people have suggested as much and, because of what he did to me and to Anne Marie, I find it hard to rule out the possibility. At the very least I believe he's likely to have known something about them. He and Dad kept few if any secrets from each other.

And looking back now I can't help but wonder if killing himself was solely because of the rape trial. I wonder if he had other things weighing heavily on his conscience – including a part to play in the deaths of some of the women Dad was charged with and Mum was found guilty of. But we'll never know. He is dead now, and his secrets have gone with him to the grave.

One more thing he and my dad have in common.

Chapter Five

Dead Man's Shoes

As soon as I feel stronger with Mum, she pulls me in. She feels me pulling away and she knows my weakness of caring what happens to her. Her letter today talked about how lonely she felt in her life with Dad. She had all the men to cope with, to please, so many she wouldn't have wished it on the Devil himself, she says. She felt so alone, but what about us kids? Who was loving us? Who has ever shown us love?

HM PRISON DURHAM

. . . the only people I could believe I stood any kind of chance of loving me, of understanding me and helping me were you children!! And of course I know just how wrong that is now – but then it was desperation . . .

I will never know how being raped by Uncle John has affected my life, especially as the majority of it has been lived after the event. I suppose I've dealt with it as many rape victims do, by putting it into a separate compartment in my mind. In a way, being so young and not understanding might have helped me be able to forget about it in a way that I might not have been able to do if I was older. I don't think I even knew it was John who was to blame and that what he'd done was a horrific betrayal of my innocence and trust. I only knew that I couldn't tell anyone about it, particularly Mum – apart from anything it might get back to John that I'd done so and I was terrified of what he might do to me. The only way I could deal with my emotions was to numb them and try to carry on as if it had never happened.

Not long after that, in December 1977, Tara was born. I have no memory of Mum telling me she was pregnant but I remember her being excited as her due date got closer. The idea of her having a baby didn't seem real to me. Then one day she took me upstairs, opened a wardrobe and showed me the baby clothes she was gathering together in readiness. There were tiny vests and cardigans and pairs of dungarees. She was like a child herself as she passed them to me, one by one, and let me hold them. I began to get really excited myself.

And when she was born I was so delighted to have a little sister and was old enough, at the age of six, to take a real interest in how Mum went about looking after her. She seemed thrilled with her new baby and, although she continued to be short-tempered and often violent to us older children, she doted on Tara. She was exactly the same with the four other children she was to have in the following few years: Louise and my younger brother and two sisters.

She encouraged me to help with all her babies as much as I could. I used to hold and talk to them, soothe them when they cried, make up bottles for them and feed them. It was hard work, especially with Tara – Mum didn't use disposable nappies for her so the old-fashioned Terylene ones had to be boiled and hung to dry. But I loved it – loved being Mum's helper – and I've always loved babies.

Heather, Steve and I noticed as soon as Mum and Dad brought

Tara home that she had brown skin and black curly hair. We asked Mum and Dad why she looked like that. They didn't seem to feel awkward about it in any way and at first didn't even acknowledge there was anything surprising about her appearance – even though the rest of the family was white.

'She's a baby, like you were all babies, all babies are different,' Dad said.

We accepted it at first but as the years passed and two more of the four children they had after Tara had similar dark colouring we asked more and more questions. Dad changed his story.

'They're throwbacks, see,' he would say.

'What's a throwback?' I asked the first time he came out with it.

'Well, it's like if you've had an ancestor who looks a certain way—'

'What's an ancestor?'

'Someone in your family's past. Like your great-great-grandfather or something. And they had a certain appearance and then years and years later you get a child in the same family that looks like them cos it's been passed down through the generations.'

We were only young and it made a kind of sense to us. 'So one of our ancestors was black?' I said.

'Must have been,' Dad nodded. 'A gypsy or a Jamaican probably.'

Neither Mum nor Dad ever acknowledged to us that Dad wasn't the father of Tara or my two youngest sisters. But they were very interested in family resemblances. They would often talk about which side of the family their two younger white children, Louise and our youngest brother, looked like.

'Louise is a West, you can see that,' Dad would say.

In the same way, Mum would say our younger brother looked

like a Letts. 'He's definitely got the look of my brothers and sisters.'

Heather, Steve and I never had any doubt that, like us, they were both Dad's children. But once we were older and the 'throwback' story no longer washed with us, we wondered about Tara and our youngest sisters. It wasn't until the trial that Mum finally admitted that Dad wasn't their father and Dad, who was dead by then anyway, never ever did. I remember children would taunt us about it at school, having seen Tara in her pram. They'd say horrible things like, 'How come you got a darkie for a sister?' or 'Your dad a Jamaican then?'

I don't think any of them had any real idea of what it meant about Tara's parentage or how she'd been conceived. No one at school knew much about me or about our family. Mum didn't allow us to bring what few friends we tried to make home. But it was upsetting all the same to hear the jokes about Tara's appear-eance, and then later our other two sisters. Of course the abuse hit them hard too over the years; Tara was especially resentful – understandably – towards people who teased her about the colour of her skin.

It seems obvious now, of course, that Tara and our two young-est sisters' dads were Mum's clients. As we grew older we started to notice that there were male callers coming to the house. We knew they weren't relatives or lodgers because they only ever stayed for an hour or so, sometimes less. They didn't use our family entrance but the separate one Dad had created for the lodgers. Some of them came regularly and, whenever they called, Mum would be upstairs waiting for them. Gradually we worked out that she was having sex with them. I'm not sure when exactly, but it was well before we reached puberty.

I knew what sex was from an early age, and not just because of what had happened with Uncle John. Dad talked about it all the time. He literally had no inhibitions about anything. He used to sit on the toilet with the door open. He was always making crude comments and jokes about people's private parts or about 'shagging'. He'd talk about how animals had sex in graphic detail. He'd frequently fondle and grope Mum and even on occasions thrust his hand up between Mum's legs then make us smell it.

'There you are, kids, that's what your mother smells like!'

We found it utterly revolting and would squirm and try to get away from him, which would only make him laugh. Mum made no attempt to stop him. She was just as frank about such things, and as uninhibited – often walking around the house naked. There was never any question of keeping her children in innocence until we were old enough to need to know about sex.

But then she also made no formal attempt to tell us the facts of life. I suppose she assumed we'd just pick them up, which we did. But I do remember, one horribly hot day when I was around seven or eight, her giving Heather and me a disgusting sort of lesson about it. We were in the lounge with her and she was sitting on the sofa. She was talking about sex.

'What you two need to realise is that for a girl to understand her body she needs to explore it,' she said.

Not understanding what she meant, I asked her, 'What do you mean, Mum?'

'Here. I'll show you.'

To our horror she lifted the front of her skirt. She never wore underwear.

'I want you to put your hands up there. You first, Mae.'

I felt sick at the thought. 'I don't want to,' I said, looking anywhere else.

'Do as I fucking well say, girl!'

This was far worse even than Dad putting his hand up Mum's

66

skirt, but you couldn't say no to Mum; she was terrifying. So we had no choice but to do it. It was so strange and I felt absolutely repelled.

'That's what you'll be like down there when you're older,' she said, matter-of-factly. 'You need to know that.'

She made out that it was the responsibility of a mother to teach her daughters such things. Perhaps in her mind it was. Or maybe she got some kind of sexual thrill out of it. I'm not sure. Whichever of those things was true, it just goes to show she was very confused about the proper sexual boundaries there should be between adults and children.

At that time Dad hadn't built the area he eventually made for Mum to work in at the top of the house – the elaborate boudoir with lace-draped four-poster complete with spyhole for him to peer and film through – but even then, in addition to the bedroom she shared with Dad, she had another for entertaining men.

Mum told me much later that Dad had very often found her clients for her. Although he was a racist he was fascinated with the idea of her having sex with black men and was obsessed with how well-endowed they were. As far as he was concerned, the bigger the better, and the more he felt Mum was used by them, the more exciting he found it.

Mum confided this in me when I was grown-up and she and Dad were going through a particularly bad patch. She insisted then that her work as a prostitute had disgusted her and that she'd only done it because they were hard up and Dad had pressurised her into it. She said the same thing at the trial, claiming that she'd flatly refused to do it at first so Dad had grabbed her by the throat and they'd fought until she'd fled the house and gone to her mother's. The prosecuting counsel cast doubt on the truth of that story, suggesting that she'd done the work willingly, and that she and Dad had never seriously fallen out and had remained in love until the day of his arrest for murder. In support of this he quoted entries Mum had written about Dad in her diary saying how much she loved him.

It even emerged that Mum and Dad had named Tara after the Tara Hotel in Upton St Leonards, Gloucestershire (now the Hatton Court Hotel) where she sometimes used to meet one of her clients – a Jamaican man who went by the nickname 'Rosco'. They thought he was Tara's dad. It must have been a little joke between them to give Tara that name and, Mum being the strong character she is, it's hard to see how she would have agreed to doing that if she'd been disgusted by how Tara was conceived there.

It also came out at the trial that Dad had been delighted that Mum had babies with a man of a different ethnic origin. The prosecution showed that over the years he'd conducted numerous amateur experiments with the semen taken from the condoms Mum had used with black men, and with the aid of copper pipes and syringes had tried to artificially inseminate her. Mum, the prosecution claimed, went along with it and it was even suggested that's how Tara and my two youngest sisters were conceived.

That seems very unlikely to me. But however they were conceived and whoever their fathers were, it never weakened or could weaken my feelings for them. I've always felt as much for them as I have for my full brothers and sisters – in fact, I became especially close to Tara after Mum was arrested and we still see each other regularly to this day. We were all just part of the same family. I loved them all and always took huge pleasure in looking after every one of them.

*

Though Mum doted on Tara when she was first born, her treatment of Heather, Steve and me grew even harsher. The new baby placed extra demands on her and she had even less time and patience for the rest of us. She became more and more violent, lashing out at us at the slightest provocation with whatever implement she could find, or throwing pots and pans at our heads, once knocking Steve out completely cold by breaking a Pyrex dish over his head.

Sometimes she threw the kitchen stools at us and on one occasion she picked a television up and aimed it at Tara. Luckily she got out of the way in time but if it hit her, she could have been seriously hurt – Mum must have known that. She didn't seem at all concerned about the risks of physical injury to us, once even grabbing baby Tara out of her high chair, hitting her then throwing her back into it, all because Tara had thrown her food on the floor.

The last time she was truly violent towards me was when I was in my early teens and she came after me with a knife. We were in the kitchen and I remember she was chopping meat with a carving knife. I was in the middle of changing clothes and was only wearing my vest and knickers. I was standing at the top of the steps that Dad had built to lead down to the basement. I must have said something to annoy her because she suddenly snapped, picked the knife up and rushed towards me, waving it.

'I've fucking well had enough of you, Mae. Do you hear?!'

I shrieked and backed away from her. 'Stop it, Mum! You're scaring me!'

'Don't tell me what to do, you fucking little bitch! Do you think I wouldn't use this on you? Do you?'

She began to make slashing movements across my chest. They cut through my vest, nicking the skin. I was petrified. I tried to dodge out of the way but she kept coming at me.

'Please, Mum! Don't! Don't!'

'Shut up then!'

But I was frozen, I think I was actually whimpering with fright. She really looked as if she wanted to kill me.

'I said shut up!'

Fearing for my life I ran down into the basement. I thought she might follow and there'd be nowhere else to run, but she stayed at the top of the basement steps, cursing and swearing at me before eventually going back to chopping the meat, snarling at Heather and Steve who'd watched in terror.

'What are you two staring at?'

Mum didn't pick on any one of us more than the others. At different times we all came in for it. Sometimes her punishments weren't just impulsive – lashing out at us with anything she could find – but were more cold-blooded and planned. It was deliberate sadism. She had a cupboard of canes and belts for those occasions. She'd take out the implement of her choice, line us up and beat us one after the other.

That was the worst thing of all. It was much harder to watch my siblings being given a hiding than it was to be punished myself. Heather and Steve felt the same way. Sometimes when Mum asked which of us had done something wrong – such as break a plate – one of us would try to take the blame and the beating that followed because, even if it wasn't true, we hoped it might save the others from being punished if one of us stepped forward and said we'd done it. That didn't always stop her. She'd just tell us we all deserved it anyway and if we hadn't been the guilty one on that occasion then she knew we would be in the future.

One of the worst occasions was when I saw her strangle Steve to the point where I really thought he was going to die. He was only little, about six or seven maybe. He'd been sitting on the kitchen counter and Mum told him to get down. When he didn't, she seemed to suddenly snap – she grabbed him by his neck and was holding him off the ground, it was beyond terrifying. His face was going purple and his eyes were all bloodshot; Heather and I were begging her to let him go but she wasn't listening, she was only screaming at us, 'Pull his trousers down! Pull his trousers down!' because she wanted to beat him. Eventually, thank God, she dropped him. When he went into school the next day, his face all covered in red blotches, she made us pretend he'd caught his neck in a tree. Mum and Dad were worried the school might ask questions about how he'd got the injuries, but – even though we had numerous bruises and welts on us over the years – the teachers never asked us how we got them. It's different now – schools are much more aware of the extent of child abuse, but back then it really felt like nobody cared what was going on behind closed doors.

Mum and Dad were also worried when – this was when we were at secondary school – Heather took one of Mum and Dad's hard-core porn mags into school. They were furious about it, obviously because it might have stirred up all sorts of questions about what was going on at home if a teacher had found it. They thought Steve rather than Heather had done it. When he got home Mum tied him to the base of a toilet and whipped him.

She never took pity on us if we cried as she beat us. In fact, she'd yell at us to stop. 'Switch those fucking waterworks off now or you'll get another one,' she'd scream.

So we learned to fight back the tears – at least until she'd gone and we were alone and could let them out. Sometimes I used to go to the bathroom after she'd beaten me, find some baby powder and pat it around my reddened eyes so she wouldn't suspect I'd been crying.

Because of that, even into my adult life, I've found it hard to cry. I sometimes think that's why, when all the crimes came out in 1994, and in the weeks and months afterwards, I couldn't give way to self-pity or tears. I'd had years of learning how to numb my feelings and never feel sorry for myself.

While we were still young children, I never thought about the reasons for Mum's frequent violence towards us, but as I got older I did begin to feel that we children might not have been the only cause of her anger. I knew that our behaviour was often the trigger for it, and sometimes we could be genuinely naughty rather than just irritating, but I could also tell she had other things on her mind. Things that were really troubling her.

I had no real idea what those things might be so I assumed it was to do with her other life upstairs in the part of the house where we hardly ever went. Different possibilities ran through my head. Could it have to do with the men who called? Or could it have been to do with the lodgers?

I don't remember Mum talking about the lodgers to us kids much but I do remember Mum telling me that Shirley Robinson – the one I can vaguely remember – had suddenly moved out.

I hardly knew Shirley, beyond exchanging a few words with her now and again but I was curious.

'Gone where?'

'I dunno, Mae. Just upped and offed.'

'Why?'

'I've no idea. She's just gone and that's that. Sometimes they're like that these young girls – they clear off without so much as a by-your-leave and you never know why.'

We'd do the clear-up when the lodgers left. Scrubbing the rooms clean.

Mum didn't say any more about it. But she'd obviously felt the need to mention Shirley's sudden absence from the house

72

to me – perhaps because she thought I would have noticed it. To an older child that might have been a clue about what had happened, but at that age I didn't have more than a faint inkling that Mum's anger and turmoil was anything to do with Shirley – or any of the other young women who passed through the house for that matter.

When I found out that Shirley had been pregnant with Dad's child when she disappeared and that she and Mum had been rivals for Dad's affection (Mum by then being pregnant with Louise), it all made sense. It wasn't just Shirley, of course, who suffered. After Mum and Dad were arrested I learned of the similar complicated sexual relationships they had with several other women who'd lodged with us over the years before apparently moving on, and the devastating truth: that my parents had sexually assaulted them and then buried them in the house and garden. I discovered that, unbeknown to us, Mum and Dad would go out in the van to lure other young women – some complete strangers – back to the house to experience a similar fate.

Could that be why Mum was violent towards me and my siblings? Because of the guilt about the nightmare going on behind closed doors at our house? Was the violence spilling over from those terrible occurrences onto us? Or was it just in her nature? To be violent to everyone and everything around her?

As it was, when I was little, I had no idea about why Mum treated us as she did. It didn't even occur to me to ask Anne Marie, who was much older and might have been able to explain at least some of it. And I realise now that she would probably have found it impossible to pass on what secrets she did know because I would have found them terrifying.

Whatever was troubling Anne Marie so badly was also largely a mystery to me until that day at the swimming pool, but I often wished I understood. I remember asking Mum and Dad once or twice why she was so unhappy, but they always had a glib answer.

'Anne Marie's like that sometimes. Just ignore her,' Mum might say.

'Women's troubles probably,' Dad would add, or, 'She's just in one of her moods. I wouldn't take any notice if I were you.'

I remember once when Anne Marie was in floods of tears at the breakfast table, I asked her why and, when she wouldn't answer, Dad said, 'It's because Elvis has died.'

I knew Anne Marie loved Elvis. I used to hear her playing his records in her room, and she had posters of him on the wall – so I believed him. I never questioned that there was more to it, or that him and Mum were the cause.

Five months after Shirley 'left', my sister Louise was born. I watched Mum feed and care for her as she had done Tara, and once again I helped her as much as I could. Mum involved me more and more with the routine tasks of baby care and despite the other complications in our relationship I never resented for a moment being her assistant.

Although she now had two infants to look after, she carried on being a mother of sorts to us older children. Despite her emotional and physical violence towards us, she did look after us well in certain practical ways. She made sure we were properly fed. We were regularly bathed and well-scrubbed and our clothes were always clean even if they were often hand-me-downs. She took particular care to make sure we were well turned out for school.

'Have you washed your hands, Mae?!'

'Yes, Mum.'

'Well do it again – I can see dirt behind your fingernails!'

74

'Brush that hair, it's in a terrible state!', 'Straighten your collar – what will people think?' 'I told you to clean those shoes!'

I used to think it was simply a matter of pride for her – that she didn't want to be seen as a bad mother. Now it seems more likely it was because she didn't want the school, or anyone else for that matter, to ask any awkward questions about how we were being brought up at home. She was doing her best to make sure there was nothing about her children which might arouse suspicion. She'd always walk us to school in the mornings, making sure we got there on time, and be there at the school gates waiting when school was over for the day. If our teachers ever found our behaviour odd they never showed it to us, never asked the kind of questions which I hope might be asked today in school when children come across as withdrawn and troubled. Sometimes I'd sit there in class, hoping a teacher might ask me what was wrong but they never did. And the truth is that even if they had asked questions I probably would have said nothing. I knew Mum and Dad wouldn't have wanted me to invite any curiosity towards the family. There was always a threat, largely unspoken but sometimes quite explicit, that if any one of us children complained about any aspect of our home life to anyone – by reporting a beating, for example – we might be taken into care and the family would break up as a result. However bad things were at home, no child ever wants that.

Yet it still beggars belief that the authorities never questioned what was going on in our house. Why didn't the school notice Heather's poor attendance record (before she disappeared)? Why didn't hospitals alert social services about the various injuries – cuts and bruises – which our parents had to take us in to have treated? Many of these injuries had an innocent explanation – the result of falling off a slide or bike or accidentally treading on broken glass – the kind of thing that happens to any normal growing child. But other injuries should have aroused suspicion and I later learned that there were over thirty occasions when Mum and Dad's children were taken to A&E and it seems extraordinary that this didn't arouse suspicion. And social services certainly received some information about the family which should have raised concerns, including anonymous tip-offs – but they didn't react until it was far too late.

In spite of my unhappiness at home, I worked hard at school – even though Mum and Dad never gave us any encouragement. They didn't even read to us when we were small and, when we were in primary school, we were told that our speech was all wrong and grammatically incorrect – as Dad's was. Nearly all of us had to go to speech therapists to have his old country ways ironed out. It made me feel second class to everyone else, but I still tried to make progress. I liked Maths, Art and English, and was a good student, but there was no support from home. Dad could scarcely read and write and Mum – intelligent and articulate woman that she later proved herself to be – also thought school a waste of time. Homework was something we had to do completely under our own initiative and had to be squeezed in between the many household chores we were given as we got older.

Despite this, I did the best I could and was always anxious to show how seriously I took my schoolwork. If I made a single spelling mistake I'd write the whole page out afresh rather than cross it out, and I even used to iron the pages of my books so they looked as presentable as possible. I tried hard and was a well-behaved and obedient pupil – not surprisingly when I think of the fear of authority Mum had instilled in me. I was rarely told off. I only remember it happening once when a teacher heard me swearing and dragged me to the toilets, filled my mouth with horrible-tasting soap from a dispenser and made me wash it out. It's a wonder that didn't happen more, when I think of the filth that came out of my parents' mouths. I hated getting into trouble then and have done all my life.

Art was my favourite and best subject. I was told I had some talent and my daughter, Amy, certainly does. I would have loved to pursue it further at sixth form and maybe at art college or university, but I always knew Mum and Dad would insist on me leaving school as soon as I was sixteen and wasn't legally required to attend. After that, their expectations of me didn't go beyond getting any old job or having babies. I ended up leaving shool with five O-levels. I was quietly pleased with myself for doing this. Even at a young age, I had ambitions for making a better life for myself than anything they envisaged for me.

I can't say I actually enjoyed school, but it was a relief at least to get away from the house – which often felt like a prison. I had a 100 per cent attendance record throughout my schooldays. Even in winter, when there was rain, sleet or snow, I still wanted to go. I wouldn't have taken a day off if I'd been dying. However unpleasant school could be, it was still much better than being at home.

What I liked most, though, was the journey to and from school. Even though Mum was with us it still gave me a wonderful sense of freedom. The walk to my primary school took us across the big park at the end of Cromwell Street. It was a place I grew to love. As we got older we'd sometimes be allowed out there to ride our bikes or just run around and play. The feeling of having escaped from home, even temporarily, was such a relief.

I used to feel the same thing even more strongly when I was older, walking back and forth to my secondary school in Hucclecote. It was a long walk – thirty or forty minutes – and Mum used to give us the bus fare but, much to her annoyance if she found out, we'd usually save it and go on foot. I would dawdle as much as I could, often with Heather. It was a way of stretching the precious time of freedom from both home and school. It was when I was happiest.

I didn't like school because I was shy and found it hard to socialise. I was never 'popular' and usually the last to get picked for team games in PE. It didn't help that Mum made me (and Heather too) wear second-hand clothes and boys' shoes – which she said were better because they were more hard-wearing. She didn't care that it made us feel odd and never part of the group. And when we were older and even more vulnerable to peer pressure, she was just as insensitive, making us wash our hair with washing-up liquid, not letting us shave our legs or use deodorant. At that age kids can be so cruel, and I can remember being bullied for that – they'd go past and sing the Rightguard advert at me: 'arms up if you use Rightguard.' Even now thinking about that is painful. And Mum always kept our hair short, so we looked like boys. She said it was easier to look after and helped prevent us picking up head lice, but we got bullied for that too.

As the family grew larger there were often remarks about how many of us children there were from the other schoolkids. People would say things like: 'Are you a Catholic?' I didn't understand why at first. Or, 'Haven't you got a telly in your house?'

''Course we have!' I'd answer before I eventually realised they were suggesting my parents were always at it because there was no other entertainment available.

Occasionally, when I was older, Dad would drop us off at school, which I found excruciatingly embarrassing. At one stage, he had a rusty white ex-security van with a big hatch at the back for the money. It was a terrible eyesore. He'd sometimes offer lifts home to my friends and if they were girls, he'd try to touch them up as they got in and out. Or he'd stop the van during the journey, get out and pee against the wheel.

When Steve was old enough, he went to the same school as Heather and me. The three of us tried to stick together as much as we could, but being in different years it wasn't always possible. I was a year below Heather and so often had the same teachers she'd had the year before. Because I looked like her, and even wore the same clothes after she'd grown out of them, they'd often call me Heather, mistaking me for her. I didn't have the confidence to correct them.

This happened at primary and then later at secondary school – which I found especially hard after Heather went missing. It was as if she'd been irrelevant to them – they'd never even bothered to get to know her, and it was a painful reminder that, for reasons I didn't yet understand, my sister had suddenly disappeared and was no longer a part of our family.

As I grew older, I became more and more aware that our family wasn't normal, which is why I find it hard when people suggest, as some who have written about our family have, that it can't have been that bad for me and my siblings because our parents were abusers and we hadn't really known any other life. Even at the age of six or seven, I knew there was nothing normal about sexually abusing a child or about the frequent beatings we received. We had TV, we saw how the parents of our school friends treated them, we walked down roads with the rest of the world – I knew right from wrong. Carrying that feeling around constantly, that your home life wasn't right, that it was different to everyone else's, was horrible.

And just as it was futile expecting our teachers to suspect something was wrong at home, there was no point hoping the neighbours would notice either. There was a rapid turnover of residents in the various houses, bedsits and flats in our street. Most people only lived there for short periods of time before moving on, and few of them had any idea who their next-door neighbours were, let alone who else was living on the same street. If anyone heard cries and screams coming from the house when Mum set about us, they never did anything about it. And when they saw Mum shouting at us as we walked down the street or across the park – which they must have done – they probably just thought, 'There goes the mad cow who yells at her children.' Who would be able to tell the truth from that small shapshot? Who wants to jump to those sorts of conclusions about people on their street? Who even imagines that those things *can* happen, let alone that they are happening?

We always knew no one would ever come to rescue us. Mum and Dad must have known it too.

Soon after Shirley Robinson disappeared Mum's father, Bill Letts, died. I didn't find out how complicated Mum and Bill's relationship was until I was grown-up and Mum let slip that he had sexually abused her from an early age, so her feelings about his death must have been mixed to say the least. Despite the fact that Dad had formed that bizarre friendship with Bill in recent years, he refused to go with Mum to the funeral. I remember them arguing about it, but he wouldn't give in so she went alone.

I don't believe Dad ever felt grief for anyone. When he received the phone call telling him his own father had died, he put the receiver down and told all the family cheerfully: 'I'm an orphan now!' So there were never likely to be tears over Bill's death. This became even clearer when, a few weeks later, he got hold of some of Bill's clothes. He never cared where his clothes came from as long as he didn't have to pay for them. He slipped on one of Bill's cardigans and then, to his even greater delight, a pair of his shoes.

'Look, I'm wearing dead men's shoes!' he said and danced around the kitchen in them. 'Waste not, want not!'

It was one of Dad's favourite sayings.

He wasn't the only one to dress in clothing that had belonged to someone who had died. At the trial it emerged that the worried parents of Lynda Gough, one of the victims, had called round to ask if Mum and Dad had seen her because she'd gone missing and they'd heard a rumour she might have lodged with us for a while. Mum answered the door. She told them she didn't know anyone by the name of Lynda Gough. But as they were leaving the parents noticed Mum was wearing a cardigan that looked like one of Lynda's. Lynda's mother remarked on it and asked Mum if she was absolutely certain Lynda had never stayed there. 'Positive,' Mum told them. The worried couple didn't challenge her any further, and went on their way, puzzled but unsuspecting.

There was a cupboard on one of the upper floors at Cromwell Street which Steve, Heather and I discovered around that time, when I must have been about eight. It was full of women's clothes and shoes. We used to dress up and play around in them. It was fun and – if she was in a good mood – Mum didn't seem to mind. She didn't usually let us wear girly clothes and there was a skirt in there that I loved; it was a bit big for me so I'd roll it up and wear it when we weren't playing, to feel smarter; fashionable for a change. Only much later did I realise that they were the clothes of young women who had been murdered in the house which Mum and Dad had decided to keep.

'Waste not, want not.'

It makes my skin feel itchy when I think about it now; I find it impossible to know what Mum can have been thinking when she saw us doing it.

I don't really believe in ghosts but there were times when Heather and I were in the bathroom – which was in an extension Dad had built – when we sensed some kind of other presence with us. There was a feeling of coldness in the air which we couldn't understand. Most of the time we used to put it down to the fact that Dad hadn't built it properly so it was cold and damp, but there were occasions when it really did feel like some-one else was with us. Long afterwards I discovered that one of the victims was buried under there.

It was around that time that the first of us managed to escape. At three in the morning, having planned it very carefully, Anne Marie got up and, taking a small bag of belongings, crept down the stairs, walked out through the front door and ran away. She was sixteen and had no plan for what she might do after she left other than take her chances on the streets of Gloucester or find a friend who'd give her somewhere to stay. Later the same day, Mum and Dad went up to her room, took down her Elvis posters, stripped it clear of all her belongings and clothes and threw them out.

'Anne Marie's gone,' Dad said.

'Where's she gone?'

'We haven't got a fucking clue, Mae!' said Mum. 'And don't ask us again!'

She was Dad's oldest surviving child, and Mum had known her since she was a little girl, and yet neither of them seemed to care one jot where she'd gone. Even for them, I couldn't under-stand how they could be so cold.

It seemed like the end of something, though I had no idea what. And I had no clue that in the first eight years of my life – between us moving into Cromwell Street in 1972 and Anne

Marie leaving – as many as eight young women had been sexually assaulted, tortured and buried under the floor or outside in the garden.

I know that Anne Marie believes to this day that if she hadn't got out when she did she would have suffered the same fate.

Chapter Six

Family

Today there was more about Dad in her letter. She calls him 'West'
– why does she do that? Who does she think she's kidding? She says
it's because he turned her into a prostitute that the police ignored her
calls for help. I don't know whether to believe her when she says she
never gave up trying to tell people about the abuse. She says because
she left us children for hours while she was out earning money for sex,
the police viewed her as a pervert, someone who didn't deserve to keep
her kids. What gets me is that us kids just saw her as a mother. She
was just our mum. . .

<u>HM PRISON DURHAM</u>

When I tried to approach the subject of abuse and
West etc. they didn't <u>want</u> to listen. Instead they
see fit to threaten me and say that I would lose
my kids . . . We were trash - my siblings and I were
and hence myself and my children were!!! . . . To them
people like us are expendable . . . hence they have no
qualms at using me as a 'scape goat!!!'

Just as I had no idea that the killing had started in the house
where I was growing up, I had no idea that it had come to an

end – but that's what happened. Eight years would pass before there was another murder – the one that left me with a grief that has lasted for the whole of my life: that of my sister Heather.

Of course, there might have been other murders that took place away from the house, the victims buried in the fields around Much Marcle or elsewhere. I've read that some experts on serial killers claim it's unusual for them to stop killing for prolonged periods. But no evidence has ever been found during those eight years to link any other murders to my parents.

Some people have suggested that the murders coming to an end was connected to the fact that Mum and Dad stopped taking in lodgers. New gas, electricity and fire-safety regulations were brought in for buildings containing bedsits. If they'd wanted to keep renting out rooms, Dad would have had to carry out further renovations to the house. These would have been expensive and might well have resulted in inspections by the authorities, which they would have wanted to avoid. The house by that time was full of terrible secrets.

There were probably other reasons they wanted to bring that chapter of their life in 25 Cromwell Street to a close, too. Perhaps they felt it was too risky to carry on, or maybe they'd simply become exhausted by their complicated and horrific emotional entanglements with the young women. They might even have been worried that, because Heather, Steve and I were getting older and understanding more about the world, we might have become suspicious about what was going on under our noses and told someone.

So the life of our house went on: as strange and abusive as ever but with at least an essence of normality, with family outings to the countryside or even the seaside. Mum would still fly off the handle, but there was laughter, too. Dad was particularly fond of clowning around. He called himself 'Teddy' and sang stupid songs. One of them began, 'I'm a little wanker!' He'd be in his overalls with change jingling in his pockets as he jigged around the room. He would have us in stitches.

He went through another daft stage when he would pretend to be what he called a 'holy man'. Whenever he saw you he'd say: 'Bless you, my child,' and make the sign of the cross.

There was a laundry room next to the kitchen with three washing machines Dad had nicked from somewhere. One day I spotted him in there up on a stepladder, changing the fluorescent light tube.

'Mae, come in here a minute!'

I did as he asked.

'Now stand still.'

And he started waving the old light tube around, as if he was knighting me.

'Bless you, my child! Bless you!'

But he accidentally cracked the side of my head with the tube. It exploded, showering me with white powder. Dad jumped down from the stepladder really worried, put his arm round me and asked if I was all right. When he realised I was, we both just burst out laughing.

Mum wasn't as funny as Dad but she did have a sense of humour. Often it was just childish little jokes, something she carried with her into prison; her letters would be full of them. Jokes like:

'How do you kill a clown?'

'I dunno, Mum, how do you kill a clown?'

'Go for the juggler!'

Or:

'What's the difference between snowmen and snowwomen?'

'No idea.'

'Snowballs!'

She'd throw her head back, laughing. As often as not she found her jokes much funnier than the rest of us did. But when she was in that kind of mood I liked her. It was a glimpse of another kind of person.

When Mum was in better moods she would also exchange banter with Dad in a way that you could only describe as affectionate. We would see this most often at mealtimes. She was a brilliant cook, serving up old-fashioned meat-and-two-veg meals – but beautifully done. Occasionally she'd branch out and make more adventurous things like curry.

'I'm not eating this shit,' Dad would say when she set it down in front of him.

'It's not shit. It's lovely. Try it.'

'It's shit. Foreign shit.'

'Try it!'

'Your mother's trying to poison me with foreign shit, kids.'

She'd laugh, 'If I wanted to poison you, you old bugger, I'd have done it years ago!'

'Don't listen to her!' Dad would flash a smile at us, 'If I'm dead in the morning, you'll know who's to blame.' Mum would flick him playfully round the head with a tea towel and he'd grin. 'Bloody dragon, she is!'

Some of what we ate was freebie stuff which came from Dad's contacts: men with allotments, or who worked at the Wall's factory in Gloucester and came round with knocked-off boxes of food for him. We used to look forward to that. At one time, I remember, we had boxes and boxes of pork pie with egg running through it. We lived off it for months until we were absolutely sick of it. I've never been able to look at one since.

But though we weren't well off, we never went hungry. I remember Mum used to bake superb cakes. We'd always have a fantastic iced sponge for our birthdays and an equally lovely fruit cake laced with booze at Christmas time. She always made a real effort for special occasions and Christmas Day was the one day when we really did all feel we were like any other family.

In the lead up to it, Mum would do a massive clean-up of the house (something I still do to this day) and we'd have to help. Decorations (which Dad would nick from somewhere) would be put up. And before the big day we were given the Argos catalogue and told we could have anything out of it up to a maximum value of £10. Mum would then go out and buy what we'd chosen, wrap it up and put the presents under the Christmas tree. When I was younger I'd choose toys such as Etch A Sketch, but as I grew older I often wanted artists' materials because I was keen on drawing and painting.

Christmas Day was also the only time when you could be sure Dad would take a day off work. After dinner, we'd all gather round to watch the Queen's speech. Dad would insist on it. He'd be on the sofa with Mum, the rest of us scattered round on the other chairs or on the floor. They were both royalists.

'Remarkable woman the Queen!' Dad would say.

Mum would agree, 'I like Queenie too. Proper class she's got.'

'And she talks a lot of sense,' Dad might add.

They were traditionalists in other ways. Dad always used to vote Conservative and he'd claim Mum did the same, although later, when I was grown-up, she confided in me that she hadn't – I've no idea if it was true.

At that time Dad was employed at the Muir Hill wagon works, a company in Gloucester that made railway carriages, where he worked on the factory floor using heavy machinery to make the various components. He supplemented that wage by doing all kinds of odd building jobs, especially for his former landlord.

He'd be out of the house long hours and many days we saw little of him.

Dad was a persistent petty thief, especially of any building materials he could lay his hands on – copper pipe, timber, even bricks. It was a compulsive habit. If he could get something for nothing by any means at all then he would. At one time we had as many as seven stolen tellies in the house. He couldn't even drive past a pile of bricks without stopping to take some, and if we were in the van he'd make us kids help him. He'd take us to the builders' merchants with him and tell us to throw extra timber, or sand or flagstones, into the back of the van while he distracted the sales assistant with his banter and jokes. Likewise, he never bought us bikes. He'd simply take us to the park and look round until he saw one that was the right size and take it. Sometimes we'd do this in the local park at the end of our road, but more often we'd go to one of the parks in Cheltenham, where there was money around and it was more likely we'd be able to steal something of better quality.

I was always nervous about helping him. I knew it was wrong and I was afraid of what would happen if we were caught. Dad thought my nerves were ridiculous. It was as if he thought he was teaching me – teaching all his kids – an important lesson about how to get by in life. Mum, who was well aware he used to get us to help with his thieving, made no attempt to stop it.

But despite that, he also worked very hard. And the money he earned, including his pay packet from Muir Hill, was all handed over to Mum who – after she'd given him a little for tobacco for his roll-ups – would squirrel it away somewhere upstairs in the house. In his spare time he carried on, slowly but surely, with his massive renovations to the house. In addition to modifications to the upper part of the house he built a large rear extension.

Mum was still working as a prostitute but – maybe because

money was tighter now with there no longer being any income from lodgers – she also started various part-time jobs, including as a cleaner. That was on top of managing the house and rearing her growing brood of children – after Tara and Louise came our younger brother and two sisters in 1980, 1982 and 1983. Five children in six years. I have no memory of her telling me each time she became pregnant, just that she seemed to be in an almost permanent state of pregnancy during those years.

With the arrival of each child she passed more and more of her workload onto us older children. She taught Heather and me how to cook and sew, not because she thought we'd find them useful skills in later life, as she'd sometimes claim, but because she needed our help. She would give us all jobs to do before we left for school and there would be more when we got home. She'd never ask us politely – it would be: 'You can wash up tonight, Steve!', 'Heather, that floor needs mopping!' 'Don't forget that fucking ironing, Mae, there's a mountain of it waiting in the wash basket!'

Around the time Anne Marie left home, Mum and Dad moved us up from the basement so that we could sleep upstairs. What prompted this, and whether it was in any way connected to the fact there were bodies buried down there, it's hard to be sure, but I think it's probably likely to have been the reason. When the police began finding bodies in the basement and Dad confessed that he'd put them there, he told them he'd been worried about the smell of the bodies decomposing because of the high water table in the area. During the years we slept down there, the basement regularly flooded: we'd wake up to find brown water up to our ankles. I remember there was a chest down there, a sort of toy box, and we'd jump onto it and pretend it was a boat while we waited for Mum to come and let us out. There was always a disgusting smell that came with it, but we didn't have the faintest idea what was the cause of it. Dad's concreting work had obviously not been good enough to completely conceal what was hidden underneath.

When we were first moved from the basement to sleep, Mum and Dad put two sets of bunk beds for us at one end of the lounge in the new extension Dad had built. They put heavy brown curtains across to separate our sleeping quarters from the rest of the room. There was also a cot in our bedroom area, which the younger children slept in. This was when Dad was still working on the upper part of the house after the tenants had gone.

It seemed like a big adventure to us to be sleeping upstairs. When Mum and Dad were out of the room we used to leap across from the top of one bunk bed to the other and have pillow fights. Sometimes Mum would catch us.

'What the fuck are you up to, you little monsters?!'

Sometimes a hiding would follow, but as time went by we grew more skilful at keeping the noise down when she was within earshot, and at listening for her approach so that we could rapidly stop our games and be lying quietly in bed when she came back into the room.

During that period, after we'd been put to bed, and the curtain had been drawn across, we'd sometimes hear Mum and Dad's voices from their end of the room. Sometimes they were simply talking to each other, sometimes they might have a visitor such as Uncle John. Or it might be a complete stranger, male or female. When we were feeling really bold we'd peep through the curtains to see who was there. If they caught us doing it, Mum would roar at us to get back into bed and go to sleep.

In the years that followed we seemed to be constantly shunted around to sleep in different parts of the house. There was one period, when I was about nine or ten years old when we were put in a room on the top floor – this was before Dad had converted that part of the house into the area where Mum entertained men. It was while we were up there that Steve, Heather and I made a little village from cardboard. We stole a Stanley knife from Dad's toolbox and, using templates we'd got from somewhere, cut the cardboard shapes out before folding and gluing them to make tiny houses with a street running between them. We were thrilled with the result until we realised we'd shredded the carpet where we'd been cutting the cardboard pieces out on – and had to hide our little creation from Mum and Dad in case they realised it was us who'd done the damage.

Later still we slept on the middle floor, in Anne Marie's old room. We loved sleeping there – in that part of the house Mum and Dad seemed to be mostly out of earshot and we were left to our own devices. Our night-time activities got even more inventive. One of them involved tying our bedsheets together, attaching a bucket to one end, lowering it out of the window and trying to entice stray cats to climb inside it so that we could pull them up into our room. We did it partly for fun, but also because we often used to hear them crying and yowling at night and thought they must be hurt or hungry. It was only as adults that we realised cats make those noises at night because they are fighting over territory or mating.

We had hated to think of those cats suffering, as we'd hated to think of each other's, though as individuals we rarely felt sorry for ourselves.

Our last move was back down onto the ground floor. This happened when Dad had finally completed his work on the upper floor, creating what was effectively a self-contained flat for Mum with two bedrooms, one for her work and another which she and Dad used. On the ground floor, Steve was given a bedroom of his own which opened into the new rear extension and was linked by a short passageway to a room at the front of the house which Heather and I shared. At that stage, the younger children were moved down to sleep in the basement which had served as a bedroom for Heather, Steve and myself when we'd been little. Although that part of the house, as we later discovered, still contained its dreadful secrets, Dad had by that time carried out some cosmetic work to brighten it up.

Heather and I felt very grown-up because this was the first time we'd had a bedroom to ourselves, and – by the standards of that house anyway – it was a nice room with a carpet, fireplace and ornate wall lights. The wall lights had red bulbs in them and one night, when the main light bulb – a standard white one – went out, we replaced it with one of the red ones. We liked the effect of lying in a room bathed in rosy light, but when Dad came home from work, he burst into the room in an absolute fury.

'What the hell are you two thinking of?'

We were really scared. Dad almost never got angry with us.

'What do you mean, Dad?'

'You can see that light all the way down the bloody street. Do you want to get me sent to prison? Get that bloody bulb out now!'

We didn't understand, 'But why, Dad?'

'Don't you know what it means – a red light in a window?'

We shook our heads.

'It means there's a prostitute working inside, that's what, you idiots! Now get the damn thing out.'

By then, of course, we knew about Mum's work as a prostitute, though as young teenagers we hadn't understood that it was illegal and might attract the attention of the police – and that Dad might get into trouble as a result.

Our new bedroom had at one stage been used by Mum

– probably for prostitution – and had a small plaque on the door with 'Rose' on it before we moved into it. Dad took this down but never blocked up the hole that was left behind. This meant we could peep out into the hallway and see Mum's clients coming and going. It was through this that we watched Dad, with Mum's help, illegally bypassing the electricity meter which was by the front door, and then remove the bypass when the meter man was due.

Unfortunately it also meant that Dad could look the other way through the door and spy on us. Because of this we used to undress in the dark and were always on the alert for him entering our room. We were getting nearer to puberty by then and Dad's sexual interest in us was growing. We sensed he was getting closer to carrying out his threat – which he had been making for as long as we could remember – to 'break us in' when he thought the time was right.

We were especially careful in the early mornings. Dad was generally the first one up in the house and we'd hear him clattering down the stairs, clearing his throat – he had a terrible smoker's cough – and spitting into the kitchen sink. We knew that if he could, he'd sneak into our room before we woke up, pull the bedclothes off us and try to grope us. Sometimes we were too slow and he did manage to get to us before we were up and dressed. He'd run a hand up our legs in a leering playful kind of way – as if he was just playing a stupid dirty little game. Eventually, to prevent this, we took to sleeping fully clothed rather than in nightdresses.

We soon realised our best chance of avoiding his horrible sexual attention was by sticking together. There was no lock on the bathroom and we felt especially vulnerable when we were in there. So we always made sure one of us stood guard at the door while the other showered or used the toilet. If we heard Dad approach we'd whisper a quick warning. Sometimes whichever of us was guarding the door would try to distract him to give time for the other to dress and get out safely.

'What's she doing in there?' he'd say, his voice betraying his excitement.

'I dunno,' we'd shrug.

'Well, let's have a look shall we?' He'd try to push past and open the door but we'd block his way.

'You can't, Dad, it's private.'

'Nothing's private in this family.'

'Using the bathroom is.'

'Hark at you giving your dad lectures.'

But he wouldn't press it. He'd just and walk away, muttering, 'Soon enough, girl. You'll get to know what's what soon enough.' He'd often grin when he made those kind of remarks, as though he was just making an idle threat, but on other occasions a dark look would flash in his eyes. It was chilling and made me realise that there was a dark side to him, that he was capable of doing things I couldn't even imagine and I had to be careful not to cross a line. Heather and I both sensed that one day he might turn much nastier and we might be unable – even working together – to fend off his advances. We just had to hope for the best.

Mum made no attempt to stop him groping us and he didn't try to hide that kind of behaviour from her. I remember on one occasion, when he was sitting in front of me he began to feel my leg and run his hand up it and she came in and saw what he was doing and just flopped down on the sofa to watch television, ignoring it completely. She saw it as just normal behaviour for Dad, and seemed to expect me to see it in the same way.

And yet strangely, although all of us children suffered in different ways at our parents' hands as we grew up, we were left in no doubt that we were part of something which mattered deeply to both of them. Both of them had grown up with a strong sense that family was important and they had brought us children up to feel the same way. My siblings and I all came to believe that, however strange and distressing things might be within the four walls of our house, we needed to stick together – especially if our family came under threat from the outside world.

The desire to instil in us such a sense of family loyalty must have been partly self-preservation on Mum and Dad's part – they didn't want us to provide help or encouragement to the police or social services when they (as they eventually did) took an interest in what was going on in our house. But it was more than that. It was as if, in our parents' eyes, our family was one big extraordinary joint creation. Not for nothing did outsiders who had picked up on our sense of family unity refer to us as the Waltons.

The family was a constant theme in the interviews Dad gave to the police when he was eventually arrested in 1994. Even when it became obvious to him that he would be charged and was facing the rest of his life in prison, he was determined to do all he could to keep the family and household together – with my mum still at the centre of it – even though he would no longer be there. Although no one can ever truly know what was in Dad's mind, I think it likely that his anger about the police taking the house to pieces and digging up the garden wasn't solely about his fear that the secrets of the murders would be exposed, but was also because he was devastated that the family life he and Mum had created there – over such a long period – was being dismantled.

*

Dad always kept a close eye on current affairs and would insist on watching news programmes whenever they came on. He seemed obsessed with them, especially *News at Ten*. We all had to keep quiet and watch with him. In hindsight, I wonder if he may have done this out of a worry, somewhere at the back of his mind, that one of the bodies had been discovered. Not the ones in the house, but the others he'd buried in the fields near Much Marcle. He had no patience with soaps and drama, which, as we grew older, we used to enjoy watching in our room – a luxury most of my friends didn't have because Dad used to steal the TVs and the electricity they were plugged into. He was especially scathing about *EastEnders*, which he refused to have on, saying there was too much violence and he found it depressing.

He'd watch videos frequently, as would Mum. Some of these were ordinary mainstream films – his favourite being *Bambi*. 'Breaks my heart, it does,' he used to say. ''Specially the bit where Bambi's mother dies.'

But as we grew older, many of the videos he'd put on were pornographic. It was real hard-core stuff, probably nicked or blagged from people he knew, but some of it also featured my mum and her clients. Dad didn't make any secret of the fact he sometimes filmed her having sex. Most of it had been done secretly, through the peephole in the wall which looked into her boudoir at the top of the house. I used to find it completely repulsive. Far from feeling embarrassed, Dad used to encourage us to watch with him, but I'd find excuses to leave the room. I'd offer to make him a cup of tea and go into the kitchen, hanging around in there as long as I could in the hope that he would have finished watching before I went back. Or I'd tell him I had homework to do and go to my room for a while.

But when I went back to the lounge he'd often as not still be there in front of the telly. Dad could watch porn endlessly. Later on, when I was with my first serious boyfriend, Rob, he even made us borrow pornographic videos. He seemed to get a kick out of the idea his family might share his vile taste in porn. He had no inhibitions about it whatsoever, and nor did Mum.

We always knew about their interest in kinky sex; they never tried to hide it from us. They'd leave porn magazines lying around the house, along with bondage gear: masks, rubber suits, whips and the like. I can remember Dad making a cat-o'-nine-tails out of strips of leather he'd found from somewhere. It was typical of him to make it himself to save money. It wasn't unusual for us kids to come across dildos, vibrators and other sex toys just lying around the house. It amused Dad, more than anything, to see how we reacted. One of the dildos was so big he referred to it as his 'Exocet', or 'the Eiffel Tower', or sometimes, even more crudely, his 'c*** buster'.

Because we became aware of the strange and perverted nature of Mum and Dad's sex lives gradually from a very young age, in a sense, we were never shocked by it. There were no sudden and traumatic discoveries – which isn't to say we didn't find it troubling and frightening. We did.

I'd known about Mum's work as a prostitute for quite a long time when she started roping me into helping her with it. She'd tell me and Heather to babysit the younger kids. The doorbell would go and she'd just disappear up to her flat at the top of the house – sometimes seeing several clients over a period of hours before coming back downstairs. By the time I'd reached my early teens I had to answer the phone, taking calls from men wanting to book appointments with 'Mandy', the name she worked under.

This would often be after tea when she was upstairs with clients. I'd have to check in the special diary she used for her work and book them in. It was almost like being her secretary. I found it very difficult and embarrassing, especially when some of them went into detail about what kind of sexual services they wanted.

'Sorry, you'll have to speak to her about that,' I'd tell them, cringing. 'I'm only taking the call. Just give me your name and tell me what time you want to see her.'

We were told to be quiet while she was entertaining clients; there was a speaker in the lounge and Mum had a microphone up in her room that she'd hiss down, 'Shut up, I can hear you!' I suppose this was so as not to upset the men, but it was hard when there were eight of us, especially as the younger kids were still so little. The men had to use a separate entrance too, with a sign saying 'Mandy' which Dad had made. One time, though, Mum must have brought one of them up to her flat without shutting my bedroom door. I was sat at the table, doing my homework, and the man with her looked me up and down and said, 'Is that one available?' I was so embarrassed and Mum got angry: 'No she isn't!'.

Sometimes she'd talk to me about her clients who seemed a very sad bunch. One of them had blown a hole in his hand with a shotgun. Another had a glass eye. She said that sometimes they just want to sit and talk and they seemed to quite like her really. Most of her regulars were white old men. One of them had not slept with his wife for years. They were lonely, she said, and in need of company as much as sex. They even gave her presents: I know because anything with the initial 'M' on it came to me because she wasn't really Mandy whereas my name began with that letter. Once she gave me a gold necklace with my intital on it which I wore until I left home, something I find very strange now.

We used to wonder what the neighbours made of all the men coming and going, but they were not the nosy kind and I only ever remember one of them complaining. He'd heard the sounds of one of Mum's sessions with a client coming from an open window. He knocked on the door and tackled Dad about it. Dad sent the man away and later that day Mum and Dad went across to his house together and, as Mum put it afterwards, 'sorted him out'. As a pair they could be very threatening indeed to anyone who caused trouble, but I can well imagine it would have been Mum who took the lead in dealing with this troublesome neighbour.

Though many of Mum's clients were regulars and local to Gloucester and men who Dad knew, others came from all over after seeing the ad for 'Mandy' which Dad used to put in national contact magazines. The regulars mostly approached the house confidently, but others looked shifty and embarrassed. She made a lot of money from it, which she used to put in her bra before transferring it to a red money box. Sometimes, after a session upstairs, she'd show me the money she'd made that day.

'Look, a hundred quid,' she'd say, waving the notes at me.

'So where's my babysitting money?'

I'd only ever dare to answer in that way if I was feeling particularly bold. But there was never any question of her paying me for my help. The money she made from the work was an important part of the family finances. She told me that over the years it amounted to thousands of pounds. It certainly helped pay for the alterations to the house, including her flat at the top.

Of all the work Dad did on the house, this was the one he put most effort into. In addition to Mum's 'work' bedroom with its four-poster bed and lace drapes, and the bedroom she shared with Dad, there was a kitchen and lounge. He even built a 'Hawaiian' cocktail bar complete with desert island murals. There was also plenty of space for cupboards and drawers for sex toys and the cameras Dad used to film Mum's encounters with her punters.

They kept this upstairs flat locked. Mum used to carry the key to it on a chain around her neck, which seemed odd in some ways since she and Dad knew perfectly well that we were aware of what was going on up there. It was a secret part of their lives which wasn't really secret at all.

Occasionally we'd sneak up there, using a credit card to spring open the Yale lock and break in. We'd look around, curious but never really surprised by what we found. It just seemed sordid and horrible. We never stayed in there long, and they never caught us.

And there were even more repulsive things. Mum kept a book in which she recorded the measurements of the men she slept with and other comments on them.

Mum's activities in the flat increasingly became part of our lives downstairs. Dad wired up a baby-listening device so that he could listen in on Mum's encounters from elsewhere in the house. Sometimes he'd have the receiver switched on when he was with us. We'd be disgusted by what we heard – horrible grunts and moans – but there was no escaping it. Dad just found our discomfort funny.

Then there were the condoms Dad would find and keep after her clients left, and even a collection of knickers Mum kept from her encounters with men. These, still soaked in semen, were placed in storage jars on her mantlepiece and, when she stopped seeing the man in question, were then taken out, burnt and the ashes put in a different jar – the weirdest of momentos. It was Dad who explained this revolting process to us, always with great relish and the sordid details left in.

At her trial, Mum went to great lengths to insist that her work as a prostitute was all done under duress from Dad, that it was simply another element of the 'hell' he inflicted on her. She said the same thing to me when I was older, and again when I visited her in prison after she was convicted: that she resented being 'Mandy' and, especially as the years went by, found the work a depressing and degrading chore. There were certain clients, mates of Dad, who she claimed especially to dislike seeing. One in particular was a family friend. 'I've got to go upstairs now and do that horrible fucking man,' she'd tell me as I washed up the evening meal – although she never actually revealed who that 'friend' was.

But in other ways she seemed a more than willing participant. The entire set-up at the top of the house seemed less like something Dad forced on her and more of a joint enterprise – there was even a cushion saying 'Mum and Dad' on the sofa on which men would sit and wait to see her. And far from being in another part of the house as you might expect it to be, Mum and Dad's own bedroom was within a few feet of the one she used for entertaining clients. Above the marital bed they shared, Dad hung a metal sign he'd made with the word 'C***' written on it. It summed up how their own sex life seemed to depend on and overlap with Mum's sexual activity as a prostitute, rather than being something they kept in a separate compartment.

What is amazing to me now, looking back on it from an adult perspective, is how easily we kids came to terms with this extraordinary aspect of Mum and Dad's lives. Of course we knew that other families weren't like that, and we did our best to help conceal as much of it as we could from the outside world because – apart from anything else – it was deeply embarrassing. But in the end we just accepted that was the kind of couple they were.

Fear of the family breaking up was one of the reasons I tried not to let it bother me too much. Heather was the same. It seemed to us that if we were quiet and obedient and tried to please as much as we could, it was less likely our home would fall apart.

Occasionally we went on family holidays. One year we went to Wales, visiting the seaside and touring Snowdonia with a four-berth caravan and tent. I remember it being really fun. We all crammed into the back of Dad's van. This was always a horrible way to travel. His tools – saws and hammers – used to be hung from the side of the van and would often fall down on us. And there were no seats so we had to perch on the wheel arches or just sit on an old piece of carpet on the floor. There were no windows or proper ventilation. I remember one occasion when we all got poisoned by fumes leaking up into the van body from a faulty exhaust. We were really sick. But when we were going on holiday we generally didn't mind the discomfort. It felt like a big adventure. Sometimes Dad would even (illegally) allow us to travel in the caravan while he was towing it. We'd bounce around inside and laugh and scream with delight.

Another holiday was at a caravan park at Craven Arms in Shropshire. Mum said she loved it so much she wanted to move there. The park had a fairground next to it, but we weren't allowed to go into it because Mum and Dad said they couldn't afford it. Nonetheless, we made friends with some other kids on the site. Heather, Steve and I were in our early teens by then and it was brilliant to be away from the house and just hang out with others of our own age. It really was a proper holiday, although us older children had to sleep in the awning which was freezing, or in the back of Dad's van. The younger children slept in the caravan with Mum and Dad. This didn't stop them from having sex, though; I remember returning to the caravan late one evening to see that it was rocking because they were at it. We were with some friends we'd made on the site and I just hoped they hadn't noticed.

One of the things I loved most about being away was the feeling of being accepted by other people who didn't think there was anything odd about us. They didn't tease or mock us. To them we seemed normal, not the weird family from 25 Cromwell Street.

Most of our breaks away from home, though, were day trips. Sometimes we'd go to safari parks. Mum and Dad would never have done it if they'd had to pay for the whole family, so us children all had to hide under blankets in the back of the van so they only had to pay for themselves. Barry Island was another favourite destination. We could get there and back in a day and, because Mum would make us sandwiches and bottles of heavily watered down squash (they never bought ice creams or fish and chips or anything like that), it was also a very cheap outing.

But the place we all loved to visit most of all was the Forest of Dean. It was a place Dad knew very well. And it wasn't far. Once there, Heather, Steve and I would usually manage to get away from Mum and Dad and walk for hours on our own. We'd deliberately get lost so they couldn't find us. When eventually they did, Mum would shout at us – but we didn't care, it was worth it.

I still love the countryside, although I sometimes wonder if I haven't also developed something of a phobia about being outside. I think it comes from a fear of being recognised as a West – something that has never really left me since the crimes came to light. Even so, I love the feeling of fresh air on my skin, of being out in the hills, and feel a special connection with the Forest of Dean.

It was a connection I think Heather felt even more strongly.

She loved being there. Somehow I felt more able to deal with the horrible things that happened at home than she did, but in that special place all the terrible anxiety and misery she felt used to visibly lift from her and she seemed like her real self again. One time when we got back home, she started writing on books and on the back of her hand some letters which mystified Steve and me.

FODIWL

We used to tease her about it, thinking perhaps it involved the initials of some boy she'd taken a fancy to. In fact, it stood for this:

Forest Of Dean I Will Live.

It was her dream to do exactly that when she was finally free of the home she'd grown up in.

I can't go there or even think of the place now without remembering that longing she had to live there, or reflecting on the fact that she was never able to do so.

Chapter Seven

Heather

Mum wrote to say she loves me. That she let us all down and she knows it. She wants me to be emotional with her, to let it all out. She says if I want to stop writing to her I can; that she can handle it now she's well enough – but she says it in such a way to make me think she still needs me, as if to remind me that she hasn't been well in the past, as if to say that none of this was her fault . . .

HM PRISON DURHAM

Mae I mean this . . . I'm not a good person and I let all you children down - especially Heather. I'm not silly, I know the damage I've done and want you to be able to tell me how angry you are with me and what a useless person I was.

As Heather and I reached our mid-teens, Anne Marie came back into our lives.

She was nearly twenty by this time and had a boyfriend. From time to time they'd visit us and sit talking with Mum and Dad in the kitchen. At the time – and more so once I understood the extent to which Mum and Dad put her through hell – I couldn't understand why, having escaped from the home where she'd been so horribly abused, she would want to return. With more perspective, I think I understand it better now. Though she'd got away from Mum and Dad physically, what they had done to her had made her emotionally a prisoner; I sometimes wonder if it can't have left her with a sort of Stockholm syndrome. I feel like that's what happened to me too, eventually.

From what I saw, her conversations with Mum and Dad were perfectly friendly – I wasn't aware of any anger or friction between them over the way Anne Marie had suddenly left home. But the rest of us were discouraged from joining them, apart from just to say hello. It was clear that Mum and Dad didn't want us to have any real contact with Anne Marie; I expect because they didn't want us to have the same idea of running away. But also I wonder if they were afraid Anne Marie might alert us – Heather and me especially – to the sexual abuse she'd suffered at their hands while she had lived at home. They may well also have worried that Heather or I might let slip to Anne Marie that Dad was taking a greater sexual interest in us – maybe prompting her to intervene in some way or even report it.

As I mentioned earlier, she did manage to warn me about the abuse that might be coming our way – that day at the swimming pool, when I had told her Heather and I were so far managing to distract Dad long enough to get out of his way.

'You might not be able to do it forever,' she said.

When I asked her what she meant, she explained that Dad had raped and sexually abused her in various other ways for years and that Mum had helped him. I wasn't particularly shocked by what she said about Dad but I didn't want to believe Mum had been part of it. It was all too horrible. I didn't want to believe that the mother I'd seen be so gentle and tender with my baby siblings could do something like that, even though we'd all suffered beatings at her hands. And because I knew Anne

107

Marie disliked Mum so much I tried to tell myself she might only be saying it about her out of spite – although I didn't want to upset Anne Marie by saying so.

Heather and I had spoken of getting out as soon as we could, but legally we were still children, so we knew that if we left home before we'd finished school we would have to go on the run and hide from both the authorities and from our parents. We knew we'd have to try to stick it out at home until we were sixteen. I couldn't help feeling that, even when I reached that age, I'd worry about what would happen to my younger siblings if I left. Whether Heather felt the same way I don't know, it wasn't something we discussed. As time passed, she became more withdrawn and depressed and wanted – she *needed* to get out as soon as she could.

I also began to realise at that time – because I could see how it seemed to have worked for Anne Marie when she brought her boyfriend home to meet Mum and Dad – that this might act as some kind of protection from Dad's advances. It was a kind of signal to him that she'd moved on and was no longer vulnerable to the terrible things he'd subjected her to over the years. She was making it clear that she didn't belong to him any longer as a sexual partner – which is how, in his perverted way, he'd come to see her.

As if to reinforce this even more strongly it wasn't long after Anne Marie reappeared that she and her boyfriend married and had a baby girl. So Dad became a grandfather. He seemed pleased about it. If he had any ambition at all for any of his daughters, it was simply that we should 'breed' and have at least as many babies as he and Mum had done.

'Making babies – it's what you're for,' he'd say. 'The more the merrier!'

Meanwhile, Dad's harassment of Heather and me grew steadily

worse. His frequent comments about it being a father's right to take his daughter's virginity had seemed like a joke when we were younger, but now we were going through puberty they became much more of a threat. He might still grin or chuckle when he was coming out with them, but it was as if he wanted us to know that it was more a case of when it would happen than if.

'Only right and proper, it is. My old man did the same to my sisters.'

We'd try to pretend we weren't listening but it made no difference. He knew we were.

'You see, I made you. You're my flesh and blood. It's only right that I get to see what I made.'

He'd lunge at us at the slightest opportunity, especially if we were wearing the skirts that were part of our school uniform. We rarely said anything about it. We knew that would probably only encourage him. We simply tried to brush his wandering hands away, or dodge them altogether. It reached the stage where we did everything we could not to be in the same room as him.

But that wasn't possible all the time. At family mealtimes we were usually forced to be all together, and the fact that Mum, Steve and our younger siblings were present didn't keep him at bay one bit. He'd talk freely about the size of our tits, the hairiness of our fannies, or the colour of our pubic hair – and he always took a particular interest in whether we were having a period.

I found out later, during the police investigation, that Mum had a notebook with the dates of all our periods. Dad would try it on no matter what, so I've never worked out why they did this. Perhaps Mum was being careful, even if Dad wasn't.

Mum would generally ignore him, or maybe just laugh and

call him a filthy pig. She really didn't care that he subjected us to this. She certainly didn't discourage him.

It became exhausting having to watch out for him all the time. I could never relax. The anxiety was enormous. It seemed to eat away at me so that, even now, all these years later, when I'm taking a shower I always have one eye on the door – even though I no longer live with that kind of threat.

And having to pacify him was just as exhausting. We had to force ourselves not to complain. Even when he did the grossest things – like walking out of the toilet after he'd urinated with his penis still hanging out and threatening to push it in your ear. Apart from thinking it would encourage him, there was always another fear – that if we did show our real feelings, shout at him, or push him away too sharply, he'd just snap and go ahead and do what he wanted to do by force.

Though there wasn't much of an age difference between Heather and me we were both all too aware that she was older and would inevitably reach the age of sixteen first – by which time Dad insisted he would have gone ahead with his plan to 'break us in'. Perhaps it was on Dad's mind too because as that date drew closer he began to focus his horrible attentions more on her than on me. And as a result Heather increasingly found it harder than I did to hide her resentment of him.

Dad began to taunt her, accusing her of being a lesbian, or 'lemon' as he put it. If she showed any kind of distress at this he'd become even nastier and more threatening.

'In a mood are we today, miss?'

'She's all right, Dad,' I'd say. 'Just leave her alone.'

'Leave her alone? Heather don't want leaving alone. She wants a bloody good sorting out by a man that knows what's what, that's what she wants.'

Heather slowly became worn out and depressed by this. She

retreated into herself more and more. She and I had spent so much time together growing up, but now she often wanted to be alone. She hardly ever laughed or smiled. She began to get into trouble at school, refusing to cooperate, smoking. And on one occasion, she even kicked a teacher.

Sometimes she used to just sit on a chair, rocking back and forth. It really upset and worried me.

'Are you all right, Heather?'

'What?' She'd be hardly aware she was doing it.

'You're doing that thing?'

'What thing?'

'Rocking. Are you okay?'

She'd shrug, 'Yeah, I'm okay.'

But she'd soon fall silent and the rocking would start up again.

I hated it. It really scared me. I used to wish she'd talk to me, but, although we were close, there were some things that we didn't tell one another. I never did tell her about Uncle John, and I sensed she also had secrets she was keeping from me.

In later years, I've asked myself whether one of these might be that Dad had gone ahead and raped her. The police certainly suggested as much when they arrested Dad. I'm still not sure. I spent so much time with her I'd like to think I would have known if that was happening, but then again I can see that her behaviour was typical of a victim of sexual abuse. Whatever the truth of that, there was no doubt that, by one means or another, Dad wore her down into a state of deep anxiety and depression. I did my best to help her but, in the end, I failed.

In the summer of 1987, when Heather finally did turn sixteen and left school, Mum and Dad began to nag her about getting a job.

'Time you started paying your way, girl,' Dad said.

'Your dad's right,' said Mum. 'You can't expect us to keep you any longer.'

Heather looked around for work and eventually lined up a job as a cleaner at a holiday camp in Torquay. She brightened up at the thought of it, she was more like her old self than I'd seen her in ages. Apart from anything else it meant that she would be leaving home – for the holiday season at least. She kept telling me she was really looking forward to it.

And yet, as the day of her leaving home drew closer, she became troubled and uncommunicative again. I wanted to ask her what was wrong because she'd been so happy about the thought of leaving, but I somehow couldn't bring myself to do it. I suspected it might be something to do with Mum and Dad, but knew she didn't want to talk about it and I was scared of stirring things up inside her. I just wanted her to be away and free.

Two days before she was due to set off, there was a party at Anne Marie's house – it was her daughter's third birthday. We all went. Heather was in a particularly bad mood, refusing to talk to people or pose for family photographs. I had no idea why. Some of the mothers of other children at the party complained to Anne Marie about her behaviour – claiming she'd been swearing. Anne Marie told Mum and Dad about it and Heather found out she'd done it and turned on Anne Marie, telling her she'd never ever speak to her again.

Then, the day before she was meant to set off for the holiday camp, her job fell through. I went to find her. She was in bed, very upset.

'It'll be all right, Heather,' I said. 'You can get another job.'

She didn't answer me. She didn't want to talk. She cried throughout the night. I'd seen her upset before but never so distressed. I felt so helpless, not being able to make her feel better.

By the following morning she'd stopped crying and just

seemed depressed and in her own world. I don't remember the last words we exchanged before I left for school, something that still makes me feel really upset, only the clothes she was wearing – black trousers and a bright pink and white tee-shirt with the word 'SPIKE' written across it. It was an outfit she'd worn for the school play.

It was a rainy, gloomy day, and I found it hard to concentrate at school, as if I knew something bad was in the air. When Steve and I got home there was no sign of Heather. Mum was very quiet and Dad – who should have been off doing a building job somewhere – said he'd had to spend the day at home because the weather had been so wet.

'Your sister's gone,' he told us casually. In fact, I'd go so far as to say he was cheerful.

'Gone where?' we asked.

'The job at the holiday camp. She had a call to say it was back on. So she went.'

'Well, that's great, isn't it?' I said, looking at Mum.

But she didn't answer. It was obvious she didn't want to talk about it.

I went to the room I shared with Heather. Steve came with me. All of her belongings had gone. It was a shock. I hadn't imagined she'd need to take everything with her.

Shortly afterwards, Dad came and found us.

'Your mother's upset about Heather going.'

We told him we could see that.

He went into more detail: 'See, what happened was, this lady at the holiday camp rang to say the job was back on and they wanted Heather to start straight away. Well, it was a bit of a shock to be honest – because your mum thought she was staying. But Heather was pleased. So we both said: "Well, fair enough, good luck to you, girl." So she just packed up her things in a hurry. We gave her some cash and off she went. This girl come to collect her. In a red mini, she was. I dunno who she was. Must have been a friend or something.'

It didn't sound like the whole truth, but then nothing Dad said ever did and we had no reason to doubt the story was basically true. I was sorry I hadn't had chance to say goodbye to her, but she'd been so sad about not getting the job that I was pleased for her that it had worked out; I accepted it, and had no reason to think I wouldn't see her again.

But in the days afterwards Mum continued to be quiet and withdrawn. She hardly spoke. I remember going upstairs and finding her in bed crying. It was very unusual. I don't think I'd ever seen her cry before.

'What's the matter, Mum?'

'Nothing.'

'Is it Heather?'

'Mind your own fucking business!'

Despite her anger, I knew I was right – that she was upset about Heather. I felt sorry for her. I don't know how to feel about that looking back, knowing what I know now. Was it sadness? Was it guilt? Was it *real*?

In the weeks that followed I expected Heather to write to me and let me know how she was getting on, but no letter came. I spoke to Dad about it.

'She's probably a bit busy what with starting a new job and all. I expect she'll be in touch before long.'

Not many days later the telephone rang at around ten in the evening. I answered the phone. There was the sound of a drunken female voice at the other end of the line. I couldn't understand what she was saying. It didn't really sound like Heather to me but before I knew it Mum had snatched the phone off me and began speaking into it.

'Hello. Who's this? . . . Heather . . . how are you?'

There was a pause and then Mum seemed to get angry. 'Don't speak to me like that!'

There was another pause before Mum replied again in similar terms. Then she offered the phone to Dad.

'You reason with her, I can't.'

Dad took the phone and began speaking:

'Come on, Heather. Don't speak to your mother like that. Show a bit of respect. She brought you up, didn't she? She don't deserve that.'

And so it went on for a few more exchanges until Dad put the phone down, claiming he'd calmed Heather down.

'Well, at least we know she's all right now, don't we?'

Steve and I had no real reason to doubt that they really had been speaking to Heather – why would they make it up?

The phone rang again a few days later. This time Dad answered. We heard him ask Heather if she was all right and they chatted for a bit before Dad put Mum on the phone. She and Heather appeared to have a friendlier conversation before Mum ended the call and told us that Heather was fine and that she'd either write soon or come home for a visit. Again it seemed pretty convincing.

I continued to wait for the letter from Heather that I felt sure would come. I was suspicious that Dad might have been finding the post first and destroying her letters so that I wouldn't find out from Heather the real reason for her suddenly leaving home, so I used to look out for the postman and try to get hold of the mail before him.

Weeks and months passed. Still there was no letter. Something began to feel very wrong but I couldn't put my finger on what. Steve and I used to talk about it from time to time. We became convinced that the story of her suddenly hearing the holiday camp job was back on and being driven away by a friend was made up and it was much more likely Heather had rowed with Mum and Dad and run away.

Without telling them, we went out into the streets of Gloucester looking for her. We even called at the Salvation Army office – which was in the city centre quite close to our house – to report her as missing and ask if they had any news or information about her. They were kind to us but nothing ever came of it.

Dad continued to claim that Heather was occasionally in touch with him. He'd be sitting down at dinner and just casually say:

'Oh, by the way, I bumped into Heather the other day.'

My heart would thump in anticipation. 'Where?'

'Just in the city. Only for a minute, like. She didn't say much but she seemed all right.'

Steve and I would exchange glances. 'Why didn't she come and see us if she was in Gloucester?'

'She had to get back.'

'Back where? Is she still at the holiday camp?'

'Probably. She didn't say.'

We'd push for more information. '*Why* was she back in Gloucester?'

'She didn't say that either.' He was always so casual about it. 'Anyway, she's all right, that's the main thing.'

On other occasions he'd come out with more complicated reasons why she wouldn't want to have contact with the family any longer. He'd say he'd heard rumours that she'd become a lesbian or a prostitute or got involved with drugs. None of it seemed believable and I made it clear the suggestions upset me, but eventually I got tired of challenging him about it.

We reached the stage where we simply stopped believing him.

Mum's explanations and excuses weren't much better. Mostly she didn't want to talk about Heather but sometimes we pressed her. We asked her why she never wrote to Heather, or had letters from her, or ever tried to visit her. Mum just said that she didn't think Heather wanted to see her and, that being so, we should all leave her alone unless and until she changed her mind.

But my worries and uncertainty about her grew. Along with Steve and the younger kids, I couldn't believe Heather would simply abandon us. We felt sure she'd know we would be worrying about her and want to reassure us. We did everything we could, even writing to Cilla Black, who at that time was doing the *Surprise Surprise* show which reunited family members who'd been apart for some time. We heard nothing back. We contacted another show called *Missing*, which tried to locate missing people, but had no reply from them either.

Eventually we told Dad that we were going to the police to report her as missing. I still remember the dark look that crossed his face.

'You better not do that.'

'Why? It's been months. We're worried.'

'Yeah, but I've heard more rumours about her. Not just drugs. Someone told me she was involved in some kind of credit card fraud. You tell the police she's missing and they'll start poking their noses into all that. You could get her into real trouble. You definitely don't want to go bringing the police into this.'

'But we're worried about her.'

'You see, I don't think you need to be. She's a big girl now. She can look after herself. And I bet you any money one of these days she'll come sailing back into this house happy as Larry.'

We didn't believe him, but we didn't want to get Heather into trouble if he really was telling the truth, so we left it. After that it really seemed as if there was nothing more we could do.

And so Heather's name was mentioned less and less in the house until it was never mentioned at all. Where once we had a sister we loved, now there was just absence and silence. It was deeply depressing.

I didn't have the slightest inkling that she might no longer be alive – and neither did my brothers and sisters. Although I was in my mid-teens by then, I'd still go out into the back garden and play about with the younger children. They had a slide, a swing and a Wendy house out there. Dad was always fiddling about out there, moving things around, laying concrete, making paths, putting down paving stones. He said he didn't want his plans for the garden interfering with. It was no wonder. His garden was a graveyard and for years we children unknowingly played on the graves. It gives me chills now knowing one of them was Heather's. Close to it, Dad had Steve dig a small pond and, in the summer, Mum and Dad would sit outside, enjoying the sound of the small fountain and watching the fish.

Both Mum and Dad changed quite noticeably after Heather disappeared. Mum kept to herself, and, although still angry at times, she was much less prone to violence. She never hit me again, but I know now that the violence continued with the younger children. I ought to have been relieved by this change, and I certainly wasn't sorry that the beatings had stopped, but it worried me too. Her mood was often dark and troubled – and I now think she was in quite a deep depression. In a way it felt just as threatening as her violence.

The biggest change, though, was in Dad. He became much quieter and less extrovert. There were times when he actually seemed to want to be kind and considerate to us. It was as if he'd somehow lost confidence in the person he was. He still occasionally attempted to grope me, but he was nothing like as persistent and determined as he used to be, even though

Heather was no longer there to look out for me and I was much more vulnerable to his approaches.

The elaborate lengths Mum and Dad went to in order to persuade us (and the few neighbours who happened to enquire after her) that Heather had left home were all designed to conceal one thing: that Dad had sexually assaulted and brutally murdered her with Mum's knowledge and, as it later became clear, probably with her assistance.

It was a terrible deception, to delude us into believing she was still alive when in reality her body had been buried in the garden where we used to play. But what they did to us can't begin to compare with the suffering of Heather. I can hardly bring myself to set down the words that follow, but it's the only way of conveying something of the horror of what happened and the two-faced nature of our parents. When Dad eventually confessed to the murder in an interview room at Gloucester police station his words were recorded. The recording was played at the trial along with other interviews. Later on, transcripts were published. This is what he said:

Right, what happened was Heather wanted to leave home, you see. She'd been knocking about with this girl with a red mini. I mean a mini-skirt, not a Mini car. We were pretty sure she was a lesbian, like. And we – me and Rose – said: 'Hang on a sec, you better think about this, girl. Give it the night, at least.' Well we talked it over most of the night, then she went to bed with Mae. She sleeps in Mae's room, see. So next morning, comes up, and she looked real rough. She been crying. So Rose says: 'Let her go.' She says: 'I'll go and draw £600 from the bank and she can have that and go.' So Rose goes off, and I'm left with Heather, in the hall with her suitcase, and she's standing there, hands on hips – you know, the big lady, like, and I says: 'How about getting a flat up the road? – then you can have girl-friends up there'. And she says: 'If you don't let me fuckin' go, I'll give all the kids acid' – she meant LSD like – 'and they'll all jump off the church roof and kill theirselves.' And I says: 'That's not nice, girl, threatening to do that to your own brother and sisters.' And she had a smile on her face, a sort of smirk – like: 'try me and I'll do it'. So I lunged at her, and grabbed her round the throat like that and I held her for, I don't know how long. You know it's surprising how long you can hold someone round the neck before you, er . . . I can't even remember to that extent what happened but the next minute she's gone blue. I looked at her from head to foot – I mean what the heck had gone wrong? I put her on the floor, tried blowing into her mouth, pumped on her chest, but she kept on going bluer. I didn't know what to do. I hadn't meant to hurt her, and Rose was due back any minute. I thought: Jeez, I've got to do something. I was scared. I looked round everywhere to try and find a knife or sommat. I mean I looked at the axe, a chop axe, a chopper, there was no way I could touch her with it. I just couldn't do it. So I looked up and see this knife sticking out. It's got like two prongs on the end, two sharp points, they got serrated edges you could saw ice with. And I got that and I tried it with the big ones first and it was terrible, mate. I was sweating. So I finally managed to take her head off then her legs. That was . . . unbearable. I can hear that in my sleep now. Then she's looking at me. If someone's looking at you you're not gonna use a knife on a person are you. And I just went like that and closed her eyes and they stayed shut and that was that. Then I thought I'd put her in the dustbin, but I couldn't get her in there. So I got the ice saw and cut her legs off – I'm telling you I lived that a thousand times since. So I finally managed to do it, to take her head off and then her legs. I mean that was . . . unbearable. I can hear that in my sleep now. I wake up very often screaming and I can hear the echoing. Then I put her in the bin, rolled it down the garden behind the Wendy house. I took her suitcase of clothes out and stuck it out behind the vet's on St Michael's Square, where everyone chucks their rubbish. Came back and Rose came in. She says: 'Oh didn't you persuade Heather to stay?' I says: 'No.' She says: 'Well, how come her trainers are still here?' And I'd forgot Heather had no shoes on. I says: 'She's gone in her shoes.' Rose says: 'Oh, all right.' Later I sent Rose out to spend the night with that coloured bloke she used to go with – 'You can make a few quid there,' I says. When she was out I went and got Heather out from behind the Wendy house and buried her . . . And I been meaning to come down here and get all this sorted before, but I never got round to it.

I don't believe half of his account of their row with. For a start, the police told me they believed she'd probably been murdered because Dad attempted to rape her and she resisted. And when Dad initially confessed to Heather's murder, he was at great pains to suggest Mum wasn't present, nor had any idea about what happened, yet later he claimed Mum had killed her and he had only confessed to protect her.

For a long time I tried to avoid learning the details about what happened. Dad's version above – however untrue – gives me nightmares; all the versions describe Heather's murder as being utterly horrific. There was never any doubt that Dad took the lead in it, and Mum was eventually convicted of the crime too. Despite her denials in court, it seemed to the jury that it was impossible she could have been out of the house for long enough for Dad to struggle with, strangle, dismember and bury Heather in the garden without her knowledge. Even if she hadn't physically assisted Dad, she must have colluded with him.

They were terrible in so many ways, but to do that to your daughter . . . No wonder he and Mum were quiet when we got home the day she was murdered. And no wonder they seemed like different people afterwards.

During the years of her imprisonment, when I was still trying to work out the truth about Heather, Mum gave me to understand that she'd made a kind of pact with Dad – that she would turn a blind eye to the terrible things he was doing to other young women in return for him leaving their own kids alone. But if that was true then surely the pact was broken when Heather was murdered? Even if Mum hadn't been directly involved, she can't possibly have believed his cock-and-bull story about how Heather came to run away. She must have known what he'd done to her – so why didn't she run then, taking the rest of us kids with her? Surely staying with him would have put the rest of us at risk of the same thing happening?

I have sometimes wondered whether Heather's murder some-how saved me. Did the trauma and horror of her death have such an effect on Mum and Dad that it was impossible for them to think of doing the same thing to another of their children? It may well have been so. It's a thought that hasn't made my life any easier. At times I've felt so guilty about being the one that survived, and that her death may have prevented mine. It's another part of the legacy my parents have left me.

Mum has always insisted that she knew nothing about Heath-er's murder. For many years, I continued to believe her: she didn't have anyone else and, ultimately, she was my mum – I didn't want to believe those awful things could be true. During prison visits, whenever the subject of Heather came up Mum would cry. Even now I believe that those tears were genuine: the police had shown her photos of what they found in the grave

– one of them, she told me, was Heather's head in a bag. Mum never seemed to get over that and her distress would always make me feel guilty about the few times when I did doubt her innocence. And if Mum was innocent of Heather's murder, then how could I allow myself to think she was responsible for any others? I couldn't betray her like that.

When Heather's remains were finally released by the authorities, I had to arrange the funeral. At the time Mum was still on remand awaiting trial in Pucklechurch, but she gave me suggestions for the service – although most of the choices were mine. I chose a church and location I knew Heather would have loved – quiet and beautiful. The vicar was really kind and supportive even when I revealed who we were. He helped me with the arrangements and understood how important it was that the press didn't find out. I chose the casket and insisted that only Heather's first name would go on the plaque and headstone. I didn't want the name West used. To do that would have defiled her memory.

Only a few personal friends and close family members attended the funeral. It was raining lightly and the morning mist was rising over a nearby stream. The service was short but beautiful. In his eulogy, the vicar referred to Heather's young age and that she had only lived a very short life. I felt strong and thought I could get through the day. It was only when the organ started up and began to play the hymn I'd requested 'The Holly and the Ivy' – one that Heather and I loved and used to sing together around the house – that I broke down crying.

After leaving the church we walked round a winding path into the churchyard until we reached the grave. They lowered her into the ground and I could see the small brass plaque with the word 'Heather' as I threw earth into the grave. I was glad at least she had a new place to lie, and that she wasn't lost any more or lying in the garden of what had been our home, but was really something from a nightmare.

In due course we had a headstone erected. The inscription was Mum's choice:

'In our hearts love will never die.'

Heather had been Mum's child and, at the time, it seemed important that she should be the one to make that choice. She even wanted to pay for it and in fact believed that she did, although in reality she had no access to her bank account, so I paid without her knowing. Part of me hates that she had a part in it now, but I still remember her crying in bed after Heather had gone; I find it hard to believe that she didn't love her. After the stone was put in place I offered to send Mum a photo. She wrote back to me to say she'd love one, and told me she'd think of me when I went to visit the grave. She also said she was glad to know where Heather finally was – it was things like this that made it so hard for me to accept that she had been part of the murder; even now it makes me wobble. But if she was, and deep down I *know* she was, to keep up this pretence, to say something like that to me, when I was burying her . . . it's so cruel, so calculated. But looking back, what really makes me so frustrated with Mum is that after these paragraphs about Heather, she brought it back to her budgies she loved so much:

Oh Mae, thank you for the budgie stuff – a Christmas stocking for budgies – have you ever heard the like!

I should have worked it out then: she cared more for those budgies than she ever did about us.

I still sometimes visit Heather, but I find it very hard. On top of the grief and the unanswered questions about what happened to her, I can't get out of my head the horrible things Dad

124

said about her after she had gone. Wasn't it enough that he had done what he'd done to her? Did he really have to rubbish her name as well? And then pretend that she was still alive when, all the while, he knew full well he had murdered, dismembered and buried her in the garden, throwing her belongings away as if they were worthless trash. I will never get my head round how you could kill your own child.

One of the things I feel sorry about most is the fact Heather was robbed of the chance to live a different kind of life from the one she grew up with – making a new family and having children of her own, as I have done. She never got the chance to escape and live the life she had imagined for herself. I don't just feel guilty about surviving. I feel that I should be doing more with the life I have, and that somehow I should live it for both of us.

Heather will never know what it is to live in the Forest of Dean as she had always dreamed of doing: carefree, without feeling the constant threat of abuse, just being herself . . .

FODIWL. Forest of Dean I Will Live . . .

All those years ago, for a brief, happy period, I thought she had got away.

Chapter Eight

Other Homes

Today Mum sent me a poem: an 'Ode to Mae'. For all of my life I've
wanted her to love me, to show me some gentleness and care – like
any daughter would – and here it is. She loved me like a part of
herself, she says. I can feel her pulling me closer with her words, after
so many loveless years . . .

> I love you like the rarest diamond
> To precious to be sold.
> Rosemary West (written in HM Prison Durham)

The irony of Heather's disappearance was that it made Mum
and me closer. I had no reason to think that Heather was dead,
let alone that she had been murdered or that Mum might have
played a part in it – all I could see was a mother who was very
upset at the way her daughter had left home. Seeing her tearful and vulnerable was something I'd never seen before, and
it triggered feelings in me towards her that I'd never had until
then. Although I knew she'd been harsh and cruel towards
Heather and done nothing to prevent Dad's predatory sexual
advances, I thought I could see genuine regret about what had
happened and even that she'd failed as a mother. I felt sorry
for her.

And as I reached the age of sixteen I began to see her as one adult sees another, rather than just as a child sees a mother. I imagine this happens in other mother/daughter relationships, especially if the mother is in an unhappy marriage. She began to confide in me. And although – for obvious reasons – the things she confided in me never included giving me an honest explanation for why Heather was no longer around, they were enough to begin to establish a different kind of relationship between us.

It was around this time that she admitted to me that she'd suffered from depression over the years, something I'd suspected – but I hadn't known how bad it had been. She thought it was something that she'd inherited from her mother, Daisy, who had suffered very badly with the illness and received various treatments over the years. One of these had been ECT (electro-convulsive therapy – where electrodes are applied to the head to deliver an electric shock to the brain). Mum told me her mother Daisy had been given the treatment when she was pregnant with her. It sounded barbaric to me. I don't know if this is possible, but it made me wonder if the traumatic procedure might have damaged Mum in some way while she was in the womb. Is that possible? I don't know.

I found myself wondering what kind of child Mum had been, especially when she occasionally got out her old photo album. It was one of those big, posh black binder type albums – with each photo mounted and protected by plastic film. Some of them were taken on the beach in Devon near the village where she grew up. She was a pretty child. There was an innocence in her face but something else too – a sadness behind the eyes. It was a similar expression to the one I can see now when I look at photos of Heather. It's almost as if she was willing people to understand there was something wrong, that she longed for someone to intervene and take her away somewhere safe. It was the look – although it took me a long time to realise it – of an abused child.

In the photographs, Mum is dressed in a girly, almost doll-like way – totally unlike the way she made me dress, with boyish clothes and shoes and short hair – as if she wanted to conceal my femininity. But Mum as a child couldn't have looked more feminine. She preferred to dress like a child even as a middle-aged woman. She wore pinafore dresses, knee socks and cardigans. There couldn't have been a greater contrast with the cheap, provocative tart's lingerie she wore for her work as a prostitute. There had to be a reason she chose to dress like that. It was as if she'd never wanted to leave her childhood behind.

There were photos of Mum's parents too in her album. I used to ask her about them. Before she'd never wanted to talk about them, but after Heather 'disappeared', treating me more as a friend now than a daughter, she did tell me things I hadn't known before. She told me her mother Daisy had an obsession with hygiene. Mum had this too to some extent. Although never greatly concerned with keeping our house tidy, she couldn't abide germs and dirt and used bleach at every opportunity. She couldn't bear to have any trace of dirt on her clothes or those of her children and washed them frequently. It was a constant source of tension with Dad, who couldn't care less what filthy old clothes he wore or how clean he was. He used to joke that he only ever took one bath a year.

But, as Mum described it, Daisy took her obsession with cleanliness to even greater extremes. She'd bleach and scrub the house endlessly, as if trying to rid it of every possible contamination, and she was constantly worried that Mum and her brothers and sisters would pick up germs. So much so that she confined them to the house as much as she could. Eventually her neurosis and anxiety developed to the point where she had a breakdown.

Mum's father Bill had to look after her. He resented it bitterly and hated being cooped up in the small council house where they lived with a mentally ill wife and several small children. He had no patience at all with Daisy's psychiatric problems, and they increasingly got worse.

And he had problems of his own. Mum told me that one of her earliest memories was of him sterilising the carpets in the house – something he'd learned how to do in his work as a ship's steward and used to do frequently when he was at home. Even to Mum it seemed over the top, but he was a man who loved precision and order and who wanted to be in control of everything.

Mum's childhood, it seemed, had been as miserable as mine. And although she didn't mention it at that stage, and I certainly didn't dare ask her, I began to suspect it had also involved sexual abuse.

And so, as I began to feel this sympathy for her which I'd never felt before, Mum seemed to sense this. Knowing Dad felt nothing of the kind, she started to depend on me emotionally. If I was blind to the truth about her then and later, it was probably this dependency that was the reason. If I doubted her, then who could she turn to?

But this change in our relationship was a gradual process and it certainly didn't cause her to show any new sympathy or understanding towards me in return. As soon as I turned sixteen I was expected to leave school and get a job – any old job – so that I was no longer a financial burden on Mum and Dad. There was no suggestion I might be allowed to continue with my studies, take A-levels, perhaps even go to university and do a degree in Art, a subject I loved and was quite good at.

Even so, I was determined to make the best of the situation, to find employment that challenged me and gave me the opportunity to learn new skills. I managed to get what turned out to be the first of a series of office jobs, doing secretarial work which allowed me to spend one day a week at college. My wage was only £3.70 an hour and I had to pay Mum £20 a week rent. Other than the extra money coming in, Mum and Dad took no interest in my work but it gave me some pride and self-respect.

Meanwhile, I met my first real boyfriend, Rob, in a pub not long after leaving school. I was really shy, standing in the corner under a loudspeaker, and he came over to me. We got talking. He was eighteen months older than I was – the same age as Heather. He'd been born only a couple of days before her in Gloucester Royal Hospital, so our mothers had probably been in there at the same time. We arranged to meet again the following night in a pub called the Tall Ship, next to Gloucester docks. From that night on we started a relationship.

I was nervous about what Mum and Dad would make of him, and even more apprehensive about how he would feel about them. As it turned out, they really liked him. He worked as a baker, and when he was on an early morning shift he would walk round to Cromwell Street and leave Mum bread and cakes on the doorstep. She was delighted, and my brothers and sisters loved him. And to my great relief, getting to know my parents didn't put him off me – strange though they must have been to him. He was always round our house, and when he fell out with his parents, Mum and Dad let him move in.

'I don't mind. He's a nice lad. He's welcome,' said Mum.

She didn't seem at all concerned about the idea of me beginning a sexual relationship, but I wasn't sure how Dad would react. After all, he'd made such a thing over the years of being the one to 'break me in' when I reached the age of sixteen.

'Yeah, let him move in if he wants,' he said. 'Mae can fuck who she likes and if they want to do it under my roof, let them.' I wasn't sure if he meant it; I worried he might still feel some entitlement to me.

But although Rob shared my room when he moved in, we hadn't actually begun to sleep together – he slept on a sofa in my room while I took the bed. It suited me for Dad to believe we had because I thought it might protect me against his horrible advances. Then one day, he came into our room without knocking. I think he thought he might catch us at it. He started to make crude remarks.

'Nice tits my daughter's got, eh Rob? Don't you reckon?'

Rob was embarrassed and so was I but it was good having Rob around. He tried not to make me feel too self-conscious about having such strange parents.

My bedroom was a sanctuary back then, but sometimes I'd not be able to escape Dad. Once, when I was cleaning my room, Dad came in and made a grab for my breasts. I pushed him away.

'Just leave me alone, will you?'

He didn't take me seriously at first. 'What's up? What's wrong with giving your dad a good old feel?'

He lunged at me again. I pushed him back. 'Get off! Get out of here!'

It was the first time I'd ever stood up to him like that. He was shocked. The grin on his face was replaced by a dark, threatening glare. Now I was scared.

'Don't you dare speak to me like that, you little bitch!'

He turned and went to the door. There was a Hoover standing just outside it. He picked it up and turned back to me.

'Do you hear me? Never speak to me like that again!'

He launched the Hoover at me. I tried to duck but it hit me

hard. As soon as he'd done it, he seemed to realise it made him look spiteful and ridiculous. He left the room without saying another word. It was as if he realised he'd been defeated. It was the last time he ever tried anything on with me.

Aside from Dad's behaviour, the other thing I worried about with Rob living in the same house was him finding out about Mum and Dad's sex life and her work as a prostitute, although that was winding down at that time. He certainly picked up on some of it. Sex was a constant thing in our house – you couldn't get away from it. We'd often hear Mum and Dad having noisy sex, or Dad would describe it to us. 'Your Mum and I had a bloody good ride last night! Do you want to know what we did?' Or he'd be watching porn and encouraging us to watch it with him.

He offered to lend Rob his hard-core videos – 'might give you a few ideas, Son' – and Mum, who was the most uninhibited person, would think nothing of walking past him on the landing with no clothes on. Luckily it didn't bother him. He was more concerned about my embarrassment and told me not to worry.

After a few weeks Mum told us we'd have to move out because the house was now too crowded. It happened very suddenly. I came home from work one day and she simply said: 'I've found you a bedsit and you're moving in tomorrow. Here's the key.' So we had to pack all our things in a hurry and get out.

I was puzzled about why she'd done this. It was a big house and Rob moving in with me hardly made a difference to how crowded it was. I soon guessed that one reason for doing it was that it would reduce the food bill. I think another was that she wanted to keep me away from Louise and Tara, because I was an adult and she didn't want them getting any ideas of independence too soon. She wanted to keep them fully under her control and that meant separating us as much as possible.

She had strict rules about my contact with them. 'You can come back on a Sunday between two and three to see them, but that's all. You're not to have them visiting you.'

The bedsit was only a couple of streets away, but moving out of the family home felt like a huge step. Rob and I weren't even at the stage of thinking of living together but it pushed us into it. I was keen to make the most of my new independent life, though. I learned to drive – something that infuriated Dad, who believed women were no more than baby machines. When I told him I was having lessons he did everything he could to undermine my confidence – claiming I'd be a danger to the public and leave a trail of dead bodies behind me wherever I drove. But I refused to be put off. Everything he wanted for me, I wanted the opposite.

After a year or so, Rob's parents helped us with the deposit to buy a house. We'd managed to work and save up enough to buy in a nice area of Gloucester – the mortgage payments amounted to no more than the rent we were already paying. We got a cat (Bhagera – 'Baggy' for short) who became my close companion for many years. So within a short space of time my life had been completely transformed. Dad was very disappointed. He refused to even set foot in the house.

'You could at least have bought somewhere in Cromwell Street, girl. Next door even. Then we'd have been able to knock through and you could have stayed part of the family.'

They wanted me to be away from the house but also to remain in control of me. Buying my own place meant they weren't any longer. But in the end they were like any other parents in that they knew that once a child reaches a certain age it becomes very difficult to control them – physically at least. I wasn't scared of either of them any more. Dad knew it, and if Mum had hit me when I was seventeen I'd have just said: 'Fuck you', and done my own thing even more.

For a couple of years, and for the first time ever, I lived what felt like a normal life – the kind I imagined other people led. I'd call at Cromwell Street now and then to see my brothers and sisters, but gradually the house came to feel like a place I'd left behind. That doesn't mean I could forget what happened to me there, or that my siblings were still very much under my parents' control. I had no fear for Steve – who left home before me – but I was worried for my sister Louise especially. Now that I was gone, I was afraid she might be next in line for Dad's sexual attention. I didn't have the same fear for Tara since she wasn't Dad's child, and as he was such a racist I was sure she would be left alone. She was also the only one out of us to have a tremendously confident character and I knew she would never put up with any kind of abuse from either Mum or Dad.

Louise, on the other hand, was white and almost into her teens. She was a quiet, thoughtful, rather shy girl and Dad seemed to have taken a particular liking to her. Before I left home I tried to warn her about Dad. Louise remembers us having the conversation as clearly as I do. We were sitting in the downstairs bathroom. It was raining and the rain was leaking in as it always did. I didn't really know how to put it to her. She was so young. Far too young to have to worry about such things. I didn't want to scare her.

'The thing is, when I'm not living here, you'll need to watch out for Dad.'

'I know,' she said, before I tried to go into any detail. 'I know what he's like.'

I wasn't surprised that she understood. She must have seen the way he pestered and groped me. I didn't ask Louise if Dad had made the same threat to her as he had to me about 'breaking me in' before I was sixteen. But I assumed from what she said that he must have done.

Louise seemed quite calm and told me she'd be all right. I hoped it was true. And on the visits I made to the house after I'd left I didn't sense that any kind of abuse was happening, just that Louise had taken over some of my role in the household, especially helping Mum with practical things such as preparing meals, looking after the younger children and shopping. Life in the house was continuing without me.

But things were changing in Mum and Dad's relationship. I'd never really understood much about their marriage – what they saw in one another or why they stayed together. I rarely saw anything resembling real affection between them. The bond seemed to be based on crude, uninhibited but loveless sex and a desire to raise a family together. But it was becoming unhappier. To my surprise Mum began to visit me at my new house. It was some distance from Cromwell Street and she used to pedal over on her bike. She didn't tell Dad, who hated my new independence. She'd sit and chat to me, drinking tea, stroking Baggy the cat, and seemed to love being away from home. It was obvious she was very unhappy.

'I envy you this, Mae,' she told me one day.

'How do you mean?'

'Having a place of your own. Decent job. Nice boyfriend. I wish I could get away from that fucking house too.'

'Why?'

'That fucking father of yours, that's why. He's made my life a fucking misery. I hate everything about him. He's a filthy, disgusting, selfish pig. A stinking, horrible bully. I wish I'd never set eyes on him.'

She told me how much she hated his constant perverted sexual demands. How she'd hated her work as a prostitute. I'd

heard her complain about that before but not in such an ex-
treme way.

'He'd still have me doing it if he could, Mae. I'm telling you
I've had enough!'

'You don't mean . . . you're thinking of leaving him?'

'Yes I am. I want a better life for myself. A life where I'm
appreciated.'

I had several conversations like that with her. Each time she
swore me to secrecy. She didn't want Dad to have any inkling
she was thinking of going. Despite the strength of her feeling I
wasn't sure she would really go through with it, but eventually
she rented a bedsit in one of the big houses close to St Paul's
Primary, where the younger children went to school. She didn't
move out or tell Dad, but after she'd dropped them off she'd
sometimes go and spend time there. She told the landlord that
her name was Mandy West – the name she'd used when she
worked as a prostitute – and that she worked as a nanny. She
sometimes took one of my youngest sisters there – claiming she
was someone else's child – to back up her story.

She didn't tell me about the bedsit. I only found out when I
went back to Cromwell Street one day. Mum wasn't at home,
but I found Dad going through the Argos catalogue.

'What are you doing, Dad?'

He told me he'd found out about Mum's secret bedsit and
what seemed to be upsetting him most was that she'd filled it
with goods bought from Argos: vacuum cleaner, kettle, toaster,
microwave.

'I wouldn't mind but it's my fucking wages she's bought the
stuff with!'

He was trying to make a joke of it but he was clearly fuming
inside.

'I asked why she's done it and she says she wants her own

space. Can you believe that? Her own space? As if there isn't enough fucking space in this house. I couldn't have made it any bigger, could I?'

I wondered whether he thought she might be seeing other men at the bedsit. I don't think he did. If he had suspected it, he certainly wouldn't have made jokes about it. Although, in the past, he'd encouraged her to go with other men, it was always for his own perverted gratification. If he'd thought she was doing it for herself, or worse still getting close emotionally to any of them, he'd have hated it.

In the past I'd seen him listen to her having sex with other men over the intercom he'd rigged up. He used to pace up and down, listening keenly, fascinated by what he was hearing, but restless and almost anxious too. He hated it if he heard her laughing when she was with her clients. He was only happy for her to have sex with other men if he felt in control of it. In fact, knowing what I know now I believe he would have killed her if he thought she'd betrayed him in that way. But there was no doubt the possibility of it worried him, and he felt threatened by her desire to spend time away from him. He felt he was losing control of her and he hated it.

In fact, she did take up with another man. She mentioned it on one of her visits to my house. I was shocked. I knew if Dad found out he'd be absolutely livid.

'Whatever you do, don't breathe a fucking word of this to him.'

''Course I won't.'

I asked her who he was. She wouldn't tell me but said she wanted to be with him but didn't see how she could ever get free of Dad. She thought this new relationship was already doomed.

'Well, it might not have worked out anyway.'

'That's not the point, Mae. I'd like to at least have had the chance to be with someone normal. Someone who appreciates me,' she said hotly.

'I can see that.'

'It'll never happen, though.'

I searched around for something to say, settling on, 'I'm sorry, Mum. You'll get over it.' It was probably clumsy of me to say it but I was just trying to do my best to be sympathetic. I didn't really know what to say. She was furious.

'How do you know I'll fucking get over it!' She spat at me, 'You've never understood me, Mae! You've always taken your father's side!'

I didn't feel that was true at all, and told her so.

'It is! You want me to stay with him and be miserable and lonely for the rest of my life!'

'I don't!'

She wouldn't listen and she didn't let me forget the conversation either. For years afterwards she would raise what she thought was my lack of support for her over this relationship, saying I'd never understood her desire to escape and be with another man. She said she found it very hard to forgive.

Looking back, I think her longing to be out of the marriage and with a different sort of man was genuine but deluded also. During the years she's been in prison she has fallen in love (as she sees it) with several men who have got into correspondence with her. One of these relationships was with Dave Glover, who was briefly the bass player with the band Slade. She became convinced they would marry. That he really was the one for her and would love and cherish her and they'd live happily ever after. Their wedding was even announced in the newspapers. It was a complete fantasy – not least because she'd been sentenced to spend the rest of her life in prison – but it was the happiest I've ever known her.

But her dream of marrying a man who would make her happy was never going to come about, not then in prison, or earlier on when she rented her bedsit in Gloucester and was still with my father. That dream came to a sudden and brutal end – and so did my new life of normality with Rob.

One day in August 1992, Mum rang me to tell me that the police had raided 25 Cromwell Street.

'The police have been here. They've arrested your dad!'

I was speechless. Eventually I managed, 'What – why?'

Mum's voice sounded petrified and furious. 'I can't tell you on the phone. I need you here, Mae!'

'I'll come round.'

I drove round there, trying to keep calm, not knowing what to expect. She was very upset. She said Dad had been taken to the police station and was being questioned about the rape and sexual abuse of one of the children.

I think my heart stopped for a second. 'Who?'

'Louise.'

I was shocked and horrified. I also found it difficult to believe because Louise was still only thirteen – barely into puberty. Heather and I had been older, approaching sixteen, when Dad's sexual advances became really threatening. I'd imagined Louise would have been safe, at least for a little while longer. What upset Mum most was that the police had brought social workers with them and the children had been taken into care.

'They think I'm involved too, Mae! They're saying I helped him to do it!'

I knew perfectly well that Mum had turned a blind eye to Dad's horrible sexual pestering of Heather and me, and I also remembered what Anne Marie had told me about what Dad had done to her with Mum's assistance. But I couldn't bring myself to imagine she would help him sexually abuse Louise. I sat with her as she poured her heart out to me, trying to console her.

'It's not that I don't know he's tried it on with you girls. But to say I'd help him do something like that. It's horrible, Mae! Fucking police, they haven't got a clue! Nor have social services! All they want to do is break up this family! They want to take my babies away from me. I haven't done anything!'

Years later Louise described to me what happened when the police and social workers raided the house. Dad had already left for work, and she and the other children were still in their pyjamas. They heard a loud banging on the door. Mum yelled at the kids not to answer it, and went to do so herself. They heard her shouting and then she ran back to find Louise and told her to keep her 'fucking mouth shut'.

They watched through a partly open door as Mum went back and tried to order the police to leave. She was swearing, kicking and punching. They wrestled her to the ground, handcuffed her and took her away. Other officers stayed while the social workers supervised the children as they got dressed. They were taken in cars to the police station. Louise was given a full medical examination and interviewed about what had happened. During that time she saw our family tree written on a whiteboard. Heather's name was on it with a question mark against it. At that stage she had no idea why. After that she was taken briefly to a holiday camp with our younger siblings and all put together in a big house in Gloucester, under the care of social workers.

After the police arrested Mum they'd searched the house and taken away a huge collection of pornographic videos, whips, dildos and other sex toys. They'd arrested Dad at work and questioned both of them separately before releasing Mum. She'd returned home to an empty house. And, knowing little of what had really happened, what I saw when I arrived that day was a heartbroken mother whose children had been taken away. The thing we'd all feared more than anything else had happened – the family had been broken up. The house seemed a desperately sad place. Mum told me that all she had left was me.

Chapter Nine

Hints and Rumours

Mum's letter was cheerful today. I never know what way it's going to swing with her: sometimes so dark and full of emotions and looking back at the past; sometimes dominated by smalltalk and clothes requests. I think on the whole she does enjoy prison life – but sometimes I wonder if she's putting a brave face on it for me. Is she finally thinking of me and the others?

<u>HM PRISON DURHAM</u>

Honestly Mae I can't believe how quick the weekends go – it's one o'clock Sunday dinner time and it still feels like Sat morning! Work again tomorrow – I've made Louise this big cosy looking white rabbit to give to Abigail for her birthday and a little heart-shaped trinket box we make in our pottery department. I hope she likes it . . .

Following their arrests, Mum and Dad were charged – Dad with three counts of rape and one of buggery, and Mum with encouraging unlawful sexual intercourse and cruelty to a child. Mum continued to deny having done anything wrong. Dad was sent away to Birmingham on remand so I never heard his version of events, and after she was put in care I wasn't allowed to have contact with Louise. She was the only person who would have been able to tell me the truth. It wasn't until years later that she was able to explain to me what had happened. Mum and Dad had only allowed me to have limited contact with her after I left home, and it turned out so much had happened I hadn't known about.

When she had been due to start secondary school, Mum and Dad decided not to send her. The education authorities asked why and Mum told them she'd gone away to live with a relative. They didn't make any attempt to verify whether it was true. Louise had been forced to be part of this lie and was even sometimes sent from home to pick up the younger children from junior school – waiting a little way outside the school gates for them so that no teachers would recognise her and realise she was still in the area.

Mum and Dad told Louise they were keeping her at home because since I'd moved out Mum wanted more help around the house. That might have been true, but a much more important reason was that Dad had started to abuse her and they were afraid she might reveal it at school. The abuse had begun in a low-key way, as it had done with me – touching and groping – but grew gradually worse until, a few months before the police raided the house, Dad took Louise to the upstairs part of the house and raped her in the most horrific way. He had kept his revolting promise to 'break her in' – the same one he'd made to me and Heather. Mum had been out of the house at the time but he raped her again soon afterwards when Mum was at home. He told her about it and asked her to examine Louise and verify that she was no longer a virgin, which Mum did. There was a third rape before he told Louise 'the job had been properly done'.

143

Dad told her that if anyone outside the family got to know about it the family would be broken up. She believed him and kept it to herself at first. But eventually she mentioned it to her younger sisters and brother and then to a friend who told her mother, who phoned the police and reported it.

When the charges were first brought against Dad and Mum I knew none of this. I only had Mum's word to go on. She insisted she knew nothing of any assault on Louise. She said she didn't think the police had any real evidence against Dad either but had found their extensive collection of porn and kinky sex gear and taken that as proof they were abusers. Knowing what I did about Dad – that what had happened was probably true – Mum's lying defence of him should probably have rung alarm bells about her own involvement. But I couldn't believe she'd been directly involved in it. She was in floods of tears for days after the children had been taken. There didn't seem to be anything fake about her grief for them. I felt I couldn't desert her.

'Thank God I've still got you, Mae,' she kept saying.

After Dad had been charged, when he was on remand in Birmingham, he was allowed to make phone calls and spoke to Mum every night. One night, before I passed the phone to Mum, he said to me 'She got no one else now, Mae. I'm trusting you to take care of her.'

He was giving me the responsibility to hold the family together. And so I moved back in with Mum. Steve did too, so that we could all feel there was something of the family left. During that time, I think perhaps because the loss of her younger children prompted her to think about it, she told me more about her childhood. Though named Rosemary Pauline, her family used to call her Rosie. In her early years they gave her the nickname 'Dozy Rosie'.

'Wasn't because I was thick or anything, Mae,' she said. 'They called it me because I used to do silly things to try and make them laugh. Not that they ever did laugh much, my mum and dad.'

That didn't surprise me. Her parents' marriage sounded miserable and violent. But she played the fool to try to lighten the atmosphere. And used her pretty looks and charm to try to pacify her father, Bill, so that he didn't hit her mother or her sisters and brothers.

'I'd climb on his knee and tease him. He liked that. I could make him forget how angry he was.'

But she hinted that there was a price there had to be paid. It was pretty obvious what she meant. I'd sometimes wondered about the advice she'd given me when I was young – that if I ever found myself in a situation with a man who wanted to touch, or do anything else to me, whatever it was, I shouldn't resist.

'Just let them get on with it,' she'd said. 'It'll hurt less and be over quicker.'

I realised then she must have been speaking from personal experience. Had her father sexually abused her?

Later on, at Mum's trial, she told the court she'd lost her virginity at the age of fourteen, when she'd been raped by a stranger. But she told me later she was twelve when it happened. I believe the 'stranger' was Bill and it was the first of many sexual encounters – a repulsive sexual exploitation of his daughter which went on for years. It was something that Dad mentioned during his many interviews with the police. He told them how it had even continued when she was married to him and living at Cromwell Street and Bill used to call round. Although Dad often lied, I believe he was telling the truth about that.

Over the years, journalists and others have interviewed my mum's family and people who knew about her early life. Put together with what my dad said and what she told me herself, this is what I believe to be true:

From being an abused child she became a wild and promiscuous teenager. She came to see sex as the same thing as affection. Men realised this and used her. They saw her, as her own father did, as fair game and that only made the damage worse. When her mother Daisy left Bill, moving out of the house at Bishop's Cleeve to live in Cheltenham and taking the children with her, Mum went too. But it was too late. The damage had been done. She went through a semi-feral phase, picking up men whenever she felt like it, sometimes having sex with them for free, sometimes for payment. When Daisy moved the family again, leaving the area altogether for a while, Mum refused to go with them and chose to move back in with Bill. I can't quite work out why she did this, considering he'd shown himself to be such a violent bully. Mabe she felt that living with him she could continue to get away with her wayward lifestyle, or even that she could keep herself safe from his violence by continuing to give in to his sexual demands. Maybe she even had that same emotional attachment to him that I worry my siblings and I experienced at her hands, despite her own treatment of us. Only she can answer that.

The arrangement suited Bill at first, but he hadn't bargained for how headstrong and disobedient Mum was becoming. She'd come and go from the house at all hours, and have sex with men as and when she wanted to. It made him jealous and angry. She was the daughter he'd created but now she was becoming her own person too, refusing to answer to one man's control. Her waywardness didn't alter when – to many people's surprise – her mother Daisy decided to return home to live with Bill, having been unable to support her younger children on her own.

The two of them were at a loss as to how to deal with Mum.

She was fifteen by then, had left school and got a job as a seam-stress in Sketchley's dry-cleaners and then at the tea rooms in Cheltenham, but she was still leading a wild and promiscuous lifestyle while being under the age of legal consent. The police began to take an interest in her, more than likely because Bill – possessive and resentful of her relationships with other men – had alerted them. The police would have seen this simply as the action of a concerned father, not the abuser he was. They spoke to Mum and contacted social services, who also got in touch with her, but no action seems to have been taken to protect her.

After a childhood like that, Dad couldn't have found a more vulnerable person when he walked into the tea rooms that day and spotted her. But her experience had made her hard too. She had learned how to stop herself feeling. Just as she'd learned to switch off her feelings about what was done to her, I believe she was able to do the same about what she did to other people.

But in the weeks and months after the children were taken into care it was the vulnerable side she showed to me. Her misery and depression seemed to deepen every day.

When I moved back in I slept downstairs on the sofa. Early one morning Mum came into the room. She seemed drunk and was mumbling to herself.

I sat up, alarmed. 'Mum, are you all right?'

She didn't answer me at first, and then she said, 'I've fucking well had enough, Mae . . . I want to finish it.'

'What do you mean?' I got up, and helped her into a chair. 'What have you done? Mum! Tell me!'

Her answer was a slurred mumble I couldn't make out. I thought maybe she'd taken an overdose. 'Have you taken some-thing?' I pressed her.

'What if I have? What do you care? What does anybody care?'

147

Panicking, Steve rushed upstairs to search around to see what she might have taken. There was a half-drunk bottle of vodka in the 'Black Magic' bar and some empty packets of Anadin by her bedside.

We called an ambulance but she refused to get in at first. Once we'd got her in it, she was rushed to Gloucestershire Royal Hospital and had her stomach pumped. She recovered and no serious harm had been done, but we were all left shaken afterwards. Some people have suggested the suicide attempt was no more than a way of faking distress – perhaps for the benefit of the authorities who were making psychiatric assessments in preparation for the court case – but I don't believe it. Whatever the cause of Mum's emotional pain at that time – whether it was guilt or remorse or grief for her children – I believe to this day it was a genuine attempt to end her life.

The events at Cromwell Street that summer put a serious strain on my relationship with Rob. He told me that if the allegations against Mum and Dad were true, he no longer wanted anything to do with them. To make matters worse, we both lost our jobs at that time. I was in a state of absolute turmoil and spending most of my time with Mum rather than at the house with him. Eventually Rob said he wanted to end the relationship. I spent months trying to win him back but failed. I was heartbroken. He had been my first boyfriend and had helped me try to break from my parents – physically and emotionally – something I needed to do if I was ever going to have a happy independent adult life.

Meanwhile, in order to try to fill the emptiness in the house Mum suggested we get a dog. I thought it was a bit of an odd choice because I knew she didn't really like dogs, but I agreed, thinking it might cheer her up. We went to a local dogs' home and found a spaniel, but it was too agressive to come home so sadly had to be put down. Then Mum found us a bearded collie, which was better behaved apart from walking in circles, and then someone else who heard we were looking for a dog rang up and offered us another, which she also accepted, so we ended up with two. She seemed glad to have them – she was desperate to have something to look after. But it felt like a poor substitute, at least to me, for her missing children.

She used to take the dogs on the train with her when she went up to Birmingham to visit Dad, where he was staying in a bail hostel. Steve and I sometimes went with her. I was startled to see the change in Mum's behaviour towards Dad when they met up with each other again. They kissed and held hands and seemed to have genuinely missed one other.

Dad seemed in pretty good spirits. There were glimpses of his old wit and dark humour. He showed us the phone boxes which he used to nick coins from and the places where the prostitutes worked – I couldn't help but thinking Dad being held in this area was like a red rag to a bull. But once he was with Mum the two of them pretty well lost interest in Steve and me. We followed them along the Hagley Road as they walked hand-in-hand like teenage lovers. Mum laughed and joked with Dad and seemed charmed by him in a way I hadn't ever seen before.

And they were desperate to have sex with each other again. On that first visit they just disappeared into the bushes to do it – more or less in public view. Steve and I were so embarrassed so we were relieved when Mum bought them a little tent from Argos for the next visit so that they could have some privacy. But that hardly improved matters. They didn't go anywhere discreet to set it up and just pitched it on a green area off the main road and disappeared inside, telling us to make ourselves scarce for a while. After that we were happy to let Mum go to Birmingham on her own.

I found it hard to reconcile Mum's changed attitude towards Dad with the things she'd said about him in the years since I'd left home. She'd been full of hatred for him, told me he'd ruined her life, wanted to leave him for another man – but now she couldn't have seemed more in love with him. And yet he hadn't changed. Far from it. He was still the same dirty, thieving, filthy-minded man he'd always been and, worse still, he was now up on a charge of raping his thirteen-year-old daughter. It didn't make sense to me. If Mum had really been as unhappy as she claimed, why didn't she take the opportunity to leave him when he was on remand and banned from visiting Gloucester?

I have a love letter she wrote to him around this time, addressed 'To my Darling' and telling him 'you really tired me out', and to hold on to the fact she loved him.

The letter had a drawing of a heart with an arrow through it, and in the centre of the heart was written 'FRED AND ROSE'.

So this wasn't a marriage in ruins; it was one that was coming back to life. Not for the first time in my life I felt completely bewildered by what was happening. I could only cope with my confusion by trying not to feel anything.

In June 1993, Mum and Dad were tried at Gloucester Crown Court. They stood in the dock together and listened to the charges. Dad was charged with three counts of rape, one count of buggery and cruelty to a child. Mum was charged with inciting him to have sex with a thirteen-year-old child and with cruelty. They pleaded not guilty.

A video link had been set up so that Louise, together with Tara and another child (who were witnesses), could give evidence against them, but before the proceedings even got under way the prosecution informed the judge that no evidence would be offered. All three children had decided they did not want to testify. The case collapsed. Not guilty verdicts were recorded. Mum and Dad embraced and went home. They were so happy.

'I told you there was nothing in it,' said Mum.

'Yeah, we can all get back to normal now,' said Dad.

It's hard to describe how I felt about the verdict. I didn't 100 per cent trust Mum and Dad, but I wasn't allowed to contact Louise or Tara – in fact, I had no idea where they were so couldn't ask them why they'd decided not to give evidence. All I heard was Mum and Dad's side of the story, which was that the charges had been trumped up, based on little more than the gossip of children and the fact that the two of them had a large collection of pornography and sex toys.

'We'll get the kids back now and carry on as we were, as a family,' Dad said.

But social services still considered them to be at risk so they remained in care. They were furious about it.

They took it in turns to say things like, 'Whose bloody children are they?' and, 'They proved nothing against us!'

That was irrelevant. Social services had legal power over the children now. They offered Mum and Dad supervised access visits. Dad was outraged.

'They're our fucking children, Rose! I am not going to sit in some fucking meeting with some fucking busybodies just to see my own children. I want them back home and that's that!'

But Mum accepted the offer. A meeting was arranged with Louise, who described it to me some time later. She was taken to a room by social workers and Mum was invited in. This was a situation Mum had never been in before and it gave Louise a sense of control. Mum was very calm, even submissive, and did everything she could to convince the social workers she was a gentle, easy-going mother. I find it frightening now that Mum knew how she *ought* to behave and yet she chose not do that all those years she actually had us in her care.

But Louise was very wary of her. She felt guilty about – as she saw it – breaking the family up and missed her siblings badly, but she was careful not to say anything that might mean she had to return home. She was afraid of what might happen to her because, as she put it, she was 'the pig that squealed'. The meeting ended with no more than an offer to Mum of a further supervised access visit. Dad's reaction was something like, 'I told you it would be a waste of fucking time! You're not going again, Rose. We'll just have to forget we ever had them and that's that!'

To my surprise Mum didn't raise any objection. She said she felt like him, that if she couldn't be in control of her children she didn't want them. They immediately set about clearing out all the children's rooms and threw their clothes and belongings away. I was amazed at how quickly they were prepared to write off five children who they'd always insisted had been such an important part of their lives.

The children had been put in a children's home nearby in Gloucester. Tara hated it and began to sneak away whenever she could to spend time at home – looking back, I find it amazing that all of us had this strange magnetism with our parents; whatever they did to us we still wanted their love. Mum and Dad didn't mind having her back in the house but neither of them had ever taken much interest in her. Her skin colour protected her from Dad's sexual attention and she was such a feisty character that Mum couldn't control her, even by the threat of violence.

With their marriage now rekindled and the youngest four children apparently gone for good, Mum and Dad took the bizarre decision to set about creating a new family. Mum had opted to be sterilised after the birth of her last baby but now decided to have an operation to reverse it so they could have more children. She discussed it with me.

I remember staring at her, wide-eyed. 'It's a mad idea, Mum.'

She didn't think so at all. 'Why?' she demanded impatiently.

'Even if they manage to reverse the sterilisation, you're nearly forty, there's no guarantee you'd get pregnant. And even if you did succeed in having another baby, they'd never let you keep it.'

'Who?'

'Social services. They don't trust you to have your other children at home with you.'

She got very angry at this. 'Fuck social services, it's none of their fucking business!'

'It's a mad idea, Mum!'

'Don't be so bloody negative, Mae. Why can't you just support me for once?'

I gave up. There was no point in me trying to talk her out of it. Her decision was already made. She booked herself in to have the sterilisation reversed and before long told me she was pregnant. But only a few weeks into the pregnancy she was rushed into hospital with severe abdominal pain. She was treated, but there was no baby after all.

Mum came home again, subdued and depressed. I tried to tell her that it was for the best but that only made her angry. I got the strong impression that, once she was feeling better, she and Dad were going to try for more babies. In the event they didn't get the chance.

Unknown to them, following their arrest in connection with the rape of Louise, the police had begun investigating what had happened to Heather. They'd asked questions about Heather during the rape investigation in a low-key way, simply saying they were trying to build up a wider picture of the family. Mum and Dad had been vague and not altogether convincing in their replies. They made extensive enquiries about Heather in the surrounding area and discovered that there was no record of her paying tax or national insurance, or visiting a doctor – in fact, no record of any kind about her anywhere in the country. It seemed highly suspicious.

The police had also asked Louise and the other younger children about Heather. They weren't reassured by their answers either. The impression they got was of a couple who had terrorised their children into silence by telling them the family would be destroyed if they told the authorities that anything was wrong. They became convinced that our home might contain other secrets.

At the same time, the suspicions Steve and I had about Heather resurfaced on a visit to Dad when he was on remand in prison. Mum had briefly left the three of us alone together to go and buy chips and he'd spoken about the rape charge. He was in a strange, unusually reflective mood.

'It ain't the worst thing I could be accused of.'

'What do you mean?' Steve asked.

'What's the worst thing you can think of that I might have done?'

'I don't know, Dad,' I said.

'Think about it.' His eyes flashed in that terrifying, dark way they could. 'Both of you. Think about the very worst thing you can imagine . . . Well, I've done it.'

I didn't want to know what that meant, but Steve pressed him. 'What have you done?'

He wouldn't elaborate and soon afterwards Mum came back. That was as far as the conversation went.

Steve and I spoke about it afterwards. We both knew Dad often told lies and spoke nonsense, and we never knew whether to believe a word he said. But what he'd hinted at sounded truly awful, and he didn't sound as if he was teasing us. He sounded serious.

'Is he saying he's killed someone?' said Steve.

'I don't know. I don't want to even think about it.'

But we couldn't get the conversation out of our heads. We kept going back over it. Later on, we mentioned it to Tara on one of her secret visits from the children's home. We giggled about it – it was a way of making it seem less alarming. Then one day, one of us – I can't remember who – suddenly said, 'Suppose Dad killed Heather and buried her in the garden?' It was said as a joke, but the more we thought about it, the more we started to wonder if – just possibly – it could be true. Deep down, we suspected it was something he could be capable of. I can't believe we could have guessed so accurately.

Without being sure how serious we were, we decided to set a trap for Mum and Dad. We played them videos of TV dramas which had similar scenarios – episodes of *Prime Suspect* and *Brookside* that featured bodies buried under a patio. We watched for their reactions but nothing about their behaviour suggested they were uncomfortable.

But we carried on talking about it among ourselves. Once we'd thought of the idea we couldn't let it go, even if most of the time it sounded completely far-fetched. One day, after yet another conversation about it between the three of us, Tara went back to the children's home and told some of her friends what we'd been talking about. Some support workers overheard them talking about it and reported it to the police.

On 24 February 1994, the doorbell rang within minutes of me arriving home at 25 Cromwell Street. The two dogs barked. Dad and Steve were out. I'd come home from work to have my lunch and Mum was asleep upstairs as she'd been on an early cleaning shift. I opened the door and there, on the doorstep, were two policemen.

'Is Rosemary West here?' the taller one said.

'What's this about?' I asked.

'Please can we come in?' They flashed their badges and walked through the front door and into the lounge.

They asked me to call Mum down from upstairs. 'Mum? Mum!' I called up the stairs, confused. The police had always been the enemy to us, but I thought this must be about one of Dad's money-making schemes or rip-offs.

After a few minutes, Mum came down the stairs in her dressing gown.

'What do you want?' Mum was pretty short with them, but not her usual swearing and shouting self.

The police officer handed her an official looking piece of paper and said they were here to investigate the disappearance of Heather West; that this was a search warrant giving them permission to search our garden. Mum stared at the piece of paper and then sat on the sofa and placed it down on the coffee table.

What? I couldn't believe it.

They asked Mum where Dad was and Mum said he was at work. He had one of those heavy yellow brick mobile phones at the time, one of the first ones to come out. Mum tried calling him on it, and also called his boss saying she needed Dad to come home straight away. Just at that moment, Steve came home to find us all in the lounge. He called Dad too and eventually, after several calls, he got through to him and told him to get home as the police wanted to ask him questions about Heather. He said Dad was eerily calm.

It was a long, uncomfortable wait and Dad took a good few

hours to appear. But when he did get home, he was friendly and subservient, calling all the police officers 'sir'. Then he took Mum off into the bathroom to have a chat. The police were just left standing there, with me and Steve. It was some time after that when the police left the house, saying they'd be back in the morning, leaving a police guard outside. Mum and Dad, inseparable, took the dogs out for a walk together, and me and Steve talked about what this could all mean.

The next morning, I was in the lounge brushing my hair ready for work, when Dad walked in. He was serious and solemn for once and said, 'I want you to look after your mother for me.'

'What are you on about? Why?' I questioned.

'Because I'm going away for a long time.' He answered. Little did I know that these were the last words we would ever say to each other.

I headed off to work as normal, but in complete disbelief of the events of the last twelve hours. What the policeman had said about Heather was on loop in my head. I just kept thinking it was all a big misunderstanding and that the police would soon realise they'd got it very wrong. Heather wasn't missing, she'd escaped the family.

I struggled through the morning at work. I could almost see Cromwell Street from our office window, making it feel so close and yet so far away. I was distracted by the sound of sirens and couldn't settle down to anything, restless with a terrible sense of unease.

Then Steve called, 'They've taken Dad, Mae, you need to get home.'

My voice broke as I told my boss that I needed to get home. I explained the situation as best I could, his eyes were wide with disbelief, 'I'm sorry, what's happening?' I had to explain it again. He couldn't take it in.

When I got home the police were in every downstairs room. I began to realise this was big.

Chapter Ten

House of Horrors

Mum wrote today to ask for pictures of Heather. She says she's ready for them. They are all that she has of her now and she would like them with her. She wants the first photo taken of her at school, where she's wearing a short-sleeved blouse and a navy pinafore. She also wants one of Heather as a teenager. One of the last photos of her alive. It's upset me a little bit; because she was so mean to Heather in those last few weeks, and yet Mum is begging for sympathy here – now she's ready for them. As if she couldn't have faced it before.

HM PRISON DURHAM

Just send them in a little parcel along with my new Sloggi knickers and they should be alright.
   Love as always,
   Mum

When the police came in and began their search in the garden, I felt as if I was entering a dream. In some ways it feels like a dream that's never ended. Up until that day – apart from the period when I lived with Rob – I hadn't known what it was like to live a normal life. Afterwards it seemed to me that it would never happen again.

The police took Dad away for questioning and Steve and I agreed to wait with Mum as the police continued with their investigations in the garden. She was predictably scornful of what they were doing. She was cursing and swearing at them, telling them they were 'useless', 'taking a fucking liberty' and 'wasting everybody's time'. When it reached early evening we were told the search had been halted but would resume the following day. They left the house, leaving only a single constable to guard the back of the house overnight. Steve's girlfriend came round and we all sat with Mum while she carried on ranting until late into the night about the police and how completely ridiculous the situation was. Eventually, we all ended up sleeping in the same room, with the two dogs and my cat Baggy.

The following morning, when the police returned to continue their search, they stuck black bin liners against the windows at the back of the house so we couldn't see what they were doing in the garden. The front of the house didn't look any different. There was no blue police tape. No indication that this was a potential crime scene. Passers-by would have had no idea what was going on inside – which Steve and I were at least thankful for.

Time passed. We didn't know what to do or think. We were just killing time, waiting. Eventually the police came to Mum and said they needed to ask her some questions. She was absolutely fuming and told them she had nothing whatever to say to them. They were insistent and, with a lot of pushing and shoving and cursing on her part, took her away to interview her.

The police also asked Steve and me some questions while they were at the house. They asked about Heather, about what happened when she left home and whether we were still in touch with her. I remember them being very cold with us, as if they thought we knew more than we were saying. They were treating us as suspects. It made me angry as well as confused. When the police asked me about Dad I pulled no punches, telling them about the sexual abuse he'd threatened me with. I didn't yet know what web was unravelling, but I knew deep down something bigger was going on and I was suddenly filled with rage against him. I blamed him for the ridiculous situation we were all in. The police were non-committal in their reaction. I was left in no doubt that they thought I might be hiding something.

Dad was being interviewed at Gloucester police station and Mum was taken to Cheltenham for questioning. Her reluctance to cooperate didn't make me or Steve think she was guilty of anything. We just knew she hated the police. She'd hated them all her life and, as far as she was concerned, it was their fault her children had been taken away from her.

Later in the day we had a message from Howard Ogden, Dad's solicitor, to say he wanted to speak to us. The police took us to Gloucester police station and showed us into a room where Howard was waiting for us. He looked very grave.

'I'm sorry to have to tell you this, but . . . I'm afraid your father has admitted to murdering Heather.'

Steve – always close to Dad in a way that I never was – couldn't believe it. His face looked grey as he said, 'You're kidding. You've got to be!'

But I remember the expression on Howard's face: he was deadly serious. 'I'm afraid not,' he said grimly.

Steve looked at me but I was too shocked to speak.

'How? How's he supposed to have done it?' Steve asked.

'He said he . . . he strangled her and buried her in the back garden. Your father's told the police they've been digging in the wrong place. He's agreed to go back to the house to show them where she's buried.'

161

You just can't prepare yourself for a sentence like that. It didn't seem remotely real. I had known Dad was capable of sexual abuse, and that he had a very dark side, but the idea of him committing murder was such a huge thing to take in. We were put in a side room and left to wait for what seemed like an age. We hardly exchanged a word. We both felt numb. Much later I would think about Heather – of the story of her leaving and how Mum and Dad described it – and I would see all the holes in it for what they really were. But at that moment in time I couldn't comprehend how what Howard had said could be true. But yet, it did all make a horrible sort of sense . . .

Later on the police drove us home. We were told Dad had been taken into the back garden and had pointed out the spot where they should dig for Heather before being taken away again. A large canopy had been erected over the area in question. More police officers and a pathologist had arrived. There was more digging going on. I felt increasingly sick.

Mum was allowed back home. We all sat together: Steve and his girlfriend, Mum and me. Mostly we were silent, although every now and then Mum would start having another rant at the police. Eventually two police officers came in. They told us that they had found a femur, and although they could not tell whether it was male or female, let alone whether it was Heather's, they thought we ought to prepare ourselves for the worst. I knew in my heart it was her. That was the moment when it ought to have become real, but it didn't. I couldn't cry. I couldn't say anything. I was on the sofa next to Mum. She was silent too, as though she simply couldn't take it in. I don't know how that makes me feel now; that she simply sat there quietly when she must have already known. The police didn't raise the question of how Heather's remains had come to be in the garden, but the implication was clear to all of us: Dad had murdered her and buried her there, just as Howard Ogden had said.

That night we all slept in the same room again. Despite the news about Heather, it was as if we were all still trying to pretend it wasn't happening. Mum remained strangely quiet and thoughtful. For long periods I lay awake, turning it all over in my head. It didn't even cross my mind that Mum was involved. I just knew that Dad had killed Heather and would go to prison. I started to go over all the lies he'd told about her to cover up what he'd done. The sheer petty nastiness of the stories he'd come up with: that she'd become a prostitute and drug dealer. I made up my mind then that I never wanted to see him again.

But, of course, I still had no idea of the real enormity of what was going to happen. That night was almost blissful ignorance. The digging resumed the following day and after a while the police came to speak to us again.

'I'm afraid we've found something else,' one of them said.

'What?' Steve asked.

'Another femur. We've now found a total of three femurs in that area. So, unless Heather had three legs, it means another body must have been buried there.' The blood rushed from my head.

They hinted to us that Dad had now confessed to two further murders. I felt sick to my stomach. I began to sense that the discovery of Heather's remains wasn't the end but only the beginning of something.

After they'd gone out, Mum started to get really angry.

'I can't believe this! That fucking man! That horrible, lying, evil fucking man! How could he do this? How could he do this to all of us? I knew he was a nasty piece of work but this . . . I'd never ever have imagined he could do something like this!'

We made her tea, tried to calm her down, but she continued to fume and curse him.

News of what was happening began to leak out. One or two people who knew the family began to call round to see if we were alright. Others telephoned. We'd always been a family that tried to avoid attracting attention; it seemed now that everyone was beginning to look at us.

The police took Mum away again for questioning. She was even more resentful than the first time. It was clear to her and to us that they thought she might be in some way involved in the murders. They asked Steve and me further questions, too, in separate rooms at the house.

'Have you ever heard mention of a Shirley Robinson?' the detective asked me, mentioning the name almost casually at first.

'Yes. She lived here once.' I answered, puzzled.

'A lodger, was she?' Again, he tried to make the question sound casual.

'I think so. I was only little at the time. Five or six.' I was bewildered by why he was asking me about a person I could barely remember.

'Friendly with your mum and dad, was she?' I realised then he was hinting at some kind of sexual connection and wanted me to say something about that, but I kew nothing so had nothing to say.

'I don't know. I hardly knew anything about her. I just saw her sometimes in the house.'

There was a pause. He made notes, but seemed sceptical about my answer.

'What about a girl called Alison Chambers?'

'Never heard of her.'

'We believe she was a lodger here too.' Again, he seemed to be getting at something I couldn't understand. I felt got at. As if he thought I was part of some conspiracy.

'I don't know. I didn't know any of the lodgers apart from Shirley and I didn't really know her.'

He didn't seem satisfied with any of my answers and he and his colleague took Steve and me to the police station and asked us more questions, about the lodgers, about Heather, about Mum's work as a prostitute, about her sex life with Dad. I found it all horrible, sickening and frightening. Steve felt the same way.

Eventually they released us and soon afterwards let Mum return home too. I assumed this meant they were satisfied that she hadn't been involved and she did nothing to make me think otherwise. And now finally it seemed as if they were turning the house into a crime scene. They told us it wasn't appropriate for us to live there any longer and that they wanted to conduct searches inside the house as well as in the garden. We were all asked to pack up a few clothes and personal belongings so that we could be moved to a safe house where the media couldn't get to us. The story was starting to become a huge one, yet the police were still saying little publicly and journalists were doing everything they could to get hold of anyone who might give them inside information.

The safe house was in the Longlevens area of Gloucester. It was very sparsely furnished and had a forlorn feel to it. We made an effort to make it homely. We put up some cheap curtains but there wasn't much more we could do and it still felt bleak and depressing. It was as if we were all under house arrest. Steve and his girlfriend shared one bedroom and Mum and I slept in the other one. Sometimes in the night I'd hear her crying to herself. She sounded so lonely. It broke my heart. She'd lost most of her children, her home, and now – so it seemed – she was having to

165

face the fact that her husband had murdered her eldest daughter and several other young women as well.

But in the daytime she was generally more angry than sad. She went on endlessly about Dad, saying how much she hated him: 'The fucking trouble he's caused me, Mae! I wish I'd never met him!'

We tried to keep her spirits up but it was very hard. The story was by now all over the papers and television and it was impossible to ignore the enormity of what was happening. Mum became paranoid the neighbours would realise we were living in the house and refused to come out to the shops with us for fear of being recognised. The atmosphere became very claustrophobic and tense.

As well as following the story on television, we were also briefed by the police most days about what was happening at Cromwell Street. The entire garden was now being excavated and the floor of the basement where we used to sleep dug up. More remains were found and Dad was making further confessions. We learned they were looking for the remains of at least nine more victims. Nine. It seemed absolutely incredible. It was so shocking that I could barely take it in. To discover that Dad had murdered Heather was a terrible shock, but the idea of him committing other murders on this scale was impossible to get my head round. From what we could tell, Dad was taking sole responsibility for all the murders though the police gave us little detail about what he was actually saying.

Events moved at a terrifying pace and yet strangely, in the safe house, time seemed to stand still. A situation that I kept thinking couldn't become worse kept doing so. It was like receiving a series of huge body blows. I felt a mixture of numbness and dread. There was no space for me to have the feelings I needed to have for Heather – to begin to grieve for my sister.

I didn't realise it at the time but the house was being bugged. Perhaps Mum suspected, I'm not sure. The police were obviously trying to find out if she knew more than she was saying and might divulge some of it to us. They also believed that Steve and I might have information we were withholding. I can understand now why they would have thought we must have known something, but it hurt a lot that they regarded us as suspects.

The press were everywhere, frantically trying to find out more about what they were now calling 'The House of Horrors'. A *News of the World* journalist got hold of Steve's mobile number from his employer and contacted him. They offered him money for his 'story', although the truth was he didn't have much of a story to tell – he knew nothing of the crimes. He didn't tell us about it but Mum found the contract in his bedroom. She was very angry. She called the police, who were very concerned that the press knew where we were.

Steve and his girlfriend had to leave the house. He sent Mum flowers but that only made her angrier still. Her anger wasn't only because of his deal with the newspaper, but because he still had sympathy with Dad. Steve had always been closer to him than he was to Mum, and since Dad's arrest he'd spoken up for him once or twice during Mum's tirades against him. She suspected he wanted to contact him, maybe even visit him in prison. To her, that would have been the ultimate betrayal. You either had to be on his side or on hers, you couldn't be on both.

Even though Steve had been sent away from the safe house, the police were still concerned the press would find us. They moved us on to an even colder and more miserable safe house in Dursley. I was becoming seriously concerned for Mum's sanity. She would go on and on about Dad, saying the same things over and over again in a shrill, shrieking voice. In almost every sentence she used my name

'I'm telling you, Mae, he's never given a shit about anyone but himself. Well, he deserves everything that's coming to him, Mae. He's caused nothing but misery for all of us. He's an absolute arsehole, Mae . . .'

It was as if she was using a form of brainwashing on me. Drumming into me by repetition what she wanted me to think and feel. And it was working. It felt I had no choice but to see everything from her point of view. And I was worried about her – I couldn't begin to see how she could ever recover from this. I wanted to help but felt powerless. It was just a case of waiting for the next terrible thing to happen.

A photographer spotted her out shopping and the next day her picture was in the newspapers. So then, on top of everything else, everyone knew what she looked like. There was no hiding place. The police moved us on to a third safe house, this time in Cheltenham. It was a police house but we didn't feel any more protected from the outside world. Yet again we tried too hard to establish some kind of normal life. We watched TV, listened to music on a cassette player, played Scrabble, trying to block out – if only temporarily – thoughts about what was happening elsewhere. It was impossible.

We had no telephone and had effectively lost all contact with relatives and what few friends we had, but the police passed some mail on. One letter was from a man who I'll call Ian, who I had once worked with. He had followed the story on the news, realised that it was my family at the centre of the extraordinary revelations at Cromwell Street and decided to try to make contact. It was a really kind letter, asking if I was okay, offering support and saying that if I needed anything at all just to ask. He began sending me books to read and also drove down from Essex to take me out for the day. He was a very supportive friend – my only friend, really – at a time when I had no one apart from Mum, which was more of a one-way relationship, with me looking after her rather than the other way round.

On Wednesday 20 April 1994, two months after they had arrived with the warrant to search Cromwell Street, the police came to arrest Mum. She didn't seem surprised, which isn't to say she gave any indication she'd done anything wrong. But with Dad still being interrogated and giving up more terrible secrets all the time, she probably thought it was only a matter of time before they took her back in. She was arrested initially on suspicion of child abuse, but she must have known they'd have other questions about the murders too.

The police waited while she got dressed. I remained in the bedroom, hating the thought she was being taken away, having no idea when I might see her again. When she was ready to go, the police allowed her to see me alone for a few moments. She whispered the instructions about her wedding ring and then left with the police. I watched from the window as she cursed and struggled as they took her away.

After the police made it clear they no longer had any obligations to me and I would have to leave the house that day, I went to the housing offices in Gloucester and registered as homeless, but they said they were unable to help, and that's when I got in touch with Steve again. We made up our differences, and after a night staying at his girlfriend's mother's house I agreed to go in with him on the book contract the *News of the World*'s publishers were offering.

My main concern at this time was still to be on hand to support Mum. I was allowed to go to Cheltenham police station with clean clothes for her and to take away her dirty washing, but they refused to let me see her. I had no idea what was happening. The police had stopped talking to me.

Then, two days later, she was charged with the murder of

169

one of the young women who had stayed at the house, Lynda Gough. She'd admitted absolutely nothing, refusing initially – so her solicitor told me – to even confirm her name and answering all subsequent questions with 'No comment'. I also learned that Dad was still insisting he had acted alone and Mum wasn't involved. I couldn't believe she was implicated, I *wouldn't* believe it. I felt the police must have got the wrong end of the stick.

Less than two weeks after she was charged with the murder of Lynda Gough, the remains of Charmaine were found beneath the kitchen floor at Mum and Dad's former house on Midland Road. Rena's remains had already been found at Letterbox Field, a few miles from Much Marcle, where Dad had grown up. That was such a shock. With the other women, it was appalling and sickening, but I didn't know how to deal with the news about Charmaine and Rena – after all the things Dad – and Mum – had said about them over years, the fact they'd shown us pictures of them, volunteered information about them – all the while knowing they had died years before. Then, in early June, those of another victim called Anna McFall were found in the adjacent Fingerpost Field. Mum and Dad were by now facing nine (it later became ten) joint murder charges. Dad was facing two additional ones – the murders of Rena and Charmaine. There has been some ambiguity about the death of Charmaine. In his early interviews with the police Dad apparently confessed to killing her a few weeks after his release from Leyhill prison having served a sentence for theft. But later he told them a different story – that Mum had murdered her after his release from prison. At other times he gave different versions, sometimes claiming he couldn't even recall when exactly she died. Some people have suggested that Charmaine died while Dad was still in prison and therefore Mum alone must have been responsible for her murder – but there has never been conclusive proof of that. And – disturbingly – the fact that her body had been partially dismembered suggests that Dad must have been involved.

With both parents now remanded in custody and awaiting trial, family divisions grew wider. While I never wished to see Dad ever again, Steve wanted to remain in contact with him. They exchanged letters and Steve visited him. At times during those visits Dad would admit the murders and at other times he denied them. Though Steve had no doubt he was guilty, he couldn't find it in him to hate Dad. In prison, he found him lonely, vulnerable and at times quite pathetic. 'He's my dad and I still love him,' Steve told me. Anne Marie took a similar attitude and also visited him in prison.

To some people this may seem as surprising as my support for Mum. But in spite of the things our parents had done to us – the beatings and abuse – we still deep down, even as adults, wanted to be loved by them and to love them in return. These feelings may not have been rational but I've since learned they are common in abused children, who often have an enormous capacity for taking the blame for the abuse themselves so that they can try to keep hold of the good parts of the relationship.

And our feelings about the importance of family hadn't gone away, even though it was falling apart. Steve – in the midst of this terrible family crisis – was about to get married and Dad took a great interest in the baby he and his girlfriend were expecting. It wasn't his first grandchild – Anne Marie had already had children by then – but because the baby was Steve's, it was the first that would really matter to him. He wanted Steve to take his wife and child back to live in Cromwell Street and was bitterly disappointed to be told that this could never happen.

Mum was disgusted at Steve's continuing contact with and support of Dad, and also to hear that Dad was trying to get messages through Steve. In one of his letters to Steve, he said that he forgave me for talking to the police and that he wanted to see me. 'Give my love to May tell her to cum and see me soon,' he wrote.[2]

I reassured Mum, quite truthfully, that I had no intention of having anything to do with Dad ever again.

I was in turmoil and desperately lonely. One day Ian called on me at my new flat. It was my birthday – we had been exchanging letters and I had told him I'd be spending it alone. He arrived with a present and champagne. He'd driven all the way from his home in Essex. I was really touched.

Ian was seventeen years older than me – in his late thirties. In hindsight, that should have been enough to make me wary of getting into a relationship with him. But to complicate things even further, he was married. It was an open marriage, with no promise of fidelity either way, but nonetheless it meant he was partly committed elsewhere. If it hadn't been for the situation I was in I wouldn't have dreamed of getting involved with him, but he was incredibly kind as well as persistent, and we started a relationship.

Although I was, in a sense, the other woman in Ian's life, I felt looked after and consoled and I'm not sure how I would have got through that period of my life without him. Over the years I have had an anxiety that men might only have been interested in me because of who I was. That because I had notorious parents who were interested in kinky and perverted sex, they might think I was somehow the same. There were times when I thought some men regarded me as no more than a notch on the bedpost. But I would never say that about Ian. Our relationship lasted only nine months but we are still in touch to this day.

*

Mum and Dad were unable to communicate directly with one another but their minds must have been turning towards the trial, neither of them certain how the other would plead or what they would say when they finally reached court. Would Dad continue to take all the blame himself? Or would he put some or all of it on her? Would she continue to deny any knowledge or involvement?

And perhaps the biggest question of all, at least in my mind, what were their real feelings for one another underneath? Did Dad still love Mum? Was Mum really as angry with him as she made out?

The answer to that – outwardly at least – came at a remand hearing at Gloucester magistrates' court in late July. They had to appear jointly and it was the first time they had seen one another since their walk in the park on the day in February when Dad was arrested and taken away.

Steve and I watched intently as Dad was led up first. He looked bewildered and anxious. We tried to catch his eye but he didn't see us. After a few moments Mum was brought up and put beside him in the tiny dock. As she brushed past him he put his hand on her shoulder and looked at her. It was a strange, imploring, almost desperate look. She pulled away from him, refusing to even look him in the eye, staring straight ahead at the magistrate. After the very brief hearing Dad tried once again to touch and make eye contact with her as she was led down, but she remained utterly cold and indifferent – as if he was dead to her. He looked devastated by the rejection and I'm not sure he ever recovered from it.

I continued to visit Mum where she was on remand. It was difficult to have any meaningful conversation with her. There were always guards within earshot. I assumed they were trying to pick up evidence. She never said anything to cause me to doubt her innocence. She was often tearful, and I was full of pity for her. No visit ended without her weeping, embracing me and telling me how important I was to her.

All I could cling onto was the hope that Mum would eventually be proved innocent, but we were warned that the trial could be a long way away because of the complexity of the case and the quantity of evidence involved. Until that day came, I knew I had to survive as best I could. Over the next few months, I moved home several more times, ending up sharing a house with Tara who by now was old enough to be out of care. I continued to see Ian occasionally. He treated me to a trip to Paris which was a wonderful, if brief, escape. He was well read and cultured and being with him always felt like glimpsing another world.

That Christmas of 1994 was thoroughly miserable, but I was cheered up by the knowledge that early in the New Year I would be meeting up with Ian again. On 1 January 1995 I set off to drive to Oxford to see him. I was listening to music on the radio-cassette but got bored with the tapes and switched to the radio. A news bulletin came on. I heard my dad's name mentioned but didn't immediately register why they were talking about him. I had to wait for the news headlines to come round again.

It said that he had been found dead in his cell that morning at Winson Green prison, Birmingham.

I didn't need to be told that he had killed himself. I already knew.

Chapter Eleven

Where No Shadow Falls

*Mum was angry in her letter today, all that anger directed at Dad.
She said he made idiots of us all, and until we can learn to face up
to our own human faults and vulnerabilities, pull together and create
a sense of community, society will be susceptible to evil and insane
monsters like Dad. They are sick, he was sick. But what was she? And
where did that leave us vulnerable kids? I can't help but thing it left
Heather dead. . .*

PUCKLECHURCH REMAND CENTRE

Sure, there's no cure for these individuals, but at
least with <u>everyone</u> aware of the potential threat we
can put a stop to them wreaking havoc on our most
vulnerable members of our society and keep them
under control!!

I pulled into a layby, stunned and shaking. I honestly hadn't
expected this. I sat there in tears, trying to take in the enormity
of it, wondering if I'd imagined it and it might not even be
true. Then Ian rang me and told me he'd also heard the news.
He could tell how shocked I was and in no state to continue
driving. He offered to drive up to me.

As I waited for him all kinds of thoughts raced through my head. Why was I feeling so devastated? Dad hadn't been a good man or anything approaching a decent father. Far from it. He was evil. He was a man who thought it was right to have sex with his own daughters. He had murdered my sister in the most brutal way. I ought to have been glad he was dead. But that wasn't what I was feeling. As well as shock, I was feeling a huge sense of loss. Not for the father I'd actually had but the one I could have had, that other children in normal families have. The father I'd wanted so badly. It was as if his death was the final confirmation I would never ever have that.

I also felt incredibly angry with him. There was no knowing how his suicide was going to affect the rest of the family: Mum, Steve, Anne Marie, Tara and the younger children. It felt like another dreadful chapter in the terrible story of all our lives. He had created carnage and now was leaving the rest of us to deal with it. It seemed like an unbelievably selfish act.

When Ian reached me he asked me what I wanted to do. I told him I needed to be with Steve. I was too shaken to drive myself so he drove me back to Gloucester. Steve was in a terrible state. He had similar feelings to me but on top of that felt guilty. He told me he'd been visiting Dad quite regularly in prison and Dad had been depressed and occasionally dropped hints about committing suicide. He felt he should have done more to keep Dad's morale up and to alert the prison authorities to his mental state.

It was a while before we got to know the details. When we found out, it only made us feel worse. Dad had collected his New Year's Day lunch of soup and pork chops and taken it back to his cell. Knowing the prison officers would then leave him alone for an hour, he pulled a sheet from his bed, tore it into strips and made a makeshift rope. He attached one end to a ventilation grille, high up on a wall and, standing on a chair, tied the other end round his neck before kicking the chair away. It would have been a slow, painful death from strangulation. Steve and I would never be able to get that terrible knowledge out of our heads.

On the wall he had scratched the words: 'Freddy the mass murderer from Gloucester'. I still don't know how this makes me feel – except incredible shame. Was he proud of it all then? Did he not have any remorse? How could he not even for Rena, and Charmaine – and Heather?

He had also left a number of letters in his cell. One of these, which he had written some weeks before and never sent, read:

To Rose West, Steve and Mae
   Wel Rose it your birthday on 29 November 1994 an still beautiful and lovly and I lov you. We wil alway be in love.
   The most wonderful thing in my life was wen I met you . . . Our lov is speshal to us. So, love, keep your promises to me. You kno what they ar. Wher we are put together for ever and ever is up to you. We lovd Heather, both of us. I wud lov Charmaine to be with Heather and Rena.
   You wil awlays be Mrs West, all over the world. That is important to me and to you.
   I havnt got a present. All I have is my life. I wil give it to you, my darling. Wen you are redy, come to me. I will be waiting for you.

We were given the chance to go to the coroner's and see his body. Steve went; although it was incredibly difficult, he felt he owed it to Dad. I didn't. I felt it would be a betrayal of Heather – and of Mum.

We were unsure how Mum would have reacted to the news. Whatever the consequences of his death, it put a violent and

traumatic end to their marriage and to the most important relationship of her life. It didn't seem possible that it wouldn't have
affected her deeply.

Steve and I went to see her at Pucklechurch Remand Centre. It
was a surreal experience. She seemed very calm and in complete
control of her feelings. Even though we were in our twenties,
she sat both of us on her knee as if we were little children. She
asked us how we were feeling and cuddled us. It felt so strange
and awkward and embarrassing. She'd never treated us like that
before – the only physical contact we'd had with her since we
were babies were the cuffs and beating she'd handed out to us.
Yet here we were clasped in her arms. We tried to explain how
confused and upset we were. She said very little about her own
feelings except that Dad's death hadn't affected her.

'It's terrible for you, both of you. I really feel for you.'

Steve and I exchanged confused looks. 'What about you,
Mum? Are you all right?'

'Oh, I'm all right. It's just you kids I'm worried about.'

I couldn't tell whether her indifference to what had happened
was genuine or if she was just putting it on. I was really puzzled
by it. When we left she hugged us both and told us she'd be fine
and to remember she'd be there for us during such a difficult
time. Steve and I talked about it afterwards.

'I can't believe that. I can't believe how calm she was,' I said.

'She's just putting it on,' Steve said. 'I swear she's cut to pieces
inside.'

'Or angry. Now she's got to deal with all this mess on her
own.'

I still found it extraordinary, though – how she could bottle
up her feelings like that, for our benefit. Sometimes I wonder
if it's just that she's incapable of having feelings for someone
who can't offer her something in return – it makes me think of

the time she lost the younger children and cleared out all their rooms as if they no longer mattered. Maybe she just doesn't have feelings in the same way that other people do.

Following Dad's suicide, Mum's legal team made a determined effort to persuade the authorities to drop the charges against her. They argued that the case against her was weak. That the evidence against her was circumstantial, that Dad had insisted during police interviews that she wasn't involved, and that he wouldn't now be able to give evidence which contradicted that. There was a court hearing to consider it all, but the judge decided there was enough evidence to proceed and he was going to commit Mum for trial. The murder of Charmaine was added to the charges against her – bringing the total number of murder counts to ten.

The funerals of the victims had begun in early 1995 and this made the question of how and when Dad's funeral should take place extremely sensitive. Although the general public didn't yet know the full details of Dad's crimes, most people were in no doubt about his guilt and that he'd been a depraved serial killer. He was hated in death as much as he had been in life. No one was sorry he was dead. There were even conspiracy theories that prison officers had colluded or even assisted with his suicide, or that when they had found him hanging they'd failed to call for medical assistance, to make sure he would die. It felt as if nobody in the country would have sympathy for anyone who wanted to give him a civilised funeral, let alone grieve for him.

His body was kept in a deep freeze for almost three months. Steve had been listed as his next of kin and eventually the authorities told him that they were ready to release the body. We had no idea what to do next. We knew that Dad hated the idea of cremation and his wish was to be buried in the family plot at Much Marcle, where there would later be room for Mum to be laid beside him. On the letter he had left for us in his cell he had even drawn a picture of a joint headstone, with the words:

In perfect peace he
waits for Rose, his wife

But that was completely out of the question. No church or other cemetery would agree to his burial and the desecration of his grave that would inevitably follow. No funeral home would accept the body.They didn't want to risk the terrible publicity. And how would we even find a minister to officiate at any service?

Stephen was still in touch with the *News of the World*, who offered to find a crematorium that was prepared to hold a funeral provided we let them report the story. I was unsure but went along with it because I didn't know what else to do. They made most of the arrangements, though it was very difficult to do it without the plans leaking out. All the cloak-and-dagger stuff depressed me deeply and, since I felt only anger and not sorrow towards Dad, I told Steve I didn't want to go, but he really wanted me there so I reluctantly agreed.

Everything seemed set, but the night before the funeral, the *News of the World* rang to say there had indeed been a leak and the plans would have to be changed. They phoned us early the following morning to give us the new details: the funeral was to happen at Canley Crematorium, Coventry. Ian drove Tara and me up there, while Steve and his wife travelled separately.

When we were almost there I had a call to say that the *Sun* newspaper and Sky TV had found out about the funeral – presumably because they had the same ownership as the *News of the World*. I was warned there were reporters already gathered outside the crematorium gates. We were told to drive straight past them when we arrived and get inside the chapel building as quickly as possible. We did so. When we got inside, Dad's coffin was already there. It had a simple plaque on the side saying 'F.W. West'. There were no flowers and the service was very short. The man conducting it said very little. There wasn't anything nice that could be said or eulogy possible. He could do little more than say the standard words of committal.

We all said 'Amen'. The coffin moved through the curtains which then closed behind it.

At some point the press had got into the building and we saw a massive flash go off and there was a scuffle between rival newspapers. In the confusion we got directed out of the wrong door and it was quite a way down a path back to the car, and the press chased us. We had to wait inside the car to collect the ashes. Ian offered to go and get them. When he returned with them they were still warm. I didn't want to hold them and insisted that Steve did so.

It was only afterwards that we heard Anne Marie had been driven up to the crematorium and was upset because she hadn't been invited. She had arrived after the service had finished and was very angry. We had no way of knowing for sure how she would have felt about attending Dad's funeral, because the police discouraged contact between us since she was likely to be a witness for the prosecution when Mum came to trial. However, I honestly didn't think she would want to be there. I knew she had visited Dad in prison but at that stage I believed she'd only done so to confront him, not to offer any support. It was only later on that I realised it was more complicated than that and she had the same ambivalent feelings towards him as Steve did.

The thing was, there had been some friction between Anne Marie and me for a long time. I had always been upset with her for telling Mum and Dad about Heather's bad behaviour at her daughter's party the day before she was murdered. It seemed to me that this added to the friction between them when Heather was at her most vulnerable. I still remember Heather crying and saying she never wanted to speak to Anne Marie again because she had got her into trouble.

Equally, I think Anne Marie blamed me for supporting Mum after the crimes came to light. But I really believed at that point that Mum was innocent – Dad had said so, Mum said so and the evidence presented was circumstantial. And I just couldn't believe she'd be capable of doing those terrible things to Heather, especially. I also knew that if she couldn't turn to me for support then she had no one. I don't expect Anne Marie to have felt the same way about Mum, knowing now the extent of the awful abuse Mum helped inflict on her, and because Mum wasn't her biological parent. To her, she must have seemed like the most wicked of stepmothers.

Another reason for the rift between us is that it has sometimes seemed to me that Anne Marie acted as though she was the only one of the children to have suffered, or at least that she has suffered more than the rest of us. The reality is that we have all suffered: just differently. All our lives have been damaged. None of us has an exclusive right to ask for sympathy.

We had no idea what to do with Dad's ashes after the funeral so Steve kept them until we could make some sort of decision. Some time later Anne Marie contacted him and asked if she could see them so that she could say her goodbyes to Dad. He agreed to meet her in Much Marcle so that she could do this, and then they would take them to the churchyard and scatter them on the grave where Dad's parents, Walter and Daisy, were buried. I wanted nothing to do with it. Everything to do with him seemed completely poisonous. I couldn't face the idea of seeing the ashes or, worse, handling them again, so I stayed at home.

When Steve arrived at the rendezvous place and went to get the ashes out of the boot of his car, Anne Marie lunged forward, grabbed them and ran off up the path towards the house belonging to another of Dad's brothers, Doug. As Anne Marie banged on the door and Steve caught up with her, the door opened and Doug appeared. There was an argument. Doug went for his shotgun and told Steve that if he didn't get off his land he would be shot. Steve had no choice but to leave without the ashes. Later, he told the police but they said they couldn't intervene. To this day, we have no idea what Anne Marie did with them.

Not long after Dad's funeral, Ian and I decided to end our relationship. The reasons were complicated but I suppose at heart I felt I wanted to be more than just a part of a man's life. Like most women, I felt I needed a partner who I could share everything with and was there for me all the time. Someone I could at least try to build some kind of future with. Ian was married and intended to remain married so it was never going to happen with him.

I tried to get on with my life, knowing that it would be very difficult as there would be a long wait for the trial. Although I had committed no crime I felt like a criminal on the run, living in a series of flats and houses, hoping no one would find out who I was, with really only Tara for moral support. Even if I was lucky enough to meet a man I liked, how and when would I tell him who I was? I could see no answer to this, and even if Mum were to be found innocent at her trial it would make no difference. I would still bear the stigma of being the child of one of the most notorious murderers that ever lived. I could see no hope of finding the kind of normal relationship most people have. The thought really scared me, because I knew I wanted my own family some day, a chance to begin new ties and loving, supportive relationships – and to have my own children. That seemed so unlikely for me now.

And then something extraordinary happened. Two months after Ian and I split up I found out I was pregnant. It was truly amazing – that out of the horror and misery and hopelessness of my situation there should come what seemed then, and has continued to be, an incredible gift.

A child of my own, another life – untouched and untainted by everything that had happened who I could move forward with into another life, even though I couldn't yet imagine what that life might be.

Chapter Twelve

Another Life

Mum's solicitor, Leo, told her about my pregnancy, I got her letter today, via him and not through the post so it wouldn't get read. She's excited for me, and she says I'm more than capable of looking after a child and bringing it up on my own. She tells me not to worry. I don't want to admit it but they are words that I find comforting, I feel especially vulnerable right now.

PUCKLECHURCH REMAND CENTRE

Dear Mae,

Just remember, look after yourself, buy yourself nice things to eat, rest a lot and don't put yourself under too much stress. Remember sometimes you have to be cruel to be kind.

My life seems to have been full of extraordinary ironies. Perhaps the greatest of these is that I would never have got pregnant and had my beautiful daughter Amy if the police hadn't raided the house, found the remains of the victims and discovered the truth about my parents' terrible crimes. It was only because all that happened that Ian got in contact with me to see if I was okay, and that we began a relationship. Even though it didn't turn into a permanent one, it was very important to me at the time. And out of it came Amy, an extraordinary gift at a time of terrible personal anguish. It's no wonder I've learned to be fatalistic about life. No wonder that, ever since that day when the police arrived at Cromwell Street with a search warrant, I felt as if I had been in a dream that showed no sign of ever ending.

The pregnancy was completely unplanned and a total surprise. Unlike Tara, who found conceiving easy, I have found it extremely difficult and later on spent years trying to get pregnant for a second time. I was twenty-three when Amy was conceived, which some people might regard as young to be having a first child, but by my mother's standards it was late. By the time she had reached that age, Mum had three children of her own, was pregnant with a fourth, and had two stepchildren. I had the impression that my own failure to shell out babies at a similar age was a disappointment and worry to them both.

I had no suspicion that I was pregnant. In fact, I only found out because Tara suspected she might be and turned up one day with a pregnancy test kit which she didn't know how to use. I told her I'd help her work it out. I studied the instructions and then tried the first indicator in the pack myself. I was astonished when it turned blue.

I could hardly grasp it at first. For over a year I had received a series of devastating personal blows. The only news I had come to expect was of the bad, often horrific, sort. Disaster after disaster. Anguish upon more anguish. Why this, and why now? I found myself thinking. And yet, before long, the confusion was replaced by something else – a feeling that this was meant to be.

I've never been a particularly religious person, certainly not a devout Christian let alone a regular church-goer and yet somehow it seemed to me that the baby was something sent to me by God, or if not God some other spiritual presence. It was as if,

186

with Dad out of my life, there was finally a space for something good. But even more powerful than that was a feeling that I had been given a child because I had nothing and it would give me a reason for carrying on. It was a new life, which would be more important to me than any other – including my own – that I would have to cherish and take care of, no matter what setbacks lay ahead.

Yet, if it felt like a blessing, I also knew it would be an extraordinary challenge. For a start, there was no possibility of me getting back together with Ian and sharing parenthood with him. We had never really been a proper couple and, in any case, he had another life – a life that I knew he wouldn't have wanted to walk out of, even with the knowledge that I was to have his baby. I had no doubt that I would have to have the child and raise it as a single parent.

I also knew that I would have to go through the pregnancy while Mum awaited trial, and then appeared in court on multiple counts of murder. Far from receiving the kind of emotional support many daughters receive from their mothers when they are expecting a child, I would have to be the one giving support to her.

Most daunting of all was the fear that, in spite of her vehement protestations of innocence, she might be found guilty. I wasn't that worried about this at the time, so assured was I about her innocence, but I worried that with Dad gone a jury might be more likely to find her guilty so that at least someone was punished for the crimes. Although I hardly knew anything of the details of the case against her at that stage, I was relieved that her lawyers continued to be confident there was nothing to link her directly with them. For the sake of my own sanity I had to keep believing in her innocence.

Her reaction to the news of my pregnancy took me by surprise

– I always knew she loved babies but her interest in me as an individual still felt very new – I didn't think she'd care, but she claimed to be thrilled for me. She saw it as a new and exciting chapter in our lives that both of us were embarking on, rather than showing any understanding of how complicated the situation really was. She wrote to me to say she was excited for me, that she *used to look forward to [her] scans. I suppose it's because the first time you get to see your baby.*

It still makes me angry now, even more so as a mother myself – how she could love babies so much but not care about us as children, or – as Heather proved – as adults. But she offered me support, which at the time I craved from her – although she didn't seem to understand how complicated the situation was:

'If anytime you feel I could do anything to help (I know it can't be much, but you never know) please don't hesitate to ask! I mean it sweetheart, I might be locked up but there are ways to do things.'

I suppose she was behaving in many ways like any mother whose daughter is pregnant. Her manner was certainly not that of a woman who was accused, let alone guilty, of being a murderess and child killer.

Yet I couldn't forget what was hanging over her for a moment. There were constant reminders. I did my best to avoid the press but sometimes it wasn't possible and if they spotted me they'd throw questions at me, trying to get a story. I had nothing to say to them, but that didn't stop them. On one occasion they ambushed me after I'd visited Mum at the remand prison, and chased me, cameras flashing and blinding me, back to the car

I'd left in the car park. They must have seen that I was pregnant and how distressed they made me.

One of the hardest experiences during that time was going to pick up what was left of the house. I don't suppose anyone thinks about what happens after a home becomes a crime scene – I certainly never had before. After the police excavated the garden and basement at Cromwell Street, they seized everything within it – including our most private belongings – and then anything that wasn't required as exhibits for the trial were taken to a huge aircraft hangar. I remember walking into that hangar – seeing our family's lifetime's worth of posessions strewn in piles on the floor – and wondering why I hadn't woken up from this dream yet.

We rooted through everything as quickly as we could: we'd been given a van and told we had an hour to take what we wanted. There were things I really wanted, of real sentimental value: paintings I'd done for my Art O level, baby things which might come in useful for the baby I was having, and family photos. It might seem strange that I wanted those but I did, and badly – it was a record of my childhood, my siblings' childhood – the only one we would ever have. I rushed round, scrambling to find and save what I could, then we were told to leave.

I didn't trouble Mum with any of that though: I thought she had enough on her plate; but I resent that now. But it was the moment at the end of our visits – she would hold onto me and there would be tears – that always kept me hanging on: 'I don't know what I'd do without you, Mae. You're all I've got now.'

She wasn't a woman who had ever found it easy to show weakness, so those moments of vulnerability had a big effect on me. The prison authorities were also concerned about her psychological state and for a period she was put on suicide watch in the hospital wing. I had no idea how serious they thought the risk of her taking her own life was, but the fact that Dad had already done the same thing must have been a factor.

The letters she sent me at that time, though, were often quite upbeat – as though she was getting used to prison life and even enjoying it in some ways. She'd tell me she'd had her hair cut, or what she was enjoying on the radio, one time it was Peter Pan: 'It's really good. There's Toya Wilcox as Peter Pan, Ron Moody as 'Hook' and loads of famous people in it. It's in four parts and it's on Radio 4.'

I wondered, though, as I have wondered many times since, what Mum really made of Dad's suicide. His motive for killing himself will never be known and he certainly never made it clear in any suicide note. To most people it probably seems like a cowardly way out of having to go to prison, but for me, the likeliest explanation is that he was already depressed that his house and family had been broken apart, that there was little prospect of Mum ever returning there and getting the family back together, and even if that did happen he would never him-self be part of it again. And on top of all that Mum had rejected him so emphatically in court that day they made their joint appearance. In doing that, maybe he thought she'd ended their relationship.

On Mum's part, I wish I'd asked her what she made of Dad's final words to her in his suicide note:

All I have is my life. I wil give it to you, my darling. Wen you are redy, come to me. I will be waiting for you.

Did she think of his suicide and these words as genuinely a final act of love? Or was he simply playing with her? Was it in fact his way of saying that, even in death, she belonged to him, whether she liked it or not?

I believe the latter is the more likely explanation, and so Mum's anger at that time was not only to do with the trouble (as she saw it) that Dad had got her into, but also the infuriating feeling that he had had the last word and that she would truly be trapped for ever in a hell of his making while he laughed at her from beyond the grave.

Chapter Thirteen

Trial

Mum is angry. Her letter is short and she can't sleep. She writes to me at 4.30am, the memories of her conviction running through her head for the thousandth time. She says the trial was unfair, that an injustice was done. Sometimes I believe her, but then . . .

HM PRISON DURHAM

Mae,

I'm in prison for the rest of my life because of that shit!!! I still can't believe it!

I'm still getting letters of support from people you know. It's really nice, makes you feel better anyway

The week before the trial was scheduled to begin I visited Mum in Winchester prison, a short distance from the court where the case was due to be heard. It was a prison that normally housed male prisoners and so they had had to build special accommodation within the male segregation unit to house her while she was on remand during the trial. Already there were serious concerns for her physical safety in prison. There'd been numerous death threats made against her and I could tell how vulnerable she felt as soon as I saw her in the room where they'd allowed us to meet.

'I hate this place, Mae. It wasn't so bad in Pucklechurch, I'd even started to make friends. Here I don't see a soul apart from the screws and my lawyers when they come.'

I felt so sorry for her. 'It must be horrible for you, Mum.'

'It is, Mae. Still, it won't be for long. The lawyers are confident I'll be found not guilty.'

She seemed to genuinely believe what she was saying. Although her words were meant for me there were, as usual, prison guards standing within earshot, no doubt listening closely for evidence which might be used against her. I thought she wanted them to hear what she was saying: that she had no secrets to hide and was confident of her innocence. I could imagine the authorities might be getting desperate for any indication of guilt from her, because I'd spoken to her solicitor who told me that in spite of all their months of intensive investigations the police had still not found anything which clearly implicated Mum in the murders.

Although optimistic, Mum spoke of her worry that Dad's death would make it harder for her to clear her name because an angry public would demand that someone should pay the price for his crimes and, since he was no longer around to do so, she might be made a scapegoat.

'Honestly, Mae, the trouble that fucking man's caused me! Anyway, people will understand the truth once it's put before them.'

'I hope so.'

'They will, Mae. And when it's all over we can start again, can't we? I've been thinking, I might move to Ireland.'

'Ireland?'

'I can't stay in this country but nobody'll know me over there.

You can all come over. You, Steve, Tara, and your children – and all the other kids too once they're out of care. We'll be a family again, Mae. One great big family. Have a farm right out in the countryside and live the simple life, eh?'

I didn't know what to say. I believed in her innocence, and I was happy that she was confident of being acquitted, but I didn't want to encourage her to live in a fantasy world.

'Let's just take one step at a time, shall we?'

'Don't be negative, Mae. I need you to believe it's going to be alright too!' she snapped.

'I know, Mum, I know it's important to be positive.'

I'd taken her clothes to wear during the trial. She'd chosen them herself from the Argos Additions catalogue and I'd ordered them for her. There were sober dresses in emerald green and black, and one dark-coloured jacket. Mum knew that the way she came across in court could affect how the jury regarded her and might have an effect on the outcome, and she was determined to dress appropriately and show a respectful demeanour. During the later stages of the trial, during the period leading up to Remembrance Day, she even wore a poppy in court. She was determined to try not to let public prejudice against her undermine her case.

I'd been living in a basement flat in Cheltenham but then Tara, who was living in Gloucester, split up from her partner and suggested I move in with her and her baby son. Although I'd come to hate Gloucester and was very reluctant to return, I was six months' pregnant and felt vulnerable and isolated. I was glad to take up Tara's offer, knowing that at least we could support one another at such a difficult time.

Living there wasn't easy. We were desperate to hang onto as much privacy as we could. We barely went out, apart from food shopping and my ante-natal visits to Cheltenham. From time to time the police called round and gave us updates about the impending trial. It was on one of those occasions that they revealed that the safe houses I had stayed in with Mum had been bugged. It was obvious that the only reason they were telling me was because they knew it would come out at the trial and so I'd find out anyway. I wasn't surprised. I was at the stage where almost nothing that happened could ever surprise me. But I felt angry, knowing that it meant the police suspected I might have knowledge of the murders which I hadn't passed on to them. In fact, it eventually became clear in court that, during all the many days they had secretly taped her in the safe houses, Mum said nothing at all that incriminated her.

I didn't attend the trial. Even if I'd wanted to I wouldn't have been allowed to as I'd been told I might be called as a witness for the defence. I was relieved not to have to go to court and sit through it. I knew it would have meant facing the media and watching Mum as the prosecuting counsels tore into her.

So I remained at the Gloucester house with Tara.

But we couldn't pretend it wasn't happening – it was being described as the 'Trial of the Century' and was being covered extensively in the papers and on TV news, and in any case we had a massive personal interest in the outcome, so we ended up following it through the media as closely as it seemed the whole nation was doing.

Mum phoned me on the first day, just before they took her on the short drive from prison to Winchester Crown Court. She seemed calm, her voice was steady, and she still seemed confident of the outcome.

'It's going to be okay, Mae. I know it is.'

She told me her solicitor, Leo Goatley, still felt the same way. Her defence team were sure the prosecution knew how weak their case was.

'It's just a matter of me being strong for a few weeks and getting through it, no matter what they throw at me. And then we can all get on with our lives again.'

'I hope so. Good luck.'

'Thanks, Mae. I love you, you know that don't you?'

'Yes, I know that, Mum.'

I didn't know it. I'd never felt it during the whole of my life. What I did know was that she needed me, desperately it seemed, and it was what she wanted to hear.

In the opening days, the prosecution set out their case. Their lead barrister, Brian Leveson QC, told the court that the victims' 'last moments on earth were the object of the sexual depravity of Rose West . . . then they were snuffed out.'

In outlining how the ten victims had died, how the prosecution believed Mum had assisted Dad with the murders and how close they had been as a couple, he also told the story of their relationship. Much of it was new to me and was so extraordinary I struggled to take it all in. Only in later years when I came to read full accounts of the trial was I able to understand all the details.

It was a story that began even before Mum met Dad, with his tangled relationship with one of the victims, his first wife Rena. She was a fiery and feisty seventeen-year-old from Glasgow who'd worked as a prostitute, and been sent to a borstal for attempted burglary. There she'd met a girl from Ledbury called Barbara. Barbara was released first and when Rena eventually got out she followed her down to Ledbury. The two girls were working at the New Inn when Dad met her. They started going out, and Uncle John began seeing Barbara at the same time.

Rena was already a few weeks' pregnant. No one knew for certain who the father was but he may have been a pimp running her when she was working the streets. Neither she nor Dad wanted a child. They tried to get rid of it. It was suggested that Dad took Rena into a field near Much Marcle and tried to perform a DIY abortion on her using some primitive implement. But the abortion failed. They were stuck with the baby. Dad told his parents, Walter and Daisy, the child was his. It was a matter of pride for him. He would have felt humiliated if they thought Rena was carrying another man's child. And he knew his parents would have hated it. They didn't like Rena. She was rough, outspoken and seemed to have some sort of hold over Dad.

With no future for them in Much Marcle, Dad and Rena decided to marry and move back to Glasgow. For Dad it was a way out of the world he'd grown up in. For Rena, having a husband helped to keep the authorities off her back, and protected her from the pimps who had controlled her when she was on the street.

When she gave birth, the child turned out to be of mixed race. They named her Charmaine. Dad continued to tell lies about her. He persuaded Rena to write to Walter and Daisy and say that she'd lost the baby she'd been pregnant with and that the child they were looking after was adopted.

Dad found work driving an ice-cream van. Rena went back to working the streets. Before long she became pregnant again, this time with Dad's child, and in July 1964 Anne Marie was born. Dad was very taken with the new baby. Rena, on the other hand, resented the fact that he didn't have the same feelings towards Charmaine and also that having another baby prevented her from working. Their relationship, which had always been stormy, grew increasingly violent. It became a struggle for control, but Rena gave as good as she got.

Neither of them was faithful. Rena had an affair with a married bus driver called John MacLachlan. Dad carried on taking sex wherever he found it. Among his other conquests, he began a relationship with one of Rena's friends – Anna McFall, another Glaswegian girl, who was only sixteen.

After his arrest Dad gave various versions of how he came to leave Scotland but all of them began with him killing a three-year-old boy with his ice-cream van. He was backing into a cul-de-sac and the little boy got in the way. In one of his versions he wrote:

I Love Workin with the public you got to know wow the Other ½ lives there ar always sumone Worse of then you. but Disaster hit me. I had a fatal accident and kill a 3 to 4 year old Boy with My ice cream Van the boy was a god customer I see him Ever day. I love him as a son. I had no son at that time. I Wonted a son but that Was no time for one. So I spoil him by giving him a Boll and Badge and allway a icecream sunday. the accideent Was on 4 November at TEN PAST three I had a firework for him. U told him I would bring them the day befor so was that Way he ream in to the back of the VAN I did not see him. I was in shock. I went backwards over a fence in to a garden sumone tuck me in their home and the police took me to hospital I was given drugs and taken home by the police.

He went on to claim that when he got back home from the hospital his house had been full of yobs and Rena was in bed with two of them. He assaulted her, was charged but then acquitted when the case came to court. As he left the courtroom the yobs that Rena had fallen in with found him and ran him out of town.

In his so-called autobiography, *I Was Loved By An Angel*, which Dad wrote in Winson Green prison towards the end of his life (with the help of Janet Leach, the 'appropriate adult' allotted to him by the police because he was unable to read or write properly), he claimed that it was Anna McFall – the 'angel' of the title – who helped him get away from Glasgow.

She sead she Wood help Me get the Girls out and back to England so I gave ana a PHON number the next day ana Rang Me and said Rena had gone out with the yobs. so I got the car and went to my home ana was ther We gopt the first out ana sead you Will have to beat Me up. I sead no way you can say I did. so we agreed ana Wood tell Rena and the yobs I had.[3]

After leaving Glasgow he returned to Much Marcle with Charmaine and Anne Marie but without Rena, and tried to persuade his mother to take them all in. Daisy wouldn't have the mixed race Charmaine in the house so he put both children into care.

Before long, Rena left Glasgow and came to find him. They went to the Gloucester area, the kids were taken out of care and they ended up sharing a caravan with Anna McFall and another friend from Glasgow, Isa McNeill. His life was becoming more and more complicated and the marriage to Rena even more violent. Often, when they fell out, Rena would go back to Glasgow, only to return to him again. It was during one of her absences that – according to Dad's memoir – he began to fall in love with Anna, who was acting as a nanny for the two children.

Anna became an obsession and, Dad told the police, she was everything Rena wasn't: gentle, kind, caring and loving – 'God's gift to me and my daughters', he called her. Anna became infatuated with Dad. She wrote letters home to her mother, saying that she wanted to marry him.

In *I Was Loved By An Angel*, Dad wrote about Anna in the same kind of romantic language he later used about Mum. I've often wondered how Mum must have felt hearing about this:

was she upset or jealous? Dad described the walks he and Anna took together, by the river, under the moonlight. But, however truthful his flowery descriptions of the relationship, it's hard to believe that, from his point of view at least, it didn't involve sex and it wasn't long before Anna fell pregnant.

Dad tried to keep his affair with Anna secret from Rena, moving her into another caravan on a different site, but Rena found out. She was furious, stealing some of Anna's things in retaliation and heading back to Glasgow yet again. The police pursued her, brought her back and charged her with theft. It was a chaotic situation. Rena now hated Anna. Anna was beginning to question whether it had been a good idea getting involved with Dad – almost certainly experiencing the violent side of him as Rena had done. It seems she wanted out.

Dad's life was in chaos. The last thing he wanted was another child, but Anna was over six months' pregnant and there was no legal way of getting rid of the baby even if Anna wanted to. In some ways it would have suited him if she'd gone back to Glasgow, but he was a man who liked to be in control of everything and so he didn't like that idea. But if she stayed and had the child and he continued the affair with her, how would Rena react? Something had to give.

Then, in early August 1967, Anna McFall went missing.

No one noticed. She was just eighteen, cut adrift from her family in Scotland, with few friends. A pregnant girl on a caravan site among people who were mostly strangers.

But, according to the prosecution, Dad knew exactly what had happened to Anna. He had murdered her. When her remains were finally found at Fingerpost Field near Much Marcle, years later, the skeleton of her unborn child was found beside her.

With Anna and their unborn child disposed of, he carried on

living with Rena and the two children in the caravan at the site near Bishop's Cleeve. He drifted from job to job, working in a mill, as a delivery man, in a bakery, indulging in whatever petty crime he could get away with. He also encouraged Rena to earn extra cash by continuing to work as a prostitute – picking up men in local pubs. He had no jealousy of the men he prompted her to have sex with. Just as with Mum later on, the idea of her going with other men excited him – provided he felt in control of it. But Rena wasn't a woman to be controlled and the pair broke up yet again, although both of them knew the break-up would probably be as temporary as all the others.

So that was his life when he met Mum: an on/off relationship with Rena, kinky and rough sex with her or wherever else he could find it, pornography, robbing and thieving, and looking after two little children in the shabby caravan. All while living in the knowledge, so the prosecution claimed, that he'd murdered his lover Anna.

Mum and Dad had described the beginning of their relationship to me as fairly innocent and almost comical, but the court was told that it had been intense and extremely complicated from the start. It was also full of lies and deception. The prosecution outlined it in great detail.

Dad had claimed to Mum that he had separated from Rena and she had gone back to Scotland, when in fact she was still living in the area. He rapidly drew Mum, who was very unhappy at home, into his world. Her parents, Bill and Daisy, were desperate to break the relationship up, especially when they found out that Mum wasn't just spending most of her time at Dad's caravan, but he'd also encouraged her to have sex with other men for payment. She was still only fifteen and Bill approached Gloucestershire social services, explaining that his underage daughter was out of control and he wanted her to be taken into care. They agreed and she was placed in a home for troubled teenagers in Cheltenham.

She hated the place, and being forbidden from seeing Dad only made her want to be with him more. She wrote him a love letter:

Dear Fred,

I am glad you came to see me. Last night made me realise we are two people, not two soft chairs to be sat on . . . about us meeting this week, it could be Sunday afternoon. I will have to get Lynda to say I am going with her. You know we won't be able to meet so often, that's why I can't get the idea out of my head that you're going with someone else . . . You told my aunt about Rena But what about telling me the whole story even if it takes all day. I love you, Fred, but if anything goes wrong it will be the end of both of us for good. We will have to go somewhere far away where nobody knows us.

I will always love you,

Rose

Both of them knew that their separation was only temporary because it was only a few months until her sixteenth birthday, when she'd be free to do what she wanted.

By the time that day arrived, 29 November 1970, Dad had been sent to prison for thirty days for a series of petty crimes, including the theft of fencing panels from an employer. The little girls, Charmaine and Anne Marie, who'd been living in the caravan with him, had been taken into care again, and instead of moving in with Dad as she'd planned, Mum was forced to return home to live with her parents.

As soon as Dad came out of prison they were reunited. Dad had found a bedsit to rent in Cheltenham where he hoped Bill wouldn't find them but it didn't take long for him to do so. He was furious and called in the police. When Mum was examined by the police doctor she was found to be pregnant. Bill's worst fears were confirmed. He suspected the child had been conceived before Mum was sixteen and wanted Dad prosecuted, but it was impossible to prove.

Mum was sent to a unit for teenage mothers where Bill and Daisy hoped she could be kept out of Dad's way. They put pressure on her to have an abortion. She pretended to agree, and Bill booked her in for the procedure. But she was desperate to have the baby. She met up secretly with Dad and they hatched a plan that when she went into the clinic, he would wait around the corner in his van and she'd run to him and they'd drive away together.

It never came to that. The night before the abortion, realising some kind of plan was in the offing, Bill went to see Mum and gave her an ultimatum. He said that she could either get rid of the baby, give up Dad and return to live at home, or she could keep the baby and go with him, but he and Daisy would disown her for good and if he ever saw her in the street he'd knife her. His threat only made her more determined. She told him she was leaving home for good to live with Dad.

The girls were out of care again by then and Dad wanted them all to get away from Mum's parents. They moved to Gloucester, rented the flat at 25 Midland Road and soon afterwards Mum gave birth to Heather.

By this time, the prosecution said, Mum knew that Rena was still in the area, in touch with Dad, possibly even still having a sexual relationship with him. Dad tried to reassure her it wasn't true, even tattoing over Rena's name, shaping the existing letters into 'Rose'. But she remained insecure and also resentful at having to look after the two children who Rena had abandoned responsibility for, as well as her own baby daughter.

But her romance with Dad was far from dead. And when he was imprisoned again soon afterwards, for theft, Mum visited him as often as she could at Leyhill prison and they exchanged love letters.

In one of them she wrote:

To My Darling
     What was you on about at the beginning of your letter. I just can't make it out for trying. Hey love thats great, three more visits, it'll take up half the time I've got to wait for you Blinking base people get's on my nerves. Darling, about Char. I think she likes to be handled rough. But darling, why do I have to be the one to do it
     Love, I don't think God wan'ted me to go to that dance. Because I didn't go after all. Darling, I think from now on I'm going to let God guide me. It always ends up that way anyway (As you may know) Ha! Ha!
     Well, Love, keep happy, Longing for the 18th.
     Your ever worshipping wife,
     Rose

Even though this was eight months before they were to marry, and Dad was still married to Rena, Mum was already referring to herself as his wife. But despite the romantic language the reference to Charmaine liking 'to be handled rough' sounded chilling and suggested Mum was mistreating her.

Dad wrote back to Mum, describing a love token he'd made

for her. It was a miniature gypsy caravan, made out of wood, which opened into a jewellery box. It had a wooden heart attached, inscribed with the words *'TO ROSE LOVE FRED'*, and on the top of the letter he'd written: **'Our Family Of Love'**.

The letter read:

To My Darling Wife Rose

Darling you forgot to write agen. Darling your caravan is at the prison gate for you I have put your assisted visits form for the 18th or 19th and for the 15th of June. Will, it won't be long for the 24 now . . . I love you darling for ever my love. You has your say from now until for ever. Darling. Will, Darling, until I see you. All my love I send to you.

Your Ever Worshipping Husband

Fred

Across the letter he'd also written 'For Heather', 'Anna', 'CHAR', 'For Rose'. And added kisses, then the words: *'Mr and Mrs West for ever'*.

She wrote back to him with a heart and the words *'FROM NOW UNTILL FOR EVER'* at the top of her letter.

To My Dearest Lover

Darling, I am so sorry I upset you in my previous letters I didn't mean it (NO joking). I know you love me darling It just seems queer that anyone should think so much of me. I LOVE you. Love I don't mind what you make me, because I know it will turn out beautifull. Darling I would like to get a horse for our caravan & put it in a showcase. We've got a lot of things to do darling in the next couple of years. And we'll do it just loving each other. Well Love, see you on the 31st, Better not write to much in case I go putting my big foot in it. (Ha! Ha!) Sending all my love & heart your worshipping wife,

Rose XXXXXX
PS Love I've got the wireless on and it's playing some lovly romantic music. Oh! How I wish you were hear beside me. Still remembering your love & warmth, Rose[4]

On 15 June 1971 she visited him again at Leyhill with the children. He was thrilled to see her and she was excited to learn that he would be released on parole on 24 June. Shortly after that visit Charmaine disappeared.

The prosecution claimed that Mum had murdered her, hidden the body in the basement and told Dad what she'd done when he came out of prison. He then dug a hole and buried the body in the rear yard, which is where her remains were eventually found in 1994. The two of them told Anne Marie that Charmaine had gone to live with her mother in another part of the country. The timeline regarding this was assumed rather than proved, which is why I wouldn't hear of it at the time. Now . . . I don't know what to think. Would Mum have done it? *Could* she? I find it hard even now to accept she's directly guilty of having a hand in this and Heather's death, but what I do accept is that my brain doesn't *want* to believe it. And that doesn't mean it's not true.

All this still left the problem of what to tell Rena, who turned up at 25 Midland Road wanting to see Charmaine and was unhappy with the lies and evasions when she asked why her daughter wasn't there. She also visited Dad's parents asking the same question. She was becoming suspicious. Dad decided something had to be done, the prosecution said. He agreed to let Rena see Charmaine and lured her to Fingerpost Field near Much Marcle, where he murdered and buried her. When her remains were recovered it was found he had buried a small plastic boomerang – probably belonging to Charmaine – in the grave with her. I feel like touches like this sum up how complicated both my parents were, how hard it is to understand them. Even when my father was at his most evil, he had at least some knowledge of what it was to be 'nice'.

With Charmaine and Rena out of the way, Mum and Dad were free to think about the future. They wanted somewhere larger to live to house their growing family, and so Mum could have separate quarters for her work as a prostitute, and they bought 25 Cromwell Street. The court was told that during the following fourteen years Dad and Mum were jointly responsible for the deaths of nine more young women and outlined what they believed had happened to them.

Lynda Gough first came to 25 Cromwell Street because she had a boyfriend who was lodging there. Her family lived in Gloucester and she worked as a seamstress. She was only slightly older than Mum and they became friends. After her boyfriend left, she ended up renting a room in the house herself. She was drawn into a lesbian relationship by Mum and then into a sexual relationship with Dad. It may have been consensual at first, but it ended with her being tied up and imprisoned in the basement for days on end, where she was tortured and sexually abused mercilessly before finally being murdered and buried. She was twenty-one.

Carol Ann Cooper had grown up in Worcester, but when her mother's marriage failed she'd been placed in care in a children's home. She was thirteen, hated the home and began to run away regularly, sometimes visiting Gloucester. At some point she got to know Dad, perhaps through someone who was lodging at the house. She started going to the house to babysit, though I was only a tiny baby at the time and have no memory of her. She disappeared on 10 November 1973. In his police interviews, Dad gave various accounts of how he'd had sex with, murdered and buried her. In one of them he claimed they'd been having an affair and she had got pregnant and threatened to tell Mum. She was fifteen.

Lucy Partington was a student at Exeter University who had come home to spend Christmas with her family at the village of Gretton, near Cheltenham. On 20 December 1973 she went to visit a friend in Cheltenham, setting off to catch the bus back home shortly after ten in the evening. She was never seen again. Dad never gave an honest explanation of how he came to meet, murder and bury her in the basement. Initially, during police questioning, he claimed he'd known her for some time, that they'd been having an affair and he was afraid Rose would find out about it. The prosecution claimed that was a lie, that she was a complete stranger who had either been lured into his van or abducted off the street with Mum's assistance, taken back to 25 Cromwell Street and subjected to a brutal sexual assault before being murdered. She was twenty-one.

Shirley Hubbard was from Worcester and the child of a broken home. On 14 November 1974 she'd run away and was never seen again. She'd been picked up by Dad in his van and taken to live at Cromwell Street. As with Carol Cooper, he claimed he'd known her for some time, that they'd had a secret affair, she'd got pregnant and was threatening to tell Rose, and that's why he'd killed her. There was no evidence that this was true, but it was believed that she too had been sexually abused and tortured before being buried beneath the floor. She was fifteen.

Therese Siegenthaler, or 'the Dutch Girl' as Dad referred to her, had actually been born in Switzerland. She had come to live in England when she was eleven and her parents divorced. She was studying in London. On 15 April 1974, she set off to visit friends in Ireland, intending to travel by ferry from either Fishguard or Holyhead. Her journey took her through the Gloucester area. Dad claimed he'd seen her hitch-hiking near Evesham and offered her a lift. He'd then gone back to Cromwell Street with her to try some form of sexual experiment which, as he put it, had 'gone wrong' and she'd died as a result. As with all the murders, he changed his account numerous times, insisting that he'd 'only wanted to help her'. Like many of the victims, he'd decapitated her before burying her under the basement floor. She was twenty-one.

Juanita Mott. Dad had also picked Juanita up when she was hitch-hiking. She already knew Dad. Like some of the other girls, she was from a broken home and had been living in various bedsits in Gloucester. She'd got to know some of the lodgers at 25 Cromwell Street and met Mum and Dad. Soon after that she rented one of their rooms but didn't stay for long because Dad threatened her that 'if you can't pay the rent you'll have to have sex with me or Rose'. But she remained in the area and Dad spotted her on the Gloucester to Newent road on Friday 11 April 1975, picked her up and took her back to Cromwell Street where he raped, tortured, murdered and decapitated her before burning her in the basement. She was eighteen.

Shirley Robinson was also from a broken home and had been taken into care at the age of fourteen, before being sent to a secure unit for teenagers. In April 1977 she left care and found a job at the Green Lantern café in Gloucester – which Mum's father Bill had bought and was running. He'd offered to let her live in the flat above. One day Dad called in there – he and Bill were getting on well at this time. Shirley was unhappy. She poured her heart out to Dad about various problems in her life, including the fact that Bill was pestering her sexually – sometimes barging into the bathroom and trying to molest her. Dad listened sympathetically and offered her a room at Cromwell Street. She was relieved and grateful. She became friends with Mum and then they started a lesbian relationship – but Dad was also having a sexual relationship with her. She became pregnant. Mum found out and was furious. She wanted Shirley out of their lives, but Dad didn't want to give her up. Shirley's due date grew near; she asked Dad whether Mum might leave him so they could have a future together. Soon afterwards she disappeared. In 1994, when her remains were found in the garden, Dad admitted to her murder quite quickly but insisted he'd acted alone, telling the police, 'I don't think Rose even knew Shirley.' He claimed he'd strangled her because she'd threatened to tell Mum the baby was his. He said Mum had been out for a walk with Heather, myself, Steve and Tara at the time he did it. When her remains were dug up, her baby was not in the place where her womb should have been, but separate from the body. She was eighteen.

Alison Chambers had been born in Germany, and lived for a time in Swansea before being taken into care and ending up at Jordan's Brook – a home for troubled teenagers in Gloucester. She got to know people who were lodging at the house and took to visiting regularly. Mum soon befriended her and became her lover, but she also fell into a sexual relationship with Dad. In August 1979, learning that she would not be allowed to leave Jordan's Brook when she reached the age of seventeen as she'd hoped, she absconded, telling a friend she was going to run away to Wales. She arranged to meet the friend the next day but never turned up. Her remains were found in the back garden of 25 Cromwell Street under the bathroom window. There was a belt wrapped round the top of her head and her jaw, clamping it

shut in order to prevent her screaming. She had been partly dismembered. Many of her smaller bones were missing – the police
thought that some of them might have been flushed down the
toilet. The evidence suggested that she had been subjected to
prolonged sadistic sexual assault and torture before being killed.
She was sixteen.

And the final victim, the prosecution said, was my sister
Heather, who had been murdered eight years later, in 1987.
They said that far from being out for a walk with Steve and me
when she was killed, as Dad had claimed, Mum had actually
been present. It was the first time I'd heard the details of how
Heather had been strangled and dismembered. I found it almost
unbearable to think about the agony of her last hours. I knew it
was information I would never be able to forget for the rest of
my life.

It was an unbelievable catalogue of horrors that had been set
out before the court. Although the police had hinted at some
of the details when I was still living in the house as they began
their excavations, most of them were new to me, especially the
way the victims, including Heather, had died. I could hardly
begin to take the enormity of it in. All kinds of emotions swirled
round in me. That Dad could imagine such awful things let alone
do them – I tried very hard not to think especially about Anna
McFall and Shirley Robinson whose babies had been taken out
of their bodies . . . I was appalled by the horror, as well as being
completely furious and ashamed that it was my own father who
had brought such terrible suffering on so many people. I felt
wretched for the relatives of the victims who, like me, were also
hearing some of these details for the first time.

I was also afraid that the anger the prosecution's case would
stir up now it was being made public would mean Mum wouldn't
have any chance of receiving a fair trial. I felt more sorry for

Mum than ever that she'd been married to this man – *loved* him in her way – and now she was having to answer to what I believed were his sick, unthinkable crimes.

The prosecution set about trying to prove that, although Dad had insisted when he was arrested that the murders were his responsibility alone, and that Mum hadn't been present or known anything about them, she was still guilty as charged. Witnesses were called, including forensic experts, neighbours, Mum's mother Daisy, sister Glenys and the mother of Lynda Gough, who described calling at the house and seeing Mum wearing one of Lynda's cardigans. It was hard to know how this evidence was going down in court, not being there myself, but Mum's solicitor got in touch and told me the Prosecution were struggling and still hadn't been able to come up with any forensic or witness evidence whatsoever that suggested she had been present at the murders or had known about them. So in the beginning, I felt reassured.

After the first week I was allowed to visit her. I didn't know what to expect. I knew she must have been under enormous pressure because of the massive public revulsion and hatred that the trial had stirred up. I found her tired but in good spirits.

'I'm all right, Mae.'

'Are you sure, Mum?'

'Yeah. They've put me under twenty-four-hour observation again in case I top myself, but no chance of that. I'm bearing up fine.'

She glanced at the guards. 'I'm not supposed to talk about the case but my lawyers think it's going well.'

'That's great,' I said.

As ever, there were practical matters she needed my help with, such as getting her court clothes cleaned, bringing new ones she'd ordered from the catalogue. I said I wished I could do more to help her, to provide moral support.

'You're doing everything you can, Mae. I'm so lucky to have a daughter like you.'

She hugged me as I left but there were no tears that time. She was feeling strong.

Things became tougher for Mum in court. Having been unable to produce anything other than circumstantial evidence that she was involved in the murders, the prosecution lawyers argued successfully that the judge should allow what was called 'similar evidence' to be heard. This meant that witnesses who had experienced cruelty and assault by Mum, which had no direct connection to the murders she'd been charged with, could be called to testify. According to the judge, their testimony could help the jury decide whether she was capable of committing the crimes she was actually accused of.

One of these witnesses was Anne Marie. I remember being very anxious about what she would say. When Mum and Dad were charged, we had taken different sides. Despite his abuse of her, she had remained in contact with him and told the police that she'd always loved him. On the other hand, I had taken Mum's side and ever since then it had felt as though Anne Marie was against us both. I wasn't in much doubt that Mum would come out of it badly when her evidence was heard. But I really wasn't prepared for just how terribly Mum treated her.

Anne Marie described the first assault which Dad and Mum had carried out on her. It happened when she was eight and they asked her to go down into the basement with them. She went willingly, with no suspicion about what was about to happen. Dad told her to take her clothes off. She didn't understand why but when she started to do so Mum told her she wasn't being quick enough and tore her cotton dress off. She said Mum then pinned her down while Dad bound her hands with sticky tape and used some strips of torn sheeting to tie her arms to a metal frame. When she asked him what he was doing, he told her it was what all fathers needed to do to their daughters and would make sure she'd get a husband when she was older.

Anne Marie still had no idea what was coming but began to scream. Mum used some strips of cloth to gag her then they raped her with a makeshift implement Dad had fashioned – a vibrator fitted inside a metal tube. She was in huge pain and distress and she became aware that she was bleeding. She then lost consciousness. They left her for a while then came back and repeated the assault.

After they'd finished Anne Marie was allowed back out of the basement and went to the bathroom to wash the blood away. According to Anne Marie, Mum followed her into the bathroom, gave her a sanitary towel and appeared to be amused by what had happened and said: 'Don't worry, it happens to every girl. It's a father's job. It's something everybody does but nobody talks about. It's all right, I won't say anything to anybody.'[5]

For years afterwards, until she was sixteen and ran away from home, Dad continued to have sex with her. She claimed that although Mum wasn't present she knew about it.

She also claimed that at one stage Dad used the same vibrator with which he'd first raped her to make another implement – a kind of belt made from metal onto which the vibrator was attached. At times she was made to wear this around the house, with the vibrator inserted inside her. She said that it made Mum laugh to see her wearing it.

I was absolutely appalled to hear the extent to which Mum and Dad had abused her; I knew how cruel Mum could be and that she had never tried to stop Dad abusing me or Heather or Louise, but I couldn't get my head round the fact she'd helped do that to an eight-year-old child. But I tried my utmost to put it out of my head – because even if she was guilty of doing those awful, awful things, it didn't make her a murderer. I knew, though, that it would be difficult for the jury to see past, and was sure it had done a lot to damage Mum's case.

It wasn't the only evidence that did so. Caroline Owens, a former nanny of Mum and Dad's, was also called as a witness.

Caroline told the court that she was sixteen when she first met Mum and Dad. She had been hitching a lift back to her home in Cinderford in the Forest of Dean one evening when they had pulled up in Dad's Ford Popular and offered her a lift. The three chatted as they drove her home, and Caroline told them about problems she was having in her life, especially with her stepfather who she didn't get on with. Mum seemed sympathetic; Caroline took to her. Dad listened with interest. They all got on well.

The following day they turned up at her house. They had Heather and me with them – I was scarcely more than a baby and Heather a toddler. Caroline's parents invited them in. They offered her the job as a nanny at Cromwell Street. She'd be paid £8 a week, have her own room, and Dad even offered to drive her parents over from Cinderford once a week so they could keep in contact. Caroline was very taken with Heather and me, and was keen to take the job at once. Her parents were more than happy with the idea too. They were impressed by Mum and Dad, who seemed a kind, friendly and considerate couple.

She moved into 25 Cromwell Street the following day. She made a good nanny, and Mum – only a few years older – came to seem like a close friend. Then things started to change. Mum would sometimes stroke Caroline's hair and tell her how pretty she was in a way that unsettled her. She took to entering the bathroom when she was in the bath and watching her.

Soon Mum and Dad tried to persuade her to join in with what they said were 'games', and she came to learn they were having sex parties in an upper part of the house. Dad thought she'd be interested. Caroline was shocked and told them she wasn't that kind of girl. She also became very concerned about the way Anne Marie was being treated, especially when she discovered the weird vibrator belt Dad had made for her to wear. Worried about the kind of people she had got herself involved with, she packed and went back home.

She thought she'd escaped them but late one evening, when she was waiting for a lift outside a pub in the Forest of Dean, they pulled up beside her in the car. They told her they were sorry she'd left and offered to give her a lift back to her parents' house. Caroline was wary, but it was a cold winter's night and she wanted to get home. She got into the car.

According to Caroline, as they drove along Mum started to feel her up. Dad watched in the rear-view mirror. She became distressed, pushing Mum away, then realised Dad wasn't taking her home but had taken a turning towards Chepstow. She began to panic. Dad pulled up at the side of the road, got in the back and together Mum and he pinned Caroline down, while Dad bound and gagged her with tape. They forced her into the foot-well of the car and drove her back to Cromwell Street.

They took her up to the first-floor sitting-room and began a violent and sadistic sexual assault on her. In order to stifle her cries she had cotton wool forced into her mouth. When Mum and Dad had finished with her, they left her trussed up and had sex with each other, after which they fell asleep. Caroline had no choice but to lie there near them throughout the night.

Early the following morning someone knocked at the front door. Dad went down to answer it. Sensing her opportunity, Caroline began to try to call for help. Mum put a pillow over her face to stifle her cries. Caroline thought she was going to be smothered to death so played dead. Having got rid of whoever was at the door, Dad reappeared. He was furious and threatened to keep her in the basement, where his 'black friends' would do with her whatever they wanted and when they'd finished he'd kill and bury her.

Mum disappeared to get Heather and me up for school, leaving Dad alone with Caroline. He raped her again and then – something Caroline said she couldn't get out of her head afterwards – he began to cry. He told her he shouldn't have done it because Caroline was meant to be for his and Mum's joint pleasure. He begged her not to tell Mum what he'd done. He told her Mum would kill them both if she ever found out he'd had sex with her on his own. In his desperation to persuade Caroline not to say anything about the rape, he suggested to her that she tell Mum she wanted to move back into the house. If she agreed to do that he'd let her go now.

Desperate for a way out, Caroline agreed. When Mum returned, Caroline was allowed to bathe and dress and they had breakfast together. She went through the motions of resuming work as a nanny and then, later in the morning, making an excuse that she needed to buy cigarettes, left the house and ran away back home.

Later that day the police came knocking. Dad was out at work and Mum, as she always was with the police, was hostile and aggressive. They began to search the house, and when Dad returned, examined the car. They found evidence of the assault, including a button from Caroline's trousers and pieces of tape. They also found a large hoard of pornographic material and sex toys. Mum and Dad were arrested. Mum admitted sexually assaulting Caroline but insisted she had stopped when asked to. Dad denied the rape.

They were tried at Gloucester magistrates' court in January 1973. Caroline was too scared to face the ordeal of giving evidence against them, and so the rape charges against both of them were dropped and reduced to charges of ABH (actual bodily harm) and indecent assault. Mum and Dad agreed to plead guilty. When the case was heard, it was suggested by a lawyer that Caroline had offered 'passive cooperation' in the assault. Mum and Dad behaved well in court, and said that it was simply a situation that had got out of hand and expressed their regret. Neither of them had any previous convictions for sexual offences and they were let off with fifty-pound fines. The prosecution suggested that after Caroline Owens' escape and the court case that followed, Dad and Mum vowed that they would never again allow a victim to survive to tell the tale and get them into trouble.

After Mum and Dad's arrest, when the police began excavating the garden at 25 Cromwell Street, they asked me about Caroline Owens. I told them I'd never even heard the name before. So it was a strange experience to find out her story and that as a baby I'd unknowingly been at the centre of it when she came to be our nanny. But I couldn't properly connect myself to it. It seemed like something that had happened to somebody else. And although Caroline's evidence was shocking and might have altered the jury's mind about Mum, it hadn't changed mine. Knowing what I knew about her, I thought perhaps there might be something in her having assisted with a sexual assault, but it was something I could barely even bring myself to think about, just as I found it impossible to believe my mum could be a murderer. And I knew that I had to carry on being there for her and, strange though it may seem, she sounded as if she was trying to support me too – although sometimes I wonder if she was saying things to convince herself just as much as me that everything was alright. Three weeks into the trial she wrote me a letter. She copied out a poem from George Elliot – although I thought she'd written it herself at the time – and told me to keep my spirits up: 'we're almost halfway through the trial now, so it won't be long and it will be all over,' she said. 'I love you very much and I am very proud of you.'

But whether it was for my benefit or for hers, it did cheer me up; it gave me more strength.

Although I was dreading giving evidence for Mum's defence, I was ready to do it – even though I knew that in doing so I might attract some of the hatred which Mum was experiencing. But I was phoned by Mum's lawyer, Leo Goatley, and told that I was not going to be called as a witness after all. He had read a proof of the book the *News of the World* intended to publish after the trial, which was put together from taped interviews with myself and Steve. Many of the interviews referred to cruelties Mum had inflicted on us both. He believed that if the court heard about these it would only strengthen the prosecution's case.

Part of me was relieved. I'd already realised that when I took the witness stand I would probably be asked about Mum's treatment of me and my siblings. I knew I couldn't lie on oath and telling the truth might make things look worse for her. But I'd wanted to say that there was another side to the story. That she'd confided in me how she'd been raped as a child, felt bullied and controlled by Dad and had been desperate at times to escape from the marriage. I didn't want to make excuses for her but I thought this might explain some of her behaviour. As it turned out, some of this did eventually emerge at the trial anyway – although in the end it didn't seem to make much difference.

To make matters worse, Leo Goatley told me he had given Mum the manuscript of the book to read. Although she had been aware of the *News of the World* contract and had said she understood why I had signed it, she was furious to read the descriptions of the beatings Steve and I had received at her hands and some of the criticisms we had made of her as a mother. She brought it up at the next visit to Winchester jail.

'I can't believe you've done this to me, Mae. I mean I'm not surprised at Steve wanting to slag me off but for you to turn against me . . . I'm just devastated.'

I couldn't look her in the eye. 'I'm sorry, Mum, I wish I'd never got involved in it.'

'Well, you should have fucking well thought about it properly then!'

I wanted to tell her that, for all I regretted what I'd done, I'd only described honestly some of the things that had happened in our house as I'd grown up. None of it was lies. And I'd only done it because I was desperate; I couldn't get a job or bear to be in the public eye because of what was happening – I had done it to survive. But I didn't have the courage to say so. She continued to tear strips off me.

'You've let me down, Mae. Now I really am on my own. The only person that's going to speak up for me at this fucking trial is ME!'

I had no answer. I felt I *had* let her down. My eyes filled with tears but she seemed indifferent to them. Worse still, she suddenly appeared to have lost all hope that she would be acquitted. I left the prison feeling absolutely wretched and that if she were convicted it would somehow be my fault.

When Mum's lawyers opened the case for her defence they insisted that there was absolutely no forensic or other evidence to show that Mum had been present at any of the murders and that the prosecution's entire case was based on nothing more than prejudice and speculation. She may have had lesbian relationships with some of the lodgers, worked as a prostitute, shared an interest in kinky sex and pornography with Dad, but none of that made her a murderer.

They said that Dad had sexually assaulted, murdered and dismembered Anna McFall in a similar way to the other victims but it was beyond any doubt that Mum hadn't been involved in her murder because she hadn't even met Dad then. This proved that he was capable of carrying out such a murder alone and therefore there was nothing to show the ones Mum was accused of had been a collaboration between them – which was what the prosecution had implied. To back this up they called as witnesses women who had come forward to say that they had been approached or assaulted by Dad and that he had been alone and the woman who stood in the dock had not been with him.

But the only person who would really be able to persuade the court she was innocent was Mum herself. When she took the witness stand she was described as nervous but determined to stand up for herself. Whenever she referred to Dad it was as 'Fred West' not 'Fred' or 'my husband' – as if trying to distance herself as much as possible from him. Did that help improve the jurors' opinion of her? I wonder if it actually might have made her come across as too clever; aware of what she was doing, trying to paint a particular picture for the jury when they knew she'd been married to him for twenty years.

She was asked about the abuse of Anne Marie. Mum's counsel had already questioned the reliability of Anne Marie's evidence because she had sold her story to the *Daily Star*. He also suggested that she had exaggerated Mum's role in her abuse because she hated her and, despite what he had done to her, still loved her father so was trying to underplay his part in it. When Mum was asked about Anne Marie she denied having any role in helping

Dad to rape her or in the sexual relationship they had continued to have for years afterwards. I so wanted to believe this at
the time. I can't believe it now.

When asked about the sexual assault of Caroline Owens she
said that the sex had been consensual to begin with, but when
Dad tried to use force and Caroline put up resistance she had
pleaded with him to stop. She told the court she hadn't wanted
Caroline to get hurt but that she also thought she had exaggerated what happened. This seemed to support what her counsel
had already suggested when he cross-examined Caroline and
established that the police doctor had found no physical injuries when she reported the assault. The counsel had pointed out
that Caroline had also done a deal with a newspaper for her
story.

When Mum was questioned about Charmaine she repeated
what she had already told the police, which was that Rena had
called at the Midland Road flat after Dad had been released from
Leyhill prison. Mum had been alone with the children and
Rena, who hated Mum, had demanded, as Charmaine's mother,
to take her away so that she could look after her. Mum said she
had had no choice but to let the child go.

Mum became distressed and sobbed in court when asked
about Charmaine and when she described returning home to
find that Dad had let Heather leave home without saying goodbye. I was told later that people in court had been moved by
Mum's display of emotion and were convinced her feelings of
grief were genuine.

When she was cross-examined by the prosecution Mum did
less well. The lead counsel ridiculed her insistence that she and
Dad led such separate lives that she couldn't have known about
the murders and her pretence that the two of them had not
shared a very close relationship. His manner riled Mum and she

became chippy and aggressive in return. It wasn't the side of her personality she needed to show.

The counsel also said her evidence had been full of lies and evasions. For example, when the police interviewed her she denied even knowing who Shirley Robinson was. Mum defended herself, saying that the first time she had been asked about Shirley was just after she had learned of Heather's death and she was in a real mess. When she was questioned again later about Shirley she did acknowledge that she'd known her.

The defence were given permission to play Dad's taped confessions to the police in court. It must have been strange and eerie for her to hear that familiar voice again. As if, even in death, he would not leave her be. And yet the content of the tapes was helpful to her as, again and again, the court heard Dad's voice saying, 'Rose knew nothing about any of this.'

To counter this, the prosecution said there had been other interviews in which Dad had indicated that Mum was involved and, on top of this, there was the evidence of Janet Leach, the appropriate adult who was asked to sit in on police interviews with him and had befriended him. She told the court that Dad had told her on several occasions that Rose had been involved in the murders and his denials of this to the police were purely to protect her. Although Mum's counsel tried to demolish Janet Leach's evidence by making her admit that she had also sold her story to a newspaper, the *Daily Mirror*, it was still damaging to Mum's case.

As the trial neared its conclusion I had another visit to Mum arranged. I was afraid, after what happened the previous time, that she would send me a message via her solicitor cancelling it, perhaps even saying she never wanted to see me again, but she didn't.

I arrived to see her feeling very nervous, and was surprised to find her in much brighter spirits. She felt the playing of Dad's confessions had been a big help to her case and she knew that if there were any doubt at all in the jury's mind they would have to acquit her. She was by no means certain that things would go her way but felt that she really did have a 50:50 chance.

I felt pleased to see some of her optimism had returned. It made me feel less guilty about not giving evidence and gave me hope too that there was a real chance that, despite the devastation my dad had caused, he would not succeed in taking Mum down with him and that we could survive with the family at least partly intact.

But as I was leaving she suddenly looked vulnerable again. She said that if the verdict did go against her she would probably want to break off all contact with the family. Even if we asked to see her she would refuse.

I felt suddenly panicked. 'Why? Nothing will have changed as far as I'm concerned. I'll still believe in your innocence. You'll still be my mum.'

'It's for your own good, Mae. I can't have your life ruined by what's happened to me.'

'But it wouldn't be your fault!'

'It doesn't matter, Mae. You'd need to cut yourself off from me. Make a life without me.'

I couldn't tell whether she meant what she was saying or if it was a self-pitying gesture intended to make me feel sorry for her.

'I won't cut myself off from you, Mum. I promise I'll stand by you whichever way it goes.'

She was pleased and hugged me tearfully as I left.

On day twenty-seven of the trial, as it neared the end, Steve and I attended court to watch the judge's summing-up. To avoid press attention, Gloucester police took us in via the rear entrance. We were ushered to the far side of the public gallery. Anne Marie was also there, sitting at some distance from us so we couldn't make eye contact – knowing there was no love lost between us, the police had made sure we sat apart.

Mum was already in the dock, wearing a suit I had bought for her, but it was hard to see her and I'm sure she couldn't see us since the dock was beneath the public gallery, facing towards the judge. We listened as the judge went quietly through the case and the issues the jury should consider. There were no new facts by this stage; everything was known, it was a matter of going through the detail one last time for the benefit of the jury and giving them guidance over what they needed to be sure of before deciding on a guilty verdict.

To my surprise he seemed fair to Mum and nothing he said made me feel she was certain to be convicted. He reminded the jury that a defendant never has to prove her innocence, it was for the prosecution to prove her guilt beyond reasonable doubt and if they couldn't do that she should be found not guilty. When Steve and I eventually left the court we felt cautiously optimistic.

Because we had signed the contract with the *News of the World*, they wanted to be sure we wouldn't speak to any other newspapers or media organisations, so for the last days of the trial they had put Steve and me up at a hotel (along with Tara, her son and Stephen's wife). It was the De La Bere, a fifteenth-century manor house with a tree-lined drive and sweeping lawns on the outskirts of Cheltenham. It was amazingly luxurious, unlike anything we had ever experienced before. The rooms were like mini-apartments set in the grounds and even had their own lounge area. We were told we could eat and drink whatever we wanted in the timber-panelled banquet hall with its huge chandeliers.

I wasn't interested. I didn't want to eat. I couldn't relax. I found it very difficult to sleep. Two journalists watched us all the time to make sure we didn't leave the hotel. It was worse than being in the safe houses with Mum. I just wanted the whole thing to be over and for her to be found not guilty so that I could try to move on and focus on the baby I was due to have in only eight weeks' time.

The first verdicts finally came through the following day, on 21 November. I was in my hotel room with Steve, and the reporters arrived saying they had some news and suggested we sit down. From their manner it was already clear what was coming. They told us Mum had been found guilty of the murder of Charmaine, Heather and Shirley Robinson. They explained that the jury was still debating verdicts on the other seven charges but these would follow. But having been found guilty on three counts it seemed inevitable that the others would go the same way.

I began to cry. I furiously told the journalists to go away and leave me alone. I didn't even want to talk to Steve and Tara. My head was reeling. It seemed like the end of everything. I couldn't begin to imagine any kind of future after this. I tried to call Mum's solicitor to find out how she was. I couldn't get through to him but spoke to his wife who told me he was shocked and devastated.

My fears about the remaining verdicts were proved right. All seven came in guilty the following day. Steve, Tara and I tried to talk about it but could hardly find anything to say. We knew that Mum would now be locked away for ever. As children we'd lost everything: father, mother, sister, house, family – even the few happy memories of our childhood had been destroyed.

That evening I told the reporters I had nothing more to say and wanted to sever all ties with them. They had got their book, such as it was, and I never wanted to speak to them or any other newspaper ever again. Tara and I gathered up our things and checked out of the hotel.

We drove home to her place in Gloucester. It was bitterly cold and we had no food in. I couldn't have been more miserable. I can't be sure what I would have done if I'd not been pregnant. Maybe I would have wanted to end it all – it's quite possible. But I knew for the baby's sake I had to carry on. In the blur of days following the trial it was the one thing I was certain of.

Chapter Fourteen

Visitor for West

Mum's mad about some rule changes in the prison; sometimes the way she talks about prison life you'd think she thought she was on a sort of package holiday – she feels so entitled. But then that's her all over: she feels entitled to me being at her beck and call now, just as she felt entitled to control us all when we were younger.

HM PRISON DURHAM

Mae, I don't believe this place . . . honestly there's no point in being well behaved and trying to just keep your head down and get on with things . . . Us long termers don't stand a chance against these people when the system takes their side. Anyway dear, now that everything has changed don't be surprised if the phone calls go to nothing!! . . . There was I like a sucker, waiting for things to get better!! Time to rethink my priorities I reckon!

A few weeks after the trial, Tara and I started renting our house outside of Gloucester where, along with her son Nathan, we hoped we could lie low while some of the fuss began to die down and come to some sort of terms about what had happened. It wasn't a great distance from Gloucester, but it was far enough for me to feel we had left the place behind – and yet not so far that I couldn't attend my ante-natal clinics in Cheltenham. We settled into the house as best we could, doing little more than hide and wait for my due date. I tried to focus on the baby, on what kind of future we might possibly have, forcing the past to the back of my mind.

Then out of the blue came a call from Leo Goatley, Mum's solicitor. He had a message from Mum. She wanted me to visit her in prison.

I couldn't believe it. I had been convinced she had meant it when she vowed that if she were found guilty she would sever all contact with the family – both for her own sake and for ours. Since the verdict, I'd been trying to shut down all my feelings about her. Of course it wasn't working – I still believed she was innocent and, apart from anything else, I was very worried about how she would be managing in prison, knowing that when the judge sentenced her he had imposed a whole life tariff, meaning that she would never ever be released. She was such a strong character and those very qualities made it seem all the more likely she'd have the determination to take her own life if she chose to. If I only needed one reason to visit her, it was to see how she was.

Soon afterwards, very early one morning, I caught a train for the four-hour journey to Durham to see her. I was full of dread and turmoil, not knowing why she wanted to see me, or how I could possibly help her. I knew that visiting Mum now would be a very different experience from when she was on remand. There would be no feeling that her imprisonment was only temporary, no positive chat about what we might do together once she was free again. Instead, there would be the grim knowledge that prison life – with its mundane routine, fear and brutality

– was her only future. There could be no cheerful words, no looking on the bright side.

'Who are you visiting?' the prison officer asked when I reached the female area.

I didn't want to say Mum's name out loud. I knew her prisoner number so I said that instead.

'I need the name.'

Why did they bother giving prisoners numbers if they wanted us to use their names?

'Rose West,' I said, as quietly as I could.

'Visitor for West!' she called out to a colleague.

Everyone heard – all the other prison officers and visitors – and turned to look at me with what felt like either pity or contempt. Despite the fact Mum was a high-profile prisoner and I'd assumed her whereabouts would have been kept secret, at least for a while, it was already public knowledge that Rose West had been imprisoned there. None of those other visitors could be in any doubt that's who I'd come to visit. I was sure they were all thinking, 'Who in their right mind would want to visit that monster?' I felt as if they were all judging me.

After my paperwork was checked I had to sit down and wait for what seemed like an age before being escorted along a series of corridors and through countless locked gates into a security-check area not unlike the ones at airports. Rings, belts and coins had to be placed in a plastic tray and sent through a scanner along with bags. Shoes also had to be sent through the scanner – shoelaces left behind as they were banned in the prison; prisoners could use them to commit suicide. There was a body search. A guard passed a scanning-paddle all over my body, another checked inside my bra, between my toes, even the back of my tongue. I remember there were spaniel sniffer dogs everywhere. I understand why they have to be so rigorous, but it all made me feel as if I too was a criminal not a visitor.

Then more corridors, more locked doors and into an open courtyard which looked up at the tiny barred windows of the cells. This was the male part of the prison, a high-security area where category A prisoners – including some IRA men – were held. I heard jeers and wolf-whistles as some of them looked down.

Then on through the male visiting area. It was a huge room. Men sat at tables with wives or girlfriends, some of them snogging – I later learned this was a way of passing drugs. There were children too – young ones, some of them, looking as bewildered as I felt. It was surreal and shocking – and noisy, the sort of noise that makes your eardrums buzz afterwards. We moved on past huge chained Alsatian dogs, into the women's part of the prison. A few more corridors – it must have been almost an hour after I'd entered the prison by now – and I was into the women's communal visiting room. And there was Mum, flanked by two guards.

We looked at one another for a moment and then fell into each other's arms, sobbing.

'Mae . . . God I've missed you! I love you so much, my darling! So, so much!'

We held one another for what seemed like an age. I thought the prison officers might pull us apart but they didn't. It was the first time in my life she had ever embraced me in that way, or expressed such depth of feeling towards me. In spite of the circumstances, I loved the feeling of being wanted and needed and valued by her.

'I love you too, Mum,' I said, wiping my eyes.

Eventually we sat down, the guards moved away out of earshot and, as she gripped my hand across the table, we began to talk.

She told me again how much she'd missed me and how relieved she was to see me. I told her I felt the same way. I expected the conversation to continue in that way, that we'd discuss serious things such as how we'd both coped with the trauma of the trial and verdict, and how we were going to face the future. But she didn't want to and, almost immediately, brightened up and began chatting about prison life.

What shocked me was that, far from feeling her life was over or finding prison unbearable, she sounded quite positive. Life inside was clearly a long way from being cushy and she'd already received abuse and threats from other inmates, and yet she didn't seem to be scared or intimidated. She explained that she'd been given category A status – reserved for those convicted of the most serious crimes and assessed as a potential danger to others. This meant that the prison officers would have to protect her from harm from other prisoners, and apparently it also meant she was allowed to wear her own clothes rather than prison uniform.

She was really delighted about this and had already been thumbing through the Argos Additions catalogue and choosing garments she wanted to me to buy for her and either post or bring on my next visit. She had a radio so she could have music in her cell – her favourite DJ being Jimmy Young. Library books were available; there was talk of giving her a job within the prison and of her receiving therapy from a psychiatrist.

'And they're even going to let me have a budgie, Mae. Imagine that! I'm not sure whether to call him Joey or Oliver. Or Jake's quite nice. What do you think, Mae? I reckon I might go for Joey. 'Course, you'll have to bring me stuff for his cage. Toys and a mirror and cuttlefish and all that. Don't want him getting bored. They say that's the biggest problem in prison – getting bored. Well I'm determined to avoid that.'

It was surreal. On my way up to Durham I'd fretted so much that she'd be distraught, I'd spent sleepless nights worrying she'd do what Dad had done, that perhaps she'd wanted me to visit so she could see me one last time before ending it all. Instead, in next to no time, we'd gone from expressing feelings of love for one another to small-talk about tops, shell-suits, bras and budgie toys that she wanted me to buy. She seemed to be in total denial of the reality of her situation, but I went along with it. I felt I had no right to depress her by reminding her of the desperate circumstances she and the rest of the family were now in – I still thought she was innocent.

Christmas was fast approaching at this point and she wanted to know about the plans Tara and I had made for it. She told me how much she was looking forward to the birth of my baby in the New Year. She'd even written out a list of names, which she pushed across the table to me.

'I always think biblical ones are best, Mae. Names that have stood the test of time. Ruth, Sarah, Thomas, James . . .'

I looked at the list. 'Well I do quite like Luke.'

'And if it's a girl?'

'I like Amy.'

'Bit plain, dear. Still, your baby, so your choice. I'll love your child whatever you call it.'

However distorted her maternal instinct was, she hadn't lost it. She went on to talk about Heather, asking what plans I had for the funeral. Saying she'd already asked the prison authorities if she could attend it on compassionate grounds but her request had been refused.

'I don't know why, Mae. It's not as if I'd try and escape. Or that anyone would need to know that they'd let me out for a day. And I'm sure you all would have wanted me there.'

This was only a matter of weeks after she'd been convicted

of Heather's murder. My view of her innocence hadn't changed and hers certainly hadn't, but I found it hard to understand how she could imagine the prison authorities could possibly think the same way. How could they allow a murderer to attend the funeral of a child they'd been convicted of killing?

When I left her, no more than an hour later, we wept and hugged one another again but there was no sense of an ending. She said she wanted us to stay in close touch and I knew I would have to go along with that. Dad had told me he wanted me to look after her but that wasn't the reason. The truth was I wanted to. She was still my mother, and although her sense of how she would continue to do some of the many things which mothers do for their daughters seemed hazy, and in many ways seemed no more than a fantasy, I had no doubt that she felt she would continue to play a big part in my future and I in hers.

I walked back to the station and caught the train home, feeling a little drained and confused, turning everything she said over in my mind. Our relationship was bound to change, I knew that, but I couldn't see how. All I knew was that it was obviously going to be just as intense and complicated as it always had been. This feeling was soon reinforced during the following weeks as I received letters and phone calls from her, many of which were about plans for Heather's funeral. Although she wasn't allowed to attend, she wanted to plan the all the details, even asking me to send her the coffin catalogue the undertaker had given to me so that she could choose one.

And in the New Year, with Heather now buried by a stream in the beautiful country churchyard which (rather than the back yard at Cromwell Street where she had lain for years) had become her final resting place, Mum wrote to me again telling me the words she wanted on Heather's headstone. I thought these words would be alright as they could come from _all_ of us,' she wrote.

She wasn't just *suggesting* the inscription for the headstone, she was making a decision on behalf of all the remaining family. As if she had no doubt she was still head of it.

I ignored her instructions, along with her plan for the funeral service and her choice of coffin. However much I didn't believe Mum had been involved in Heather's death, I knew that in her last days and hours Mum had treated her atrociously. She was my sister. I felt I had to protect her in death in a way that I hadn't been able to in life. All the same, I couldn't bring myself to tell Mum I hadn't carried out her wishes. She still had a claim on my loyalty that I couldn't even think about resisting.

When I told her Amy had been born and we were both doing well she seemed thrilled. I sent her photographs and she wrote back to me to say she was beautiful, that she couldn't wait to hold her. But then of course, slipped in between these phrases were requests such as, 'Oh by the way don't bring anything with you for me, it's much easier this end to have things posted in,' and that she'd sat on someone else's headphones: 'Luckily it didn't do too much damage and one of the officers fixed them for me. I was so embarrassed!'

But luckily, I wasn't completely alone. I had Tara, who, as a young mother herself, could give me support and advice in those first months with Amy – and Amy's father, though we hadn't been a couple for some time, was kind and supportive too. I didn't want to dwell on Mum's absence or give in to self-pity. I knew I had to not only survive, but to think about making a life for both myself and my child.

We remained at the rented house with Tara and Nathan. I won't lie: money was a constant worry at that point. I didn't know how I was going to support Amy and myself. I had what remained of the *News of the World* fee but it was dwindling rapidly. I couldn't imagine how I'd get a job because it seemed inevitable that any employer would find out who I was. Who could possibly want to employ a daughter of Britain's worst female serial killer? I was also constantly in fear that people in the small town would discover my identity and so, as soon as I could, I changed my surname so that it was the same as Amy's – who had her father's name. I felt it gave me some chance of anonymity.

Mum treated all of her children differently and our experiences of both her and my father varied wildly. The family broke up when the younger children were taken into care and was shattered completely when the murders were discovered, so in many ways we were left in ignorance of what each of us had been through. As we became older, however, and my siblings and I re-established contact we began to learn more about our separate experiences.

Tara is by far the most extrovert of us three older girls and has never held back on her opinions of Mum and Dad. Unlike Louise, Dad hadn't sexually abused her. Why this should be I don't think anyone can explain, but the fact dad was racist I expect factored in it to an extent. But being spared that kind of attention from him – and seeing little of his dark side – has left Tara feeling much angrier towards Mum (who beat and bullied her as she did the rest of us) than Dad.

When Tara, Louise and the younger children, were removed from Cromwell Street by social services following Louise's rape allegation, Mum and Dad told Steve and me to forget all about them. That was their attitude to the children they'd lost and they expected it to be ours too. I found their mindset bizarre and shocking. At the time I didn't understand it at all and now, as a mother myself, it's unthinkable. If their feelings for the children had been genuine, how could they suddenly switch them off?

'They've only got themselves to blame, haven't they, for telling a load of fucking lies,' Mum would say when I raised it with her.

'But they're so young. They'll be frightened.'

'I don't want to hear any more about them, Mae! They're gone and that's that! I've told you, haven't I? Forget them!'

But I never stopped wondering what life was like for them – who would be looking after them, whether they'd be kept together or separated. I knew that in some ways they'd be relieved to be out of the house, but I was sure they'd be bewildered and frightened too, and I knew from my own experience that when a child is abused – as they had been in different ways – it doesn't necessarily mean bonds with a parent are broken. The feelings of wanting to be loved and parented, no matter how badly, don't die. That thought haunted me.

Whereas I'd had some contact with Tara after she'd been taken into care because she'd often broken her care orders and found her way home, I'd had none with Louise. But after Mum was convicted she managed to get in touch. She'd got my phone number from Tara and phoned me one night from a call box. I was so happy to hear from her but she was in a desperate state.

'I can't stand this any longer. I want to go home!' she cried.

I didn't know what to say and in a moment of brutal honesty I found myself also crying, 'We haven't got a home any more, Louise!'

'I know we haven't!' she sobbed.

She poured her heart out to me. Her experience in care had been hell, she said. Social services had placed her with a series of foster parents who regarded her as nothing more than a pay cheque.

'Three hundred quid a week they get for having me but make it as clear as they can that they resent me being there. They're all the same. They don't want me, just want the money. I've told social services I've had enough, I want out. I thought now I'm sixteen they'd let me go but they say the order lasts till I'm twenty-one! Can I come and see you, Mae?!'

My heart fell in my chest. 'I don't think you're allowed to see me,' I said quietly, 'because I'm in touch with Mum.'

'Please! I feel so alone. I've got no one else to talk to who'd understand!'

'I know, I know, but I reckon it would get you into trouble and make things worse.'

I tried to calm her down but nothing I said made her feel better. I felt so sad and helpless when the call ended. I'd always worried Louise might think I'd chosen Mum over her, but it wasn't like that at all. I'd felt I had to support Mum because she had no one and no future. I also thought at that time she hadn't known Dad had sexually abused Louise. I'd hated being separated from Louise and my younger siblings and would have loved to see them if I could. It was heartbreaking to know she wanted to see me again now but if I agreed I'd only make her situation even harder.

Then, a few days later, she just turned up on my doorstep. I was so shocked by her appearance: she looked skinny, miserable and completely lost. I had to tell social services where she was – I was afraid they'd set the police looking for her. They reluctantly agreed to let her stay with me for a few days. I felt so sorry for her. She seemed so deprived of love and affection and so glad to be with family again, even if only temporarily. She even asked me to make meals like Mum used to make us – chicken soup or sausage, cabbage, mash and Marmite gravy, followed by plum sponge and bread pudding.

I was thrilled to have the chance to do it, to try in what small ways I could to look after her. It was so touching to see her play with Nathan and hold Amy. And I listened to her, for hours on end, as she told me what life had been like for her after she had been taken away from home. The worst thing of all had been the guilt she felt towards our younger siblings.

'It's because of me, because I told what Dad had done to me, the others lost their home, their mum and dad.'

'Don't be ridiculous,' I told her. 'You didn't do anything wrong. All you did was tell the truth about something horrible that had been done to you.'

'No,' she said, pleadingly, 'it wasn't actually me. I told a friend, she told someone else and before I knew it police and social workers were asking me about it. I didn't mean to get Mum and Dad in trouble! And I never wanted to break the family up! But I did, didn't I?'

I told her none of it was her fault, she was a victim here, and all the nightmarish things that had happened since – the discovery of the bodies, Mum and Dad's arrests, his suicide, her trial and conviction – none of these were the fault of any of us children. If anything, it all might have saved a lot of people.

But everything about her experiences with the authorities had encouraged her to have feelings of guilt – even the abuse itself felt like her fault. She'd been separated from the younger kids the moment the police started questioning her about what Dad had done.

'They grilled me and grilled me and grilled me. I was sitting in this office while they took statements off me. I could see the other kids in another office through the glass. I just wanted to be with them. The police told me they were going to be taken horse riding and as soon as I'd given them what they needed I could go too. I just wanted it all over and done with so I could be with my family again. So I gave them the statement. I told the truth.'

'And you were right to do that,' I told her. 'You mustn't keep blaming yourself.'

'I can't help it, Mae,' she cried.

I wasn't sure if she'd want to tell me what happened with Dad, but eventually she did. She told me how, when she'd turned eleven, and begun to have periods, both Mum and Dad had encouraged her to have boyfriends. Then, when she was thirteen, Dad raped her. It sounded beyond horrific. He'd taken her upstairs to do it. The younger children, down below, had heard her screaming. Terrified, they'd gone up to hammer on the door to try to make him stop whatever they were doing. He'd popped his head out to ask what they wanted. They couldn't bring themselves to ask him to stop doing whatever it was that they didn't really understand to Louise, and they just mumbled something like: 'We thought you might want a cup of tea, Dad.' He told them he didn't. Closed and locked the door and carried on.

He raped her vaginally and anally on two other occasions, telling her after the first time that he needed to do it again because he hadn't done it right the first time and she'd have medical problems if he didn't do it again properly. Hearing these details for the first time made me feel physically sick and so sorry for Louise. I asked her if it was true Mum had helped. Louise told me that, during the second time, Mum had been in the house and Louise had gone to talk to her about it afterwards in the bathroom. She said Mum had shown her no sympathy, and more or less said it had been her own fault. When she first told me all this, she played down how horrible Mum had been, knowing I was still in contact with her, but in years since she's been much angrier about Mum not doing anything to intervene when she almost certainly could have done.

I couldn't listen to Louise talking about all this without feeling guilty myself. Had I done everything I could to protect her? I'd warned her to watch out for Dad. That as she reached puberty he'd begin to take a sexual interest in her as he had done with me. And I knew that she'd have needed to use the same strategies I had to distract him or fend him off. I assumed somehow that's what she'd managed to do. If I'd known Louise was being raped by Dad I would have done something about it, but I didn't know. And I'd believed, up until that point when Louise had finally had a chance to explain what happened, that though Dad must have assaulted her, Mum hadn't known about it. Now I was learning otherwise and that Mum hadn't just ignored his sexual interest in Louise but casually stood by. Louise told me she even used to check her 'down below' by putting a hand between her legs to see how sexually developed she'd become. I look back and wish I'd come back to the house more after I'd left home; wish I'd got Louise on her own and asked her to tell me if everything was okay; wish I'd shouted more at Mum and Dad to leave all the kids alone. It's so easy, though, in hindsight to think you could be so strong, when in reality, Mum and Dad were not the type of people you reasoned with.

The guilt deepened the more I heard from Louise and thought about the consequences for her of giving that statement to the police. She said Mum and Dad had done everything they could to intimidate the younger children into not backing up her story, telling them it would break up the family. Their loyalties were torn, and it threatened to wreck Louise's relationship with them. Eventually, despite his lies and denials, Dad was charged with rape and Mum with 'causing or encouraging the commission of unlawful sexual intercourse with a girl under the age of sixteen' and with 'cruelty to a child'.

Louise had been so brave to take things that far, but in the end the charges were dropped anyway because neither she, nor our younger siblings, could face the ordeal and trauma of going to court and giving evidence against their parents. But that left Louise feeling it had all been for nothing. The abuse may have ended but the emotional suffering caused by the break-up of the family was only just beginning. When she and the younger kids had been taken into care, they'd been told they wouldn't be split up, but that promise was broken and over time they ended up in different places, so Louise lost her brothers and sisters as well as her parents.

They were, however, kept together after Mum and Dad's arrest following the discovery of the bodies at Cromwell Street. The authorities put them in a hotel to prevent them from seeing or hearing anything about the case through the media.

'They rigged the tellies so that there was no news,' Louise told me. 'Just *Bambi* playing twenty-four hours a day. Didn't matter which channel you switched on, it was always *Bambi*.'

The choice of film was such an irony. After Dad was arrested he apparently told someone *Bambi* was his favourite film, and that the famous scene when Bambi's mother dies broke his heart and brought him to tears whenever he saw it. But making the children watch *Bambi* all the time wasn't going to prevent Louise and the others finding out about the murders for long. Nor was anything else social services tried to do. The news spread everywhere over the following days, weeks and months. When Louise did find out, and the press began describing our old home as the 'House of Horrors', it felt as much beyond her comprehension as it had been mine and Tara's. It was the same when she heard about Dad's death. She was by that time living with the worst foster parents she'd ever been placed with.

'It was snowing,' she said. 'I was about to sneak out to go sledging. Looking forward to getting out of that house for a few hours – then, out of the blue, it came on the news. "Fred West found hanged at Winson Green prison. An investigation has been launched."' Having had such mixed feelings about it myself, I asked her how she'd felt about it.

'Nothing much at first. Just shock. It seemed totally unreal. Then it started to sink in. I'd lost my dad. Whatever everyone else thought about him, he'd still been my dad.'

We spoke then about him, and how in many ways he'd been the parent we liked best. The one we'd all have chosen to go with if our parents told us they were going to divorce. Extraordinary as it sounds, aside from the sexual abuse, in many ways he'd been quite kind and even funny. He'd sometimes intervene when Mum punished us with an 'Ease off, Rose!' She was the one who terrified us. The one who dominated us and, as far as we could see, wore the trousers in their marriage. In some ways he'd been the kind of husband many wives might want. Worked hard, didn't gamble, didn't really drank, ploughed all the wages he brought home each week into the family home or handed it over to Mum for the housekeeping. 'Just kept the shrapnel for himself to buy tobacco for his roll-ups and the odd Mars bar,' as Louise put it.

Louise was doing her GCSEs while Mum was on remand.

'Not ideal,' she told me and Tara, in her understated way, 'when you call at the newsagent's on the way into school and your family home's all over the papers, the House of Horrors, with pictures of your mum and dad on the front pages. Yet in a funny way it didn't feel connected with me at all. It was the same when the trial was going on.'

'How did you feel when Mum was found guilty?' I asked.

'Same, in a lot of ways. Like I knew she was my mum, and I didn't disbelieve that she'd helped kill those women, but she didn't feel part of me. All I knew was my life was a mess and I didn't know how I'd ever get out of it. I just went out and got blind drunk and ended up throwing up in a friend's car.'

Louise was absolutely exhausted, going over all this with us. Tara and I got her to bed and over the next few days we continued talking and catching up. Everything Louise told me should have made me want to cut ties with Mum then – I can see that looking back now. But I was still so young, so in need of her, so grateful to be needed in return.

When I had to drive Louise back to where she'd been living and hand her over to social services, she really didn't want to go, and I really hadn't wanted to take her. But I knew that any breach of the conditions of her care order could land both of us in trouble. She was in tears when I left her, and it was no surprise when a few days later she ran away from her foster home and turned up on my doorstep again. She was even more desperate this time. I persuaded her to go back but it kept happening. Her foster parents and social services became very angry but Louise stuck to her guns, insisting she wasn't prepared to stay there any longer, care order or not. They told her that the only way she could get free of the order was to go to court and ask for it to be lifted, but they warned her that if she managed to do that, their responsibility towards her would end and she'd be homeless.

Nothing was going to stop her, though, and she set about getting the order quashed. While those legal proceedings were under way she came to stay with Tara and me for a few weeks before the local council found her supported accommodation nearby. I'd have preferred her to live with me and Tara but the authorities weren't happy about that.

When Louise's care order did end there was no longer

anything preventing her from having contact with Mum, and I asked her and Tara if they wanted to visit her with me. Neither of them wanted to but I persuaded them because I still felt an obligation to support her and I thought that seeing them again would help her. I somehow also felt it might help Louise and Tara, because although there was every reason why they'd feel angry with her, I sensed that in some ways they missed her. I also explained to them that I thought Mum had changed since her prison sentence began – she had seemed genuinely affectionate, cuddled me frequently and was upset and tearful when I left. They were surprised and interested in this and wondered if they too might now have a different kind of relationship with her. So they agreed to do it and I wrote to Mum and said we wanted to visit and she replied saying she'd sort out the visiting orders and would be so excited to see us all.

We made the four-hour journey to Durham together, taking Tara's son and Amy with us – prison rules prevented older children visiting but it was permitted at that time to take little ones (although later the authorities banned Mum from receiving visitors under the age of eighteen).

Though she'd had some contact with Tara, Mum hadn't seen Louise for years. She'd been hardly more than a child when they last saw one another at an access meeting with social services but she was now a young woman. Louise told me she noticed the astonishment on Mum's face, seeing the change in her.

'Just look at you, Louise. I can't believe it. Been such a long time, hasn't it? How's everything been going anyway? You must tell me all your news, Louise . . .'

Mum kept repeating Louise's name throughout the visit and Tara said the same thing. For as long as I could remember she'd done this with me too – sometimes it seemed like she ended every sentence with my name – but it was really striking hearing my sisters say she did it with them too. I hadn't really thought about why. Later on, Tara and I spoke about it. 'It's just a way of controlling us, isn't it? Like brainwashing.' I could see what she meant.

Though Mum made friendly conversation with Tara and Louise about what had been going on in their lives, and cooed over Amy and Nathan, she seemed far more interested in talking about herself. She told us she was settling into prison life more, explained about the routine, gossiped about prison officers and other prisoners. There was no sign she felt any kind of responsibility towards Louise, Tara or anyone else in the family about what had happened and the suffering they had been through. Everything was either the fault of Dad or social services.

'We'll just have to stick together now we're all back in touch, won't we? Look after one another like families should. It won't be easy, but if we do that we'll be fine, won't we, girls?'

She still seemed in complete denial of the reality of her situation and ours. She spoke in platitudes. Tara, never shy about saying what she thinks, only just managed to hide her annoyance; Louise couldn't seem to find any feelings at all. She just wanted to get out as soon as she could and go home. When we eventually did leave there was no sign of the distress or vulnerability Mum showed when I'd visited her on my own. There were no tears, there was no clinging, none of the, 'I've missed you so much, Mae, you will come back soon, won't you?'

The friendly tone she'd shown that day just seemed like a front to Tara and Louise. Mum showed no real concern over how they'd get by as young adults with such a terrible past. There was no practical advice about money, accommodation or anything else. No sense at all that she could at least now help them by finally being honest. I shouldn't have been surprised. Beneath that front, her real attitude to Tara and Louise, as she revealed it to me, and to them, on other occasions was negative at best and often hostile. I knew, as the three of us took the train home, that reconnecting my sisters to Mum had been a mistake, and was only ever going to cause them anguish. I felt really guilty about that.

Mum used to say she saw something of herself in Tara, but the only resemblance I ever saw was that Tara wasn't afraid to speak her mind. There was nothing cruel or dark in Tara's personality. She was just a young woman trying to live her life, making some mistakes along the way as everyone does but doing the best she could. Mum didn't see that. She thought Tara was never going to make anything of herself, that she'd make a terrible mother to Nathan and any other children she might have. This seemed an especially cruel thing to say a young woman who has just had a child and is new to motherhood. But Mum had no qualms about telling Tara this – even to the point that she said Tara would end up having her kids taken away from her just as she had.

She could be just as negative about Louise, telling her that because she was such an emotional wreck she'd never make a success of work, relationships, and especially motherhood. As Louise began to try to make a life for herself out of care, Mum discouraged her from having children because she thought she wouldn't be capable of bringing them up properly and they too would end up damaged. It was as if she was damning Tara and Louise when their adult lives had hardly begun.

I'd stand up for both my sisters when Mum came out with things like that. Tell her that what they needed was help and support, not this stream of negativity. Whatever I said in their defence didn't seem to make any real difference to Mum, though she continued to go through the motions of being a mother to them, sometimes giving advice, directly to them if she could, or through me. Louise never visited Mum again after that first time because she said had seen nothing to suggest she felt any genuine remorse towards her over the horrific sexual abuse she'd suffered. Tara made only a few more visits although she would sometimes take part in phone calls I had with Mum. Mum also continued to send birthday cards and sometimes presents to them, and to their children as the years passed. Going through the motions of motherhood with Tara and Louise, even though her relationship with both daughters had pretty well died.

With me it was different. She made it seem as if I was the one who understood her and would support her through thick and thin – in her eyes, a kind of soulmate. While she knew my own life was a huge struggle at that stage, she would urge me to see the problems I faced as solvable, even if the solutions she suggested were confusing or unrealistic or hopeless. She claimed to dote on Amy and started to give me advice about how best to bring her up. Her attitude to me and my future was, so she made out anyway, much more concerned and in some ways positive than it was towards Tara and Louise.

If Mum had been normal, or anything like it, I might have seen some good in this. But since she was the person she was, being her favourite child just made my life incredibly complicated. I didn't feel I could ever abandon Mum, and despite my sisters' hostility to her, I didn't think at that time that they wanted me to either – they still felt some kind of bond with her, however strange. And the truth was, somewhere inside me, I still needed her.

Tara and I continued to live together, with Louise nearby – trying to remain completely anonymous. It was hard not to worry about people finding out who we were. It would only take someone to stare at me in the street or in a shop for me to wonder if they suspected or had even somehow found out. At times, however unfairly, it felt like we were criminals, but I knew that for Amy's sake I just had to keep my head down and work towards some kind of future.

Anonymity became even more important to me when, only nine months after Amy was born, I was summoned to go to court in Bristol as a witness in my Uncle John's trial and testify about how he had raped me as a child. After Uncle John killed himself, his suicide was all over the papers. The *News of the World* pursued me, wanting a story, but the last thing I needed was that kind of attention. All I wanted was to keep out of the public eye and focus on my life with Amy.

One person outside the family who did know my identity and remained supportive was my health visitor, Barbara, who continued to call at the house for some time after Amy was born. She was an older lady and enormously kind and became like a friend. She was in a really unhappy marriage and used to talk about that sometimes.

This was something that happened to me more and more over the years. People would find out who I was and, knowing I'd had a very difficult life, somehow felt they could then pour out their own problems to me. Maybe they felt it would make me feel better, knowing that other lives could be full of pain too, but often I felt it was a burden. I had enough stuff of my own to carry without taking on other people's. Though it has been reassuring, if sad, to discover that many, perhaps even most, lives are full of secrets, guilt or shame.

But with Barbara it was different. Her compassion seemed genuine, and she never spent hours pouring out her soul about how hard her life was for selfish reasons – she was just honest about it. Nor did I have any feeling that she was spying on me – looking out for the slightest indication that I was a child abuser like my parents so that she might, if necessary, alert the authorities who would take Amy away. This was a real fear for me then and continued to be so for a long time afterwards. She helped me begin to feel I could be a good mother.

I have often thought that without such occasional kindness from people outside the family I couldn't have survived.

I remained in frequent touch with Mum, by phone, letter and visits, but increasingly I began to dread the sound of the telephone ringing on Sunday afternoon; the noise the envelopes made hitting the doormat; the journey to Durham and the invasive searches followed by Mum's stories. It was stressful and exhausting and such was her emotional control over me that when she didn't call me, or there was a long gap between letters, I would become anxious – worrying that something had happened to her or, worst still, she was rejecting me. And I hated the dishonesty which keeping in touch with Mum forced on me – such as lying to Amy about the real reason for my visits to Durham. Years later, when Amy was about ten or eleven, she was telling me a story of 'that time we were on holiday, and we went on that boat on the river.' I didn't know what she was talking about, but the more she described it, the more I realised she was talking about one of our trips to Durham. 'Yes, love,' I said, feeling my heart break a little inside that I couldn't tell her the truth.

And the visits themselves were so emotionally demanding – never knowing what mood I'd find Mum in – emotional and clingy or flippant and childish. The prison officers always trying to eavesdrop so that no conversation was ever really private. Sometimes there would be a security alert and they'd put the prison on lock-down which meant all visitors had to leave the building and return later to resume the visit, going through the same security procedures once again. When I came home from each visit I felt emotionally violated and also somehow physically dirtied by being in the prison, so much so that I would always take a bath when I got in.

Mum had sought to appeal her sentence but unsurprisingly it had been turned down. She was angry about that, denouncing the unfairness of her conviction but, when I was with her, her anger seemed to quickly evaporate and she would be back to telling me the latest gossip bout her life in prison, or asking how I was getting on.

She was full of advice, sending me leaflets about state benefits I could apply for or about help available for single parents. But the truth was that the contact we had was more about me helping her than vice versa. In one letter she asked me to send her Shirley Bassey's 'This is my life' on cassette; saying she liked the top I'd sent her; and *if you can spare an odd tenner you can send me it for Xmas to buy some extra things'.*

I had very little money to spare so helping her out by buying her clothes and occasionally sending cash wasn't easy – I was never sure if Mum ever appreciated this or if it was just not in her interest to notice. But I knew that the help, alongside the support, I gave her was really important to her. She had little or no contact with my brother Steve, who she continued to blame for siding with my dad.

Barbara realised how withdrawn I was becoming and encouraged me to try to get out more. I didn't know how to go about it. If I became friends with anyone, how could the friendship progress? I would either have to lie about who I was and live with the fear of being found out. Or I could summon up the courage to tell the truth and wait for what I expected would be inevitable rejection. Either way, though, the friendship would be ruined.

The same was likely to be even more true of boyfriends. What man would want me, knowing who I was? Probably only freaks and weirdos, I felt. How could I risk making myself vulnerable by developing feelings for a man only for them to reject me?

Tara was more resilient about these things. She has always been tough and outspoken and has been less concerned about disguising her family background. If people teased or abused her for who she was she would give it back as good, if not better, in return. She has always been like Mum in that way. Tara quite often went out in the evenings, sometimes returning to Gloucester to see friends or to go out with men. I envied the freedom her looks gave her, her mixed-race features didn't single her out as a West.

But Barbara persisted in telling me I needed to make an effort and, knowing I couldn't face going out to pubs and clubs, suggested I try a dating agency. So, at the age of twenty-five, I summoned up the courage – having finally lost the baby weight I'd put on with Amy – and wrote to one. This was before online dating or any of those apps, so a lady came to the house, took my details and together we wrote a profile. Of course, I didn't reveal anything that gave away my background. I just had to hope that if I did meet someone I got on with, I'd find a way of explaining who I was without scaring them away.

I was sent a few men's profiles, and met up with one, which didn't go any further. The next was a divorced man who was thirteen years older than I was. He had a good job and, on paper, sounded nice. I was quite attracted to the idea of an older man, hoping it meant he was more likely to be confident and reliable than someone younger. I really didn't need a relationship with someone who was immature. We met for dinner.

His name was Chris and he came across as a warm, gentle, quiet man. We began dating and I soon reached the point where

I felt I owed it to him, and to myself, to tell him the truth about my past. He seemed to react well and said that it didn't make any difference to his feelings about me. But a few weeks later, he told me he'd mentioned it to some friends and they'd advised him to dump me immediately because I would bring terrible baggage to the relationship. I was really upset, not just at his friends' reaction but at the fact he'd told them in the first place. I said I felt betrayed, but he calmed me down, told me he had no intention of taking his friends' advice, that he was serious about me and wouldn't dream of ending our relationship.

However, not long afterwards, he called and said he too had something important to tell me. He sounded anxious. I asked him to come round to my place, we sat down and eventually he revealed that he had multiple sclerosis. I didn't really know much about the disease, so he explained a little about it and that his diagnosis had been made a few years earlier. He played it down, saying it hadn't affected his life badly and that sometimes it progressed very slowly and some people remain relatively un-affected by it for many years. He told me he was afraid I'd want to end the relationship but I told him I understood what he said and that I accepted him for who he was just as he had accepted me for who I was. In a way, both our revelations to each other seemed to deepen the bond between us.

Things moved quickly after that. Within eighteen months Chris had sold his house and bought a new one in a town some distance from where I lived with Tara, and Amy and I moved in with him. It was a nice house; the first time in years that I had found some stability in my life.

Mum seemed pleased about my new circumstances although I got the impression that most of the time she had no proper sense of the reality of my life. This became even clearer when she got it into her head that she should change her name from

Rose West to Rose Harrison (which was the surname Amy and I used). She wrote to me to explain her reasons:

Then at least you can say Nanny Harrison instead of Nanny West! Then later when your kids are older you can say we all changed our names together for obvious reasons. And also if they should hear anything about Rose West as they get older it won't click to them (until you want it to of course.)

Her suggestion about changing her name was as crazy and impossible as it was useless. Of course Tara and I (and later our other siblings, if and when they had children) would have to face explaining their grandmother's absence, and even more importantly their family history, when the time came – but Mum changing her name wasn't even going to begin to help.

But I did feel that in her own way she was trying, and I was tactful about the way I explained to her that there was no point pursuing it. Although largely wrapped up in her own life, she continued to take an interest in mine and, however limited this was, I was still glad of it.

A couple of years after Chris and I moved in together his MS worsened and he began to struggle getting up and down stairs. In order to make things easier for him we moved to a single-storey barn conversion in a rural location. It had a big garden and looked out across open countryside. It was a lovely house and Chris at least found he was able to manage his mobility difficulties better there.

Life was a long way from being from being easy but it had become more settled. I knew I had some way to go, though, to face up to reality. Chris was a very generous man but it had been important to me from the age of sixteen onwards to earn my own living. I realised I wanted to re-establish my financial independence, which meant getting a job and facing the world in a way that I hadn't needed to before. Amy also was coming up to school age and she too would soon need to emerge from the protective cocoon of our home.

So together, mother and daughter, we entered a new stage of our lives.

Chapter Fifteen

Fallout

Mum's changed her tune about prison again: sounds like she's been having a laugh, cracking jokes left right and centre. She's keen to arrange our next visit. The new child protection law means our visit with Amy will be the last for a while. She said something that struck me – that I seem like a good mother. What does a good mother look like? Can't help but thinking I wouldn't know.

HM PRISON DURHAM

Dear Mae,
    Anyway you looked well and you had a funny kind of motherly presence about you I haven't noticed it that much with you before.

I'm not sure which I was most nervous about – Amy starting school or me getting a job.

From the day Amy was born I knew there was a risk of me being overprotective. Because of the childhood I'd had, no one could have been more aware of the risks young children face. My determination to see my daughter safely through that period of time, physically and emotionally undamaged, was ferocious, but I was aware that I couldn't keep her under my wing forever.

I would have to gradually let her go, learn to entrust others with her care and allow her to learn to trust others in return.

There was another worry. I was never quite sure how much the various official bodies you have to deal with in life knew about me. Although I was no longer called Mae West I knew that the police, hospitals, social services and schools often shared information, and it always seemed possible, sometimes even likely, that anybody working for these organisations might find about my family background.

What if Amy had a fall at home and went to school with bruises? Would they believe it had been an accident? I sometimes even used to wonder how I would react if Amy injured herself at home badly enough to need an ambulance. Would I hesitate, fearing my explanation about how it happened wouldn't be believed? Would social services be informed? Or the police? If that happened there would be no chance of keeping my identity secret. Or maybe they already knew? It was hard not to feel paranoid at times that I was being watched. Were they just waiting for me to make a mistake so they could have the excuse to take Amy away from me? I found the thought of that unbearable, but I knew that's what would happen if they thought they saw the slightest evidence of abuse.

I was also still trying to find my way with being a parent with a young child. Sometimes I used to watch other parents for an idea of how I should treat Amy. They all seemed relaxed about letting their children mix with other kids. I knew that was the right attitude to have and yet I found it difficult to allow my own child that freedom because Mum – always concerned about outsiders knowing what went on in our house – had barely ever allowed us to play with other children. I knew that was wrong, that it would be unhealthy for me to treat Amy like that or she might grow up un-socialised and withdrawn, but I didn't know how much social contact was too much.

Whatever freedom other parents allowed their kids I felt I ought to give to her. If her friends' parents were letting them go to parties or, when they were older, sleepovers, I thought I should do the same. And yet this often went against my instincts because I felt so protective of her. And it involved me having social contact – even if just to make practical arrangements with the other parents – which I preferred to avoid. I didn't want to give anyone the opportunity of asking me awkward questions about my life.

But I tried to make myself do it as much as I could. I wanted to be like other parents. Often, I didn't succeed. I'd watch other mothers at the school gates, chatting or laughing or inviting one another round for coffee and think I should try and be like that, but I knew that I couldn't.

And I was constantly fearful for Amy. When she told me she wanted to do some activity away from home such as a school trip, which seemed like it might put her at risk, I'd often want to say no. I sometimes found myself in turmoil about it and one parents' evening I broke down in front of a teacher. She asked me what the matter was.

'I don't feel I can get fully involved in school activities,' I said, hiding how my past kept me from getting too close to people, in case they guessed who I was. The shadows of the past remain.

'Maybe you feel a bit cut off and isolated yourself? How about if Amy joined the Brownies? I run the local pack myself. That way you'd meet other parents and Amy would be able to social-ise more out of school.'

She could see the doubt in my face and probed a little more. The school was in a prosperous area and I said something about feeling awkward because other parents seemed to be much better off than me, going on about their nice cars and conservatories and holidays in the south of France, and I wasn't from that kind of background. Then there was my broad Gloucester accent, which I felt made me stand out among their posh voices.

I could see the teacher sensed there must be more to it than that and, to my amazement, I suddenly found myself telling her who I was. I couldn't believe I'd done it and regretted it immediately. She wasn't sure how to react. She made sympathetic remarks but seemed more embarrassed than anything and never mentioned it again. I don't blame her. How are people supposed to react when you say: 'I'm the daughter of Fred and Rosemary West'? It's more than likely to be a conversation-stopper.

Every time you see that person afterwards you sense that's probably what they're thinking about it. And no matter how much you may have stressed you want them to keep it in confidence you just can't be sure who else they'll tell.

I ran into similar problems at work. I'd managed to get a job by this time. It was with a large company in a nearby town. I started out in the sales department which, although I'd picked up considerable office skills in my previous employment, wasn't the kind of work I'd ever done before. I hated it. I didn't have the pushy manner that sales people need. Sometimes I felt I was selling people things they didn't need, which felt wrong. I also couldn't cope with the aggression and abuse from the public that sometimes comes with that kind of job. I respected people who could do it – the way they could shrug off the hassle, win people over and make the sale. We worked in an open-plan office and I'd look around and see how much better the others were doing. In particular there was a man called Pete who sat nearby. He was younger than me and seemed particularly brilliant at it. I used to look at him, listen to his bright and cheery telephone manner with potential clients and really admire him.

Feeling I wasn't really up to the job, I went to our supervisor who was called Paula and told her I wanted to hand in my notice. She was sympathetic and said she didn't want me to leave. She arranged for me to move into the renewals section, which was less stressful, and then shortly afterwards told me there was a vacancy in the HR department which she thought would suit me well as I had secretarial skills. I was really grateful and ended up sitting near her and got to know her a little.

One day she happened to be writing her date of birth down: it was the same as mine. We were struck by the coincidence and got talking and I found I really got on with her. She wasn't nosy about my life, nor was I about hers, but over a period of time, in the normal way of things, we began to find out a little bit about one another. On one occasion, I mentioned, without thinking, that I hadn't always had my current surname.

'What was it before?' she asked.

It too was an open-plan office and I couldn't bring myself to say 'West' in other people's hearing so I wrote it on a piece of paper and pushed it across to her. She looked at it.

'So did it change because you got married?' she whispered.

It would have been so easy to say yes but I liked her and my instinct was to tell the truth. I shook my head, took back the piece of paper and wrote 'Fred' in front of 'West'. She understood immediately but there was little awkwardness or embarrassment. It was such a relief. She continued to treat me exactly as she had done before. It was the beginning of the strongest friendship of my adult life and it continues to this day.

I've never had any fear that Paula would divulge my past to anyone – not unless I wanted her to – and I've found that I could talk to her about pretty well anything. People who don't know me might assume that I'm totally preoccupied with the horrors of my past and my relationship with my mum, but that's far from the truth. There are times when those things are in my mind because they continue to have such an impact on my life, but the truth is that much of the time I am dealing with the same issues – relationships, kids, work – that most people spend their time dealing with.

That's the kind of thing I would talk to Paula about. Naturally, from time to time, my childhood or my parents would come up, or I'd talk about Heather, or my surviving brothers and sisters. She was often surprised, as I guess most people would be, that not all of my family life had been misery. There had been love and affection – between me and my siblings at least. She seemed most surprised to discover that I had a sense of humour – and perhaps that had helped me survive.

When I first went back to work I was very quiet and with-drawn, but my confidence grew – partly as a result of my friendship with Paula. I began to really enjoy the social aspect of work: office banter and occasional get-togethers with colleagues outside work. Apart from discussing it pretty freely with Paula, I kept the details of my home life mostly to myself. I was begin-ning to feel the job was helping me to rebuild my life.

Then one day the head of HR took me aside and told me she no longer wanted me to work in that department. She was vague about the reason but I felt upset and disappointed, assuming it was a reflection on the quality of my work. I was moved into training. It was nice in one way because Paula was involved in that too, and I was given the job of organising the course mate-rials and assisting her with the courses she ran. But something kept nagging at me about why I'd been moved.

It was some time before I discovered the real reason – I found out from my colleague, Pete. He told me that someone in the sales department had come across a book about the Cromwell Street murders and had seen a picture of me on the back of it and recognised me. This person had mentioned it to colleagues and it had become a source of gossip for some of them. Although others, like Pete, had refused to join in, saying my past was none of anybody else's business.

I suppose I knew it would get out eventually. I spent a lot of time puzzling over why the information about my past would make me unfit to work in HR. I couldn't see any logical reason but obviously it meant that in some way management felt I wasn't to be trusted. It wasn't rational but I couldn't help feeling at fault for what had happened. Nor could I help wondering whether it would always be like this: the past always catching up with me, always being made to feel somehow guilty by association because of who I was.

I didn't share much of this during my continuing visits to Mum. I didn't want to discuss my problems with her in great detail – apart from anything else, rather than being able to help, she was the cause of them. And in some ways my life was going better than it had in a long time.

She continued to take an interest in Amy's progress and was upset that the prison authorities wouldn't allow me to bring her on visits any more due to her age. She still seemed determined that she should remain at the centre of the family and, although she saw Tara and Louise much less often than she saw me, always wanted news of them and of our younger siblings. The only relationship with any of her children that she seemed to have written off was with Stephen, who never visited her or wrote and whose support of Dad, rather than her, she had never forgiven him for.

'Sometimes I can hardly believe he's my son!' she'd say, before adding, without any conviction at all: 'Oh don't worry, I still love him very much.'

I didn't believe she loved him at all. And though she wanted to feel at the centre of her children's lives, her effect on us – even in prison – continued to prove toxic in a way that I found devastating.

Since we had made contact with one another again, my relationships with Tara and Louise had been very important to me. It wasn't always easy. Though it had been so good to have Louise back in our lives, she sometimes found it hard to fit in with me and Tara. I guess this can often be a problem in families where there's a close triangular relationship between three siblings – there is a danger one always feels left out. I tried as best I could to be even-handed, giving as much time and attention to Louise as I did to Tara, but still found that jealousies and resentments arose. And when any two of us fell out, the third found it hard to stay impartial, especially when both sisters were putting pressure on her to take their side.

As time went on we had a number of rows and upsets, but always managed to patch things up and become friends again. But all three of us were damaged and vulnerable and there was always the risk of a much bigger fallout, which is what eventually happened.

I don't want to go into too much detail, but it all came to a head over a photo Tara and I decided to send Mum which included Louise. We hadn't checked with her first, and when we told her she was very upset. It was a very private photo, and I can understand now why we really shouldn't have sent it, but we didn't really think at the time. Louise ended up having a big row with Tara about it. I tried not to take a side but because I'd sent the photo too and wasn't sticking up for Louise, she felt I'd picked Tara over her. I hoped it would all blow over – I gave it a few weeks, then, hoping Louise's feelings of anger and betrayal might have subsided somewhat, I went to her house to see if she was all right. I rang the doorbell but no one answered. I tried phoning her mobile but she didn't pick up. I went back home and continued to call her that day and on numerous occasions afterwards but still couldn't reach her. I didn't know what else to do.

Weeks turned into months. Tara too felt bad about what had happened and also tried to contact her without success. Eventually her mobile didn't even ring when we tried it and seemed to have been disconnected. I drove over to her flat on several more occasions and still couldn't raise a response from inside. Then, on one visit, I peered in through the window and saw a baby's pram. I came to the conclusion that Louise must have moved and someone else was now living there.

Tara and I felt awful. In the months and years that followed, we thought and talked about Louise often, hoping she might get back in touch with us, but it never happened. We kept wondering where she might have gone but had really had no idea. It seemed we had no choice but to accept we'd never see her again.

We had already lost one sister. Now, as well as Heather, we had lost Louise, too.

Chapter Sixteen

A Better Kind of Person

Mum's letter is filled with fire. She writes that I've got to find someone I can trust as this whole nightmare should be a wake-up call. I have to make the right choices for me and Amy – be a strong adult figure for her – and let go of the past. It's hard to accept her advice as she sits in prison with so many secrets. She is my past, my violent and terrible past. And a part of me doesn't want to let her go: she's all the memories I have.

<u>HM PRISON DURHAM</u>

<u>YOU</u> need people in your life you can put your trust in. <u>AND</u> as you yourself are a trustworthy person others will automatically be able to trust you <u>AND</u> appreciate it!! By for instance lending you some money.

Later on, I came to see that at the heart of the fallout with Louise was Mum: it was who she was and what she'd done that had pulled us apart, but at the time I didn't. I blamed myself. I continued to find it hard to be angry with Mum. Sometimes I'd feel that emotion welling up inside me, but when I eventually came to write to her, or speak to her on the phone, or visit her, the anger had usually melted away and was replaced by pity.

Although she had adapted to prison life quite well in some ways, it was still painful to think of her locked away there for good. I continued to visit her regularly – usually once every month or two at least, though finding the money for the rail fare, and sometimes for a cheap B&B if I had to stay over, was often a struggle. Every visit to her began and ended with tears – and they seemed as real as mine. The regime at Durham, especially for category A prisoners, seemed to vary according to the whim of the prison authorities. Sometimes it seemed to be relatively relaxed. At others, perhaps due to drugs found in cells or a general rise in tensions, it seemed to be much more harsh. I felt certain that at times, although Mum could be hard, and hated to show any weakness to those in authority, she was finding it tougher than she sometimes let on.

From the tone of some of her letters you wouldn't have guessed it; she'd write about her work making toys. Her day sometimes sounded less like she was in prison and more like she was working in a sort of factory or commune far away:

The time go's so quick, I get up in the morning, shower, quick cup of tea and off to work. Back on the wing for 12, have dinner, collect post, have a cuppa and a fag with the girls. Maybe try and get to the washing machine (which doesn't happen very often) and before you know it, it's back to work! Back on the wing for 4, have a cuppa and a fag with the girls again and catch up with all the news and have tea Off to the gym at 5.15 until 6.15, another cuppa & fag (and maybe a laugh too) and that leaves an hour before they lock-in!

She took various classes, she went to church on Sunday, 'to thank God for my wonderful children and my beautiful grandchildren! and even met the Bishop. But I thought a lot of that tone was her putting on a front for my benefit, or perhaps to convince herself all was okay. I knew how good she was at denying reality, and things she revealed on visits and in other letters painted a very different picture. Some years into her sentence there was a change of governor who introduced a tougher regime, on top of which Mum felt that she was being singled out for special treatment:

I'm being treated with more contempt than ever, mainly because I will insist on protesting my innocence of these convictions all the time. I won't conform, I won't sit and have their nice cosy little chats with them, I won't misbehave, I won't inform on others ... they don't know what to do with me. And because I've been told I will never be released they can't threaten me with getting 'more time' or 'never getting out'! They can't punish me for misbehaviour because that just doesn't happen, and yet they deal with me in the only way left open to them, 'sheer contempt'!! I've been put through some horrifying searches just recently, that's why I've had to send all my stuff to you. I gave away most of my things after the first search, which led them to putting me back on 24 hour watch. They said I was acting funny, I was acting funny!!

Because she was a category A prisoner, the searches were particularly thorough in her cell, with dogs going through all her things: she was really upset, and angry that it meant she had to bunk in with another prisoner one night while this was taking place, something that apparently never happened between

Cat As. She even let the budgie go because the searches were so frightening, she said. Essentially it sounded as if there had been a lot of rule changes under the new governor, and she was receiving the brunt of them and didn't like them – she'd been so settled before.

And because my contact with Mum was usually frequent and regular, it used to worry me if there was a lag in hearing from her and if I wasn't being sent visiting orders. I was sure that some of the other prisoners would have it in for her and that the prison authorities would make life very hard for her if she retaliated. I knew Mum had never been afraid to take people on – physically if necessary, if she thought they were bullying her. She also believed the authorities were concerned that, because the evidence presented against her at the trial had almost all been circumstantial, she might eventually mount a successful appeal and get her sentence quashed. For that reason she believed she was under close surveillance, that her mail and phone calls were being closely monitored and, possibly even, her cell bugged. Sometimes, on leaving the prison after a visit, I'd even be asked by prison officers if she'd revealed anything 'of interest'.

In the outside world, I too was entering another difficult stage in my life. I'd turned thirty and had been with Chris for five years, but our relationship was beginning to break down. Partly it was the age gap between us, but mainly it was becoming clear that we'd got into the relationship because we were both carrying serious baggage (my family history and his serious illness) rather than for more positive reasons. On top of this I was starting to want more independence and he too felt that he wanted to do things with his life (travel, go on holidays with friends) while he was still well enough to be able to do them. He was a lovely man, brilliant with Amy, and that made it even harder, but reluctantly we made a mutual decision to separate.

The break-up was amicable and we remained friends afterwards, which helped, I was suddenly starting all over again. I moved out of Chris's house, found a flat in a nearby town, which at least allowed me to keep my job and Amy to remain at the same school, but I really wanted to find what most other people seemed to have: a secure home, a stable, happy relationship, and the feeling that the past is not always going to keep catching up with you and ruin the present.

I did my best to be a good single parent. I took Amy to Disneyland Paris. This was a big step for me. I'd never been much of a one for holidays, preferring to spend most of my time indoors when not at work, and I had never been abroad on my own before. I felt proud of myself for making the trip, even though I was only doing what other parents do for their kids all the time. I still felt, though, that I wasn't giving Amy the life she deserved and that there was something that wasn't psychologically healthy about one parent sharing a small space with a child. I was probably keener to meet someone else than I would have liked to admit and it wasn't that long before I did so.

His name was Richard. I met him in a pub in town. Like Chris, he was older than me – this time by ten years. The relationship turned out to be a huge mistake. There were various reasons why it was never going to work out and why I ignored the warning signs that were there from the beginning – especially what I came to see as his controlling nature – but I leaped into the relationship because I simply felt glad to be wanted.

The truth is there have been a number of times when I have felt almost grateful that anyone wanted me. I always felt as if I was starting on the back foot because I was a West. Most depressingly, some men seemed to regard me as an object of sexual curiosity, a notch on their bedpost – even wondering if I might know kinky sex tricks taught to me by my notorious prostitute mother.

All this led me to take decisions in relationships based on my need for security rather than love. Older men seemed to offer this and yet when I got into the relationship I wasn't happy (and neither were they) because there wasn't really enough between us to build on. It was like that with Richard and things were made more complicated by the fact that he had two daughters in their early teens. In getting into a relationship with him I would effectively become a stepmother – and this at a time when I wanted to concentrate on being the best parent I could be to my own child.

Despite all this we were pretty soon into a serious relationship. I was able to confide in both Tara and Paula about it, which helped to some extent. At that period it would have been impossible to get sensible advice off Mum as, extraordinarily, she had plunged headlong into an ill-advised 'romance' of her own.

Over the years, many people have befriended Mum – fellow prisoners, prison visitors or people she didn't even know who wrote letters to her. Some of these have been from well-known people: writers, criminologists, even celebrities. Some have been from total strangers who were simply fascinated by her, often for very suspect reasons.

At around that time she received one from Dave Glover, the bass player with the band Slade. Before long she became completely smitten with him like a teenage girl with a crush and developed a postal romance with him. To others this might seem hilarious but from the start I was worried about the psychological effect on her. I felt such a deluded romance stemmed from the dreadful sexual abuse she'd herself suffered as a child and a feeling that ever since neither my dad nor any other man had ever loved and cared for her in the way that she wanted. Now when she sent me her all-too-often clothes request, she'd also ask for things for Dave too:

Ah Mae it's brilliant talking to you on the phone - I love our conversations.

Right, Cat no for trousers, Argos Additions.

Stretch satin trousers,

Gx0547 Black

Size 18 £15

Mae, I was wondering if you would get a card for Dave too?

What the prison authorities, especially the psychiatrists working with her, made of the relationship I don't know. They must have been aware of it because all her correspondence was intercepted and read. If they weren't very concerned then they should have been, because although the situation might have seemed comic, Mum was taking it all very seriously. She believed Dave had feelings for her which were just as strong as hers for him and she was convinced he believed in her innocence. She sent me photos of him asking 'what do you think?' and poured her heart out to me about him in letters which were full of adolescent yearning. She began to talk, quite seriously, about the two of them getting married. Predictably, the relationship began to unravel when prison officers, who over the years have often leaked things about Mum's life in prison, tipped off the press. She wrote to me to explain what had happened, in her eyes at least, saying she'd spoken to him a lot trying to give him support and, *as I was speaking to him the press was trying to break the door down and pushing notes under it!'*

At this point though she was still besotted and seeing a future for the two of them: 'He calls me Sweetheart!! I cried after I read that!! This man is the light of my life, my soul mate, my best friend and the 'love of my life'. Love is definitely worth it!'

Of course, I never knew exactly what Dave's feelings for Mum were, but it was an extraordinary relationship. What more unlikely pairing could there be than a convicted serial killer and a member of a glam-rock band? She started planning their marriage at that point. I suppose I should have found the prospect of her remarrying beyond bizarre, but I had reached the stage that nothing in Mum's life could surprise me.

Then, quite suddenly, Mum called the wedding off, issuing a brief statement via her solicitor Leo Goatley explaining that she 'wanted to give this young man his life back'. I was never convinced that was the real reason. She may well have felt sorry for Dave, caught up in a ridiculous media storm, but I think the real reason was that it suddenly dawned on her that the whole thing was a complete fantasy. She may have still nursed some small hope of being released from prison one day, but it was a long way from being an expectation – so what prospect was there of any kind of normal fulfilling marriage between herself and a man she had never even physically met?

When Leo Goatley issued the statement on her behalf he commented that Mum had sounded to him 'flat but not distressed', but I was sceptical of that. I suspected she felt foolish and, in her own way, very upset at the collapse of her fantasy. I did my best to support her through it – again in some ways as a mother would help a daughter deal with a broken teenage romance – but this was all happening at a time when my own need for emotional support had grown. Richard and I had moved in together, despite some reservations I still had. I told

Mum I'd made this leap of faith. Despite the ongoing turmoil in her own life she wrote to me with advice about how I should approach this new stage in mine, and especially deal with the challenges of family life and becoming a stepmother.

'They need someone to love them and they need a friend. They will need you to try to understand their needs and to be there for them,' she said. *Where* she got this from I have no idea, considering the sort of stepmother she herself was. Again, looking back, what makes me angry is that she clearly knew how she *should* behave, and chosen not to. 'I'll be thinking of you especially, and I'll be here if you should need me,' she wrote. And oh how I wanted to believe her.

Chapter Seventeen

Breaking the Bonds

Mum's letter was full of smalltalk today. Films she'd watched, how much she's going to the gym – that sort of stuff. She was being nicer to Tara, too, than she normally is. But then of course she follows up all of this with a request for one thing or another; I can't help but wonder if that's what she's really after when she's kind to us . . .

I'm making the very best of things and oh boy, they certainly know Rose is around. I've got lots of support and we have a real good laugh (most of the time).

I'd appreciate it if you could send me ten pound a week from now on. But please don't worry about missing the odd week, I'm never really that desperate for money.

Within a year of our first meeting, Richard and I were married. I was so pleased. I'd begun to fear I might be single for ever, and I wanted marriage for the sense of normality and security it would bring. Richard was the first man I'd met who wanted to marry me and I felt thrilled and flattered.

We were living in Richard's house, which was only just round the corner from my old flat. When I'd first visited him there the place was just as it had been when his first wife left him: it seemed rather stuck in a time warp, with Laura Ashley wallpaper and old-fashioned furnishings which I didn't like. I had some savings and we used these to do the place up. I've always enjoyed decorating and DIY – perhaps the only useful thing I learned from my dad. It was satisfying to be making a new home again.

There'd been signs, though, from early on in the relationship that should have caused me to think more carefully before making such a huge commitment. I found Richard possessive, which in some ways I liked, especially at first – it made me feel wanted. But as time went on, it began to feel oppressive and suffocating. He didn't like me going out without him or even talking to other men. Yet I'd given him no reason at all to think I'd be unfaithful and started to resent what felt like attempts to control me.

The fact he was quite a lot older than me and seemed to be still quite emotionally involved with his first wife didn't help. And I obviously was facing challenges that were hard for him to understand – being the best mother I could be to Amy, as well as dealing with the huge issues I was carrying from the past. Eventually, tensions between Richard and me became too much for either of us to deal with and I left him.

In the ten years since the Cromwell Street crimes had come to light there had been many times when I thought that things simply couldn't get any worse. Yet that's what seemed always to happen. Soon after my marriage to Richard ended I fell out with my brother Steve, something it wouldn't be right to go into here. He and I had always had a complicated relationship but he'd always been important to me. We'd been through so much together and, apart from Tara, he was the only person I had left in my life who could understand how difficult it was to live with the terrible legacy our parents had left us. As an adult he'd faced similar challenges in trying to build a life for himself. I ought to have been able to turn to him at that point in my life, as I would have hoped he could turn to me, but unfortunately he did something which really upset me and left me feeling betrayed and badly let down. I had already lost my sisters, Heather and Louise, and now it seemed I'd lost my brother too.

After I left Richard, Amy and I moved into a new flat across town and it seemed like the lowest point yet. While there had been more obviously traumatic periods in my life, I can't remember a time when I felt more demoralised by the accumulation of setbacks and less confident that I could build a new life for myself. 'Life's a bitch and then you die,' Mum sometimes used to say to me. It wasn't the most inspiring reflection on life but there were times when it seemed all too true.

But there were a few reasons for hope that I clung onto. The flat I found across town was bright and cheerful; I still had my job and my friendship with Paula; I had the support of Tara who was living fairly close by. Above all I still had Amy, who remained a joy to me and whose presence in my life always encouraged me to carry on and stay as positive as I could.

There was something else beyond that which, as I've said before, I can't define very easily. It isn't a religious faith, certainly not a conventional belief in God, and I've never been a regular church-goer. It's just a feeling that there is some other presence in the universe that is keeping an eye on me and will see me through. So even as I was faced with a present fraught with problems, and a very uncertain future, I continued to feel that presence, whatever it was. I hung onto the feeling that someday, at some unknown time in the future, things would be okay.

The ongoing routine of school for Amy, and of work for me, helped – as did a relationship which began in a low-key way not long after I split from Richard. It was with one of my work colleagues, Pete, whom I'd known and liked for some years. He was several years younger than me and that alone put the relationship on a different footing than any of those I'd had before. There was no sense at all that I was attracted to him simply because I thought he'd take care of me.

Nor was he pushing for that either. He lived at home with his mother and, like me, had no desire to rush headlong into a serious relationship. It suited us both. What's more, he'd known about my past for some time, as had a number of people at work since someone spotted my picture in that book. I had nothing either to hide from him or to frighten him with. That alone was a huge relief. We took things steadily. The relationship was exactly what I needed.

After the collapse of my marriage to Richard and the fallout with Steve I began to feel increasingly resentful of Mum. Much of that was because it brought home to me yet again how useful a mother's support might have been during that time, whereas our relationship was much more about me providing support to her. On top of that, as I became more confident and independent due to my relationship with Pete, I was becoming more and more aware of just how much she manipulated me into feeling her happiness was down to me. But instead of voicing my anger at her refusal to take responsibility for the pain and turmoil in all her children's lives, I fought it back and remained loyal to her, still visiting her and putting up with her demands which sometimes felt intolerable:

I'm sorry dear but the underwear will have to go back. The bra is just not the right style and the knickers are too low in the waistline.

I tried not to feel taken for granted. Every letter she sent me seemed to contain lists of items she wanted, which grew ever more complicated and specific and could take a considerable amount of my spare time to fulfil. And then there was the expense. As a single parent on a relatively low income I had to watch every penny and the train journey to Durham to see her alone created a big hole in my monthly budget. I had very little spare cash to buy her things.

These might seem like relatively trivial matters but to me they signified a growing selfishness in her. She had always had this trait and it was made worse, over the years, by the people she made friends with from the outside world while in prison. Some of these were total strangers who wrote to her saying they were convinced of her innocence. Others were prison visitors who likewise offered moral support. They were often well intentioned, like Sister Paul, who had befriended her when she was first on remand at Pucklechurch, or like Mike (or 'Mick the Vic', as Mum called him) who was the prison chaplain at Durham, or Mike's wife Mary, who was a prison visitor there – Mum said they 'adopted' her as their daughter. But their effect on Mum, so far as I could see, was often unhelpful, encouraging her feelings of self-justification over behaviour which I (and Tara too) thought selfish. And she used them to play stupid games with us, trying (sometimes successfully) to make me feel jealous and resentful of her relationship with them. I'd often get, 'Well you might not agree, Mae, but Mike and Mary think I'm right.' I found it extraordinary and cruel that Mum felt able cut herself off from us, her real family, as and when she wished and become a kind of daughter to two people who she didn't know well and had no previous connection to. I was certainly not able to simply cut off emotionally from the mother I had.

As time wore on it was as if she sensed that I now had so much against her, I might want to break the bonds between us altogether, and so more and more she would play the victim and the little girl. Prison visits still always ended with her in tears, which would invariably rip me apart and trigger mine. We'd weep and hold onto one another. Whatever she had done to annoy or upset me, I felt that beneath her anger and self-pity and selfishness, she was still lonely and vulnerable.

I thought this might change when she was transferred to HM Prison Bronzefield in Kent. It was a relatively modern top-security prison for women where the living conditions, especially for category A prisoners like her, were much better. Mum was delighted at the move and I felt relieved that she was finally out of the hellhole that was Durham jail, but the change seemed to make no real difference to our relationship. Though there was less hardship in her daily life, it was obvious that underneath she still felt the same sense of grievance at being – in her opinion – locked away for life for crimes she did not commit. And she still made sure I knew she felt unhappy, lonely and vulnerable.

And her game-playing got worse, especially in her dealings with Tara and me. I started to feel as if she might be trying to destroy my relationship with Tara – which was just about the only family one I had left apart from with Mum. Things came to a head when Mum came into some money inherited from Dad's estate. It wasn't a large amount and she wasn't allowed to keep it for herself, but she was in a position to share it among her children and grandchildren. Even in prison, she'd always tried to remain at the head of the family and suddenly she felt in an even more powerful position. Instead of deciding to distribute the money equally, she held onto it and began to hint at giving this or that amount according to who was currently in her favour.

I brooded on this and became increasingly angry. I suddenly saw – in a way that I'd never been able to before – how poisonous her behaviour was and how much was at stake for what remained of the family. I talked it over with Tara who felt exactly the same way. Tara had always felt Mum was one thing and one thing alone: evil. I summoned up all my courage and wrote to her:

Dear Mum,

I have spoken to Tara and she has said that she does not want the kids to have the money; she feels she will give the kids all they need for their futures. I have had a long talk to her and she has made me see sense in a lot of what she has said.

Firstly I want to tell you how I feel. You may not agree with any of it but I still think it needs to be said. I feel that you separate us all and you treat us differently, take Steve for instance. He has never felt that you really ever loved him.

Sometimes I feel unless we are making something of our lives you don't want to know us. If we go to work, bring our kids up well, own property etc., then you want to know us, but if we struggle – and let's face it I think with what we have been through the likelihood is that we were never going to be able to live a normal life – then you just shy away. Maybe it makes you feel better to know that at least one or two of us made good but the truth is all of us have made something of our lives however small. It's as if you judge us and we feel you have no right to do that.

It's like this money, you did not sit down and think I have 7 children (8 if you want to include Anne Marie) and say well I want to give them all an equal amount, however small, because they are my children. No you judged us over whether we criticised you in the press, got compensation or just never stuck by you and we all got written off. But I suppose you can write us off and hope the grand-children make more of their lives and you can feel good about what you did for them. Oh and I only mean a select few of them as well, because of Steve, his kids lose out and so on, it's just a power thing at the end of the day. Well none of us want it.

I hate doing this but it's time I stuck up for myself and for the family. Ever since we were kids you have tried to separate us. When it suited you the family had to stick together, but individually if we wanted to spend time with each other it wasn't allowed. I won't turn my back on Amy no matter what she does. Like I am with you, Mum, when you love someone it should be unconditional, I have always been there for you ever since I was young, even though you can be so hard sometimes. You should be less judgemental and more parental. It's not about the money but what it could have symbolised – that for once we all counted and we were all equal.

Mae

I was in turmoil when I posted the letter and waited for an answer. I had no idea how she would respond. I knew she would be deeply hurt. I suspected she would be furious too. It seemed more than possible I would never hear from her ever again. But her reply came after only a few days. She thanked me for being honest and said she wished she could explain face-to-face. She wrote:

When I came to prison I never intended to try to become a 'parent' to you children. I know that with all that has happened in my life and later in 'our' lives that I would never be capable of such a 'feat'. I was never a 'parent' and could never be now! You have always been 'there' for me and I have counted myself as a very privileged person indeed!! I was hoping and I still do now - that it was a choice you made rather than a feeling of expectation - that I could 'live up' to your hopes of having a 'good' mother.

But she said it ultimately wasn't something she was capable of being, and that she was sorry about the money. And then she signed off as she always did:

Love as always,
    Mum xxxxx

I read the letter over several times. I was amazed. It seemed to be the most honest and insightful communication I'd ever had from her.

I'd be lying if I claimed I didn't have conflicting feelings about what to do. Yes, I was angry with her. I knew I'd reached a turning point and could no longer put up with her manipulative and dishonest behaviour. But to abandon her for ever now, after all the years of support I'd given her, and knowing she had no one else who could take my place, felt like a huge step. If I turned my back on her now it would break the last bond she had with the family and cut her adrift. So I replied. I didn't mention her letter to me – I didn't know what I should say in response to any of it. Instead I told her about Amy's new secondary school uniform and some other bits of smalltalk: I wanted to be nice. She didn't reply. I have never written again, or seen her since.

Does it make me angry that I didn't get the last word? No, because it's reflective of who we are as people. It's our relationship all over: I cared. She didn't.

Chapter Eighteen

Another Family

I didn't know for sure at first how she would respond to my new silence. I couldn't be certain that she might not backtrack and try to draw me into her life once again. For some time, I half-expected a letter or a phone call from her – pleading for help or sympathy or saying that life without contact with me was unbearable for her. Every time a letter fell through the letterbox or the phone began to ring I'd find myself holding my breath.

Though I often used to dread the arrival of her letters, with all their complicated emotional and practical demands, I missed them too. I'd kept all the old ones and sometimes I'd get the box out and read through them. Although I'd finally reached the stage where I understood the expressions of affection and love she used towards me in them couldn't have been genuine, I felt sad at the thought there'd be no more like this:

Perhaps you don't realise what a wonderful job you are doing for us all. I'm always boasting about you. You really are an angel darling and that's no bull-shit. We all love you very much, even if we don't always tell you so.

I felt sad, too, that because our relationship had ended, there would never again be an opportunity for Mum to tell me the truth about all the things she'd been accused and convicted of – the sexual abuse, the rapes, the torture and murders. Of course I never seriously believed that would happen, but while Mum and I were in touch, at least it was a possibility. Because, while it had taken me over ten long years, I could no longer hand on heart think Mum was innocent of the crimes. I had heard too many of her lies, listened to too many of her riddles and warped accounts, heard too many stories from Tara and Louise to believe she hadn't been involved in some way. I shall never know the truth, and I still want to believe that she's innocent, but I just can't any more. It makes me angry, because if she could find it in her to be honest about all that, although it would have been dreadful knowledge to have, at least it would help me and my family move on, and just as importantly if not so, perhaps help the surviving family and friends of all the victims too.

Those people were often in my thoughts, all the more so as time passed, and if I could ever have done anything to ease their dreadful pain I would have done it. As it was, I was simply left with the knowledge that my mum and dad had caused it and I was powerless to make amends.

Because it only gradually became absolutely certain there'd be no more letters from Mum, it felt like our relationship died slowly, without a clear ending, and as a result there was no real grieving process. I felt caught in a kind of limbo, unable to move on.

Soon after our final exchange of letters, though, I did experience a bereavement which left me full of grief. My cat, Baggy, died.

I'd had Baggy for sixteen years, from well before the terrible secrets of Cromwell Street began to emerge in 1994. He had been my constant companion throughout all of the subsequent trauma and turmoil. He had lived everywhere with me: the house with Rob, Cromwell Street, the safe houses with Mum, the houses and flats I'd shared with Tara, Chris, Richard, and during those times when I'd been on my own with Amy.

I was absolutely distraught at his death. It may sound ridiculous and fanciful but I had always had the strange feeling that Baggy was sent to look after me by Heather. It had been only eighteen months after she disappeared that Rob and I bought him and his spirit always seemed to be somehow connected with hers. He became so precious to me. He was more than just a companion who made sure I never felt completely lonely – I felt that so long as he was around I would be protected.

Once, he was in a really bad accident and when Dad saw him he said: 'God he's fucked, better have him put down.' I was furious at his callous attitude and told Dad so. I took Baggy to the vet myself and begged him to do whatever he could to save him. He had been hit by a car and his face was smashed up, his jaw hanging down, and he had lost his front claws. I told the vet I'd pay whatever it cost to save him and, somehow, they managed to do it.

Strangely, although I had grown up in a house that turned out to be full of death, I had never seen anyone die or even a dead body before. Baggy was the first time. The pain of his going was excruciating. After he died, I had him cremated and took his ashes to the churchyard where Heather is buried and scattered them on her grave. Whenever I go there now I know I am remembering both of them.

Pete was a rock for me at this time, as was my friend Paula. And with the door slowly closing on my relationship with Mum it felt like I was once again at the beginning of a new chapter in my life. I was fearful, not knowing what it would bring, though even with Baggy gone I found myself again drawing strength from a feeling that there was some other benign presence watching over me, looking after me, which would see that one day I came through.

As Amy started secondary school the elephant in the room grew bigger and bigger: what should I tell her about my past, and about Mum and Dad?

Dad was much the easier of the two. From early childhood I simply told Amy he was dead. She never asked awkward questions about how he'd died, or when, she just seemed to accept it and we never discussed him. With Mum it was much harder. I told her what I felt were white lies: that she was not well and in a type of hospital, where I could visit but children were not allowed. The phone calls I received from Mum were mostly general – we would talk about everyday things like what we'd seen on TV, so I knew if Amy was ever listening she'd be none the wiser. I also hid Mum's letters from Amy because they had the prison heading on the notepaper. Sometimes I would just rip the top off so there would be no address at all on them.

It was hard because I didn't want to lie to Amy, and I tried to keep the information I gave her as close to the truth as I could without revealing the full terrible reality about her grandmother, and for that matter of my own past. If she got to know all that, how would she, as a child, have dealt with it? And how could I help her process it when in many ways I was still doing that, trying to get my head around my mother's guilt. And even if she was able to take it in, she would have been forced to hide it from other people, to lie just as I had done for a great part of my life, and I didn't want that. Not telling her the truth seemed like the lesser of two evils.

Once, when she was nine or ten, and we were living on our

own, a reporter from the *Sun* newspaper came to the door. It was to get my reaction to one of the many stories about Mum which got into the papers from time to time. I've no idea how he even tracked me down. He stood at the door and began talking about Mum and Dad in a loud voice. I was furious. I ushered Amy into her bedroom and then went back to the reporter and gave him a piece of my mind, saying I had nothing whatsoever to say to him.

But it was getting harder and harder to keep it a secret from her. She started to ask me questions which I found difficult to answer. And then there was my brother Steve who, before our terrible fallout, came to see me occasionally. He's never felt inhibited about talking about our past and would do it quite freely. If Amy was in the house, I would have to put her in another room and ask him to keep his voice down. Once she saw his Visa card on the table and noticed his surname was West. I had to admit it had been my name too at one time, but explained that I'd changed it so she and I could both have the same surname as her dad.

I realised she couldn't be left in ignorance about it forever but didn't know what to tell her or when to do it. I was afraid another child at school might somehow discover the truth and tell her. I knew that could be devastating to her and potentially very damaging to our relationship. I felt paralysed and yet was reaching the point where I absolutely knew I would have to take the bull by the horns and explain everything to her. In the end I found I didn't have to.

Amy is a very private person who tends to keep her feelings to herself. I had learned, over the years, that if she had things on her mind, her behaviour would change and she would become even more uncommunicative. Instead of telling me what was bothering her I would have to prise it from her. During one of these spells when she was going through the usual repertoire of difficult but typical teenage behaviour – changing her appearance, getting moody, slamming doors – I knew something was going on and decided I had to find out.

I picked her up from school one day, drove her home and, while we were still outside in the car, asked what was bothering her.

'Nothing's bothering me, Mum,' she said.

'There is. I can tell there is. What is it?'

'Honestly, there's nothing. I'm all right.'

'That's not true. Tell me, Amy. What is it?'

There was a long silence, before she said, simply, 'I know.'

'Know what?' I had no idea what was coming.

'I know who my grandad and grandma are.'

I was in total shock. I couldn't speak at first. Eventually I just whispered: 'How do you know?'

She explained how she had worked it out. She'd become more and more puzzled about why I was evasive when I spoke about Mum and Dad, and also my childhood. She knew my family name was West and, though I'd barely ever mentioned Mum and Dad's first names, she'd picked them up. One day she had decided to type the names into a search engine on the internet and was immediately faced with countless links to the story of the crimes of Fred and Rosemary West from Gloucester (and she knew that was where I was originally from). Suddenly, my unwillingness to talk about it through the years all made sense to her.

Though Amy told me this quite calmly I could see it had been a massive shock to her. I felt full of guilt. I explained that I really hadn't wanted her to find out in that way, that I knew I should have broken it to her before so that she learned the truth in a less shocking way.

'It's not your fault, Mum,' she said.

'What do you mean?'

'What they did. It's nothing to do with you. You didn't choose your mum and dad. And I've read a bit about it now. Not just the murders, but the way they treated you. It must have been so horrible for you, and your sisters and brothers.'

I felt tears coming. I tried to fight them back but I couldn't and I saw she was crying too. I took her hand and she told me again it was all right. It was such a weight lifted from both our shoulders to have it all out in the open at last. I asked her how she felt about her own biological connection to my parents and she told me that since she'd never felt any emotional bond with them, it didn't trouble her. I told her that if she ever had any questions about it in the future I would answer them as honestly as I could, and that she shouldn't bottle up her feelings about it. I made it clear to her, as I always have, that I would be there for her whenever she needed me.

It was such a huge relief for me not to have to lie and hide things from her any longer. From then onwards, we found that we were able to discuss the subject quite openly and, while I knew that was bound to have an effect on her life and on her relationship with me, it didn't seem to have damaged her emotionally. I felt as if the curse of the West legacy was beginning to lift.

I felt liberated by this knowledge and it gave me cautious hope for the future which, since abandoning direct contact with Mum, I had dared to think about more and more. It was in that optimistic frame of mind that, having talked it over carefully, Pete and I decided to move in together. Amy and I once more felt like we were part of a family.

Chapter Nineteen

Ghosts

Mum copied out a prayer and sent it to me today. It's a lovely prayer, reading it made my eyes well up. But then she does this quite a lot: copies things out and sends them to me as if she's written them herself. It's telling of who she is, I suppose: she knows the things she should be saying, but they're not true to her.

<u>HM PRISON BRONZEFIELD</u>

YOU ARE VERY SPECIAL

In all the world there is nobody like you. Since the beginning of time there has never been another person like you. Nobody has your smile, your eyes, your hands, your hair. Nobody owns your handwriting, your voice, you're special. Nobody can paint your brush strokes. Nobody has your taste for food, or music or dance or art. Nobody in the universe sees things as you do.

    You're special,
    As always,
    Mum

Just because you lose direct contact with someone it doesn't mean they are no longer part of your life. That was bound to be true of a mother like mine. I still, of course, had incredibly strong and confused feelings about her and couldn't help wondering from time to time how she was getting on. I also had physical reminders of her: boxes of letters and photos. Mostly I left these untouched, not wanting to stir up emotions which I was trying to put behind me. Sometimes, though, I would come upon them and find myself going through them. There were old snapshots of the family, taken around the house, or on holidays in Wales, or outings to Barry Island and the Forest of Dean. When I looked at them and the past they brought back memories which seemed somehow unreal, as if my younger self and my family were now ghosts.

Among the letters I'd kept was one Mum had sent me with the words 'YOU ARE VERY SPECIAL' at the top. It seemed like a kind of love letter. At the time I received it, I was moved, thinking she had composed it herself. Soon afterwards, I found out it was actually a copy of a widely used prayer, written by someone else. How Mum came across it, I don't know. Yet even if she hadn't written it herself, I wanted to believe she felt the emotions expressed towards me in those words, which she had carefully written down.

But then again, did she? Over the years I have become less and less sure about what Mum truly felt about anything. What she claimed she felt and what she really did were obviously sometimes very different things. How could she really have felt the grief she claimed to feel for Heather if she had colluded with or helped in her murder? How could she have truly loved any of her children if she had been responsible for the horrific death of one of us? Or sexually abused us? Or helped Dad do so? As time has passed, those doubts have grown.

And though from time to time she'd tell me that I could ask

her anything and she would try to answer honestly, I came more and more to question whether she ever had. It seemed that, like Dad, she only ever told partial truths and often complete lies. So often, when I asked her anything difficult her response would be to blame Dad, suggesting that she had only ever done bad things because he'd forced her to and, if she hadn't helped him, he'd have done even worse things to us children. But when it came to answering questions about what part she had actually played herself in the sexual abuse she was always defensive and evasive. It was the same whenever I probed her about all the murdered women found at Cromwell Street and elsewhere.

Those unanswered questions continued to cast a big shadow over my life. My physical relationship with Mum had ended but an emotional one still existed between us. But gradually that shadow began to diminish, and I started to feel a degree of freedom and relaxation I'd never really felt before. A lot of this was to do with my relationship with Pete. He made me feel looked after and secure. Often he'd show it in small ways, such as making me laugh at myself by taking the mickey out of my Gloucester accent, which I'd always felt so self-conscious about. Or he'd tell me how much he loved the old-fashioned medical remedies I'd suggest he use which Mum taught me, such as putting butter on bumps and bruises. Things like that made me feel that I wasn't such an abnormal person after all.

I'm sure it was no coincidence that, not long after my contact with Mum came to an end, I found out I was pregnant again. I was astonished. I can't get pregnant easily and as a result have never really taken precautions. Pete and I had been seeing one another for several years and I was pretty well convinced we would never have children. When we found out, we were both, in our different ways, elated.

I felt sure that it would never have happened if I'd still been seeing Mum. It was as if the closing of that door had opened another. And it felt like yet another development in my life that made me feel there was some kind of unseen presence that was looking after me.

Not that I wasn't anxious about the thought of becoming a mother again. All those doubts I'd had when I'd been pregnant with Amy came back. And the anxiety grew even more intense when I went for my sixteen-week scan and was told the baby was a boy. I tried to hide my feelings from Pete because he was overjoyed to find out he was going to have a son, but away from his sight I wept. I didn't want a boy because most of the men in my life had let me down and I had no confidence I could successfully bring up a male child.

And there was an alarming omen. They gave me my due date: 29 September. It was Dad's birthday – a day I had come to hate. Was this going to be another terrible twist of the knife? The curse of being a West coming back to haunt and damage my life again?

The worry that my son would be born on Dad's birthday remained with me throughout the pregnancy. I couldn't bring myself to tell Pete at first. It would have shown a continuing obsession with my terrible past that he had done so much to help me get over. But as the date approached I grew more and more certain that the baby would be born on the due date, so I did tell him. Being a practical kind of person and not at all superstitious, he told me not to worry, that it might not happen and even if it did it wouldn't matter, but I was convinced it was a bad omen.

I waited and waited, fearing the worst.

Just before the due date, the baby seemed to stop moving. Even though the same thing had happened with Amy, I was afraid he'd died, even fearing that it was my anxiety that had caused it to happen. They took me into hospital, examined me and told me the baby was fine.

'Are you quite sure?' I asked.

'Absolutely,' the doctor said. 'He's got a good strong heartbeat and babies often do stop moving as much as birth approaches.'

I told her I was still sure something was wrong and blurted out that I was desperate for the baby not to be born on my due date because something terrible had happened on that day. She asked me what, but I told her I couldn't say. She probably thought I was mad. She told me again not to worry and I was sent back home to continue waiting. But I would do everything I could to avoid a date that could bring bad luck into my baby's life.

The due date arrived and dragged by so slowly. I was on tenterhooks all day long, expecting my waters to break and the contractions to start. Thankfully, as I paced up and down, midnight came and there was still no baby.

In the end he was two weeks late and I had to be induced. Because it was an induced birth, I was in labour for a long time. I wanted him to be born on 4 October. I've always been superstitious about dates and numbers. I was born on the first of the month, Amy the second, Pete the third, so if the new baby had been born on the fourth it would have been 1, 2, 3, 4, which would have felt lucky. As things turned out he arrived on the fifth. Pete was with me, so although it was a difficult labour it was a much better experience for me than with Amy.

We called the baby Luke. Although I had been so concerned about having a boy, I loved him to pieces from the very beginning, just as I had done Amy – and unlike when she was born I had a proper home to take him back to. It was wonderful to feel

I was bringing him into the heart of a loving family. What also helped enormously in those early weeks and months, and still does to this day, is that my friend Paula had a child at almost exactly the same time and so we have watched our babies develop and go through the same stages together. We have shared the fears, anxieties and joys of motherhood and that, as well as having Pete to share the parenting, has made it so much easier for me.

I can't claim that being a parent to a second child has been without many challenges. Unlike Amy, who was such a quiet, obedient child, Luke is much more full of himself. But I am learning to be more relaxed about his school life now; we have playdates and I chat to other mothers in the playground. Learning not to be too hard on myself, to see problems and then blame all of them on my personal failings because of my past, has always been a challenge, but I am making progress with it. Luke is a wonder and a miracle to me, just as Amy is.

When Luke was barely more than a year old, something equally wonderful and miraculous happened.

I called, by chance, into a branch of Sainsbury's where I now live. It wasn't a supermarket I normally used but Christmas was approaching and I needed to buy Amy one last present. I parked outside, put Luke in his pram and went inside. As I hunted for the present I caught a glimpse of Louise moving along the aisles ahead of me. I froze, hardly able to believe my eyes. It was as if I'd seen a ghost. It was years since I'd seen my sister and, to the best of my knowledge, she'd left the area.

She was with another woman and had a teenage girl and two young boys with her. As I moved after her, she happened to look in my direction. I looked down quickly, embarrassed, hoping to avoid direct eye contact, but I knew she'd seen and recognised me too. From her reaction I felt sure she didn't want to acknowledge or speak to me.

She moved away, into a different aisle, out of sight. My heart was racing, I started to tremble. I didn't know what to do. After a few moments, I realised that, no matter how hard it might be, I would have to try to speak to her. I also knew that if I told Tara I'd seen Louise and not even made an effort to talk to her, she would be furious with me. It was an opportunity that might never come again. I searched the aisles and finally spotted her again, approaching from behind, not knowing what on earth I was going to say.

'Louise, this is stupid!' were the words that tumbled out.

She turned, looked at me and at Luke in the pram and answered.

'I've got nothing to say to you.'

She started to walk away. I could hear the children who were with her saying: 'Who is it? What does she want?'

I knew there was no going back now. I had to get her to speak to me. I followed her.

'Come on, Louise, this is silly. I miss you, you're my sister!'

I put my hand on her trolley to stop her moving on. She looked at me. I could see she was crying. 'I don't want to do this,' she said.

I took the tears as a sign she must really care. The teenage girl who was with her saw that I had left Luke's pram a little way behind. 'Shall I get the baby?' she asked, and without waiting for an answer did so. By now both Louise and I were in tears. Other shoppers were staring. God knows what they thought. We didn't care.

Louise looked at Luke and asked if he was mine. I told her he was. I looked at the children who were with her and she said they were hers.

It turned out that Louise had never left the town and had even carried on living for several years in the same flat where we'd had that last terrible row, the one I'd assumed she'd moved out of. It was so strange and surreal to be with one another again, but I didn't want to push things any further so I gave Louise my mobile number so she could call me if she felt she wanted to see me again.

I went back out to the car and called Tara, explaining what had happened. Tara asked if Louise wanted to speak to her. I told her I wasn't even sure she wanted to have any more contact with me, and that we'd just have to wait and see whether she wanted to stay in touch. As it turned out, Louise called that same evening. We spoke for a while, she gave me her new address and I called round soon afterwards with some Christmas gifts.

I've remained in touch with her ever since, and so has Tara. It's taken a while to rebuild our relationship after the painful way it had seemed to end, but we have both come to agree that, looking back, the break was right for us. During the time we'd been apart we'd both moved in different ways, facing different challenges, forming new relationships and having children. A big issue for Louise had been that she hadn't wanted to have a relationship with Mum after coming out of care, but had felt obliged to because I was still so involved with her and had encouraged her to do so. When she found out that I was no longer in contact with Mum she felt happy to have me back in her life.

She told me that she had also felt the same way about my contact with Steve, because he still had the surname West and had never bothered about hiding from people who he was – often talking to the press – so she felt she needed to protect her kids from him. I explained to her that after the huge fallout I'd had with Steve, I now had only minimal contact with him, so that gave her even further reassurance that she could remain in touch with me.

Since re-establishing our relationship, Louise and I have supported one another. She listens to me and gives me good advice and I try to do the same for her. Although we live different lives, she faces similar problems and challenges. Some of these are of the kind that any woman and mother might face. Others are unique to us, and a result of our complicated past. Both of us were physically and sexually abused and as sisters we share a particular determination to bring up our children in a safe environment, free from the abuse, fear and terror which we experienced.

And through contact with Louise I also re-established contact with our three youngest siblings. With Dad long dead and with Mum no longer in our lives, it began to feel as if we had rescued those parts of our family that were salvageable. Set against the many setbacks we had faced, it was no small achievement.

Chapter Twenty

Moving On

The house at Cromwell Street is no more. A few years after the bodies discovered there were laid to rest, the council demolished it. There was talk for a while of having a memorial there; personally I'm glad there isn't one. I don't want to remember Heather where she was unhappy – I remember her when I'm strolling through the Forest of Dean or listening to A-ha on the radio; when I'm in places and doing little things I know she loved. Now, instead of our childhood home that brought misery to so many people, there is a walkway. It seems fitting somehow: you can travel through it, you can move on.

I know the story of the Cromwell Street murders will never go away. That it's one of the most shocking in the history of crime, and that Fred and Rosemary West will for ever be regarded as among the most notorious serial killers. Psychologists, criminologists and others will forever analyse the crimes and explore the motives of my parents, tabloid newspapers will keep returning to their story and there will always be TV documentaries about the subject. I sometimes watch these, curious to see how accurate they will be, and wondering if they might provide any new insight.

The faces of the victims still haunt me. Not only Heather, but all of them: Charmaine, Rena, Lynda Gough, Carol Ann Cooper,

Lucy Partington, Therese Siegenthaler, Shirley Hubbard, Juanita Mott, Shirley Robinson, Alison Chambers, as well as Mary
Bastholm who many people believe was also a victim. I find it
impossible to see them without thinking about what they went
through, the futures they were robbed of and the grief their
loved ones had to suffer as a result.

Knowing your parents are regarded by most people as evil
beyond belief is incredibly hard to live with, especially when
your own experience of them has been more complicated and
you've seen a side to them which makes them more than simply
monsters. As I've tried to show, both of them had a side which
seemed, at times at least, like other people. Mum could be
tender and gentle with very young children; she had a sense of
humour. Dad could be friendly and make us laugh.

But I realise that many people will never be able to regard
them as human in any way they understand. I also know that, no
matter the facts, there are some who will continue to stigmatise
myself and my siblings. Regard us as no more than weird curi-
osities, children of freaks who came to regard the behaviour of
our parents as normal and never learned the difference between
right and wrong. Over the years I have had people suggest that
we would laugh at the crimes of our parents, relish the details
of their perverted sex lives, play with the bones of their victims
and even use their kneecaps as ashtrays. Though I can see why
what happened in the Cromwell Street house has attracted such
ghoulish interest, I've found it very hard to deal with the as-
sumption some people have had that my sisters, brothers and
I grew up to think our parents' cruel and bizarre behaviour was
normal. That couldn't be further from the truth. None of the
physical violence or sexual abuse we suffered ever seemed anything other than terrifying and repulsive and wrong. Far from
revelling in the details of our parents' sex lives, we found their

behaviour absolutely revolting. When Dad used to sit down and watch videos of Mum having sex with her clients, we'd leave the room if we could or do our best to ignore what was happening in front of us.

I'd sometimes thought about getting counselling of some kind. I always held back from it, feeling somehow that I wasn't deserving of that kind of attention, and I had no idea how to go about finding it. I also couldn't face the idea of contacting someone out of the blue, having to explain who I was and why I needed help. Despite feeling I'd moved my life on in many ways, I still clung in every way I could to anonymity. Also, I kept thinking, what counsellor would want to take on such a case? Most people have emotional baggage – divorces, bereavements and the like, but mine, by any standards, was surely extraordinary. It would be hard to even know where to begin.

But eventually, because I wanted to try to move forward with my life and also for the sake of my future relationships with my partner Pete and my children, I decided to take the plunge and contact Victim Support. I had to summon all my courage. I felt so nervous making that first call, and just as vulnerable as I'd imagined I might be when I revealed my identity and explained the nature of the issues that had caused me to seek help. Luckily, I was able to find someone who wasn't afraid to take me on and prepared to help me try to find ways of dealing with my past.

It's not been easy. Talking about intimate and extremely painful memories has been a huge challenge. My instinct has always been to consider other people's feelings before my own – those of my partners, my children, my brothers and sisters and my mother. I've tended to hide my own or at least try to. If others close to me had a problem at any time I would immediately take it on myself to try to solve it. I felt I wasn't just a big sister to my younger siblings but in some ways, because they'd never had a proper mum, a mother to them too. Trying to accept that it shouldn't always be down to me to sort things out for other people goes against all my instincts.

It took me a long time to understand that the origin of the problem lies in my relationship with Mum. She manipulated me from early childhood, making me emotionally dependent on her, despite the cruelty and violence, and when I was older making me feel that, because Dad was such a terrible husband, she needed constant emotional support from me. I could never switch off my feelings of obligation towards her.

Our relationship has never been more intense than it was when I was with her in the safe houses after Dad's arrest for the murders. For days and weeks, we were shut away together and I had to listen to her day and night, justifying herself and complaining about Dad. The police secretly recorded her:

'Of course I'm angry with him, Mae, what do you think? I mean, look, if I got near the bastard now I'd put me fucking hands round his throat and somebody would have to fucking pry them off. Mae, he's taken your sister's and my daughter's fucking life. This is something you don't fucking forgive. I'd never forgive that. You don't forgive that. You never forget it.'

It was absolutely relentless. I didn't want to be shut away with her but I had no way of escaping it. As Tara suggested later, it was a kind of brainwashing and, in many ways, it was success-ful. It was like being held hostage. I felt fear, and anxiety, but also as if the outside world didn't exist. And although it was the police who had put us there, it was as if Mum had imprisoned us there together, not them.

Later I read about Stockholm syndrome, where a person can become emotionally dependent on the person who is holding them hostage. I can see now that I was always an emotional hostage to Mum.

Talking to Victim Support has helped me to see that and also to recognise some of the consequences. I didn't have a normal childhood. It was so abnormal as to hardly be a childhood at all. I've had to try to accept that no matter how much I relive what happened in my mind and wish it had been different, nothing can change that now. And that it's okay to mourn for the childhood I never had or the person you're never going to be.

I'm also learning to understand better how it's affected my relationships with other people. I have a fear of rejection. I've spoken about this with my siblings who also feel it strongly. You might be watching a movie with a partner and reach out to touch them on the hand and because they pull their hand away you take it as a full-on personal slight, rather than recognising they may not be in the mood for personal contact at that moment because it's a really engrossing movie, or whatever other minor reason. You start to overanalyse. Doesn't he love me or even care about me any more? So you pull back, withdraw into yourself and your partner asks why and when you explain they think you're making a mountain out of a molehill, and find it hard to reassure you.

I've realised I spend too much time thinking and overthinking things. Measuring people's reactions to me, even in tiny encounters like saying hello to someone in the street, or paying for something in a shop. I'll wonder why a person has seemed to look at me in a certain way when probably they were barely even thinking about me at all. At the back of my mind, my worry is often that they're wondering: is that Mae West?

I'm trying to learn to conquer my anxiety about people finding out who I am. I don't think it'll ever go away completely, but I am starting to see that if they do find out it isn't the end of the world. I've made mistakes in my life as all people do, but there's no reason why I should feel ashamed of being me. In the past I've tried to avoid starting conversations, even trivial ones, with strangers or people I don't know well, for fear it might lead to awkward questions. I've realised that's a mistake; it only makes me feel different and isolated.

Another challenge is trying to come to terms with the fact that my siblings had very different experiences of my mother, and saw her for the person she really was long before I did. I feel angry with myself for being so naïve and gullible. I know I was manipulated but that doesn't make it any easier to come to terms with. I know it will take me a long time to deal with the anger I feel towards myself over that.

Recognising that other people, outside my family circle, have problems – something I didn't used to consider all that much – has been helpful too. Everyone has baggage: relationships gone wrong, serious illness, bereavement. If I'm in a public place now, the street or supermarket, and I look at other people, I'm more inclined to think it is their own lives, their own problems they're having to deal with. They aren't likely to be looking at me, wondering what mine are.

So, what of the future?

It feels like I've been on a very long journey, but I am still only in my forties and, with luck, there is a lot of life yet to come. Like everybody else, I don't know what the future holds. What I do know is that I am in a much better place than I have ever been in my life and have something good to build on.

There will always be damage. Things are far from perfect between myself and my siblings. I'm not in contact with Anne Marie and don't expect to be ever again; there have been too many wounds in our relationship and I don't think we'll ever see the past in the same way.

I still see Tara and Louise regularly. The three of us are in intermittent contact with our other brother and two sisters, even though they're scattered far and wide across the country, have new identities and are leading their own lives. I haven't seen Steve for some time and our relationship is limited to occasional text messages, but I believe that he's in a new relationship and seems okay and is aware of my new happier circumstances.

I would never, ever wish the painful things that have happened to me on anyone else, but I have learned from some of them. I look at my mum and dad's lives and can see that certain behavioural traits have been passed down through the generations. I don't know whether this is to do with nature or nurture, or a combination of both. I know the abused can become abusers, and in my parents' case that was true. However, I strongly believe this doesn't have to be the case. The cycle can be broken. My own children have grown up free of the terrible consequences of physical or sexual abuse. They have also grown up in a secure environment of love. I feel confident that this will also be the case when my own children become parents.

I count myself as lucky. Things could have worked out very differently. But I have ended up within a stable home with a husband who understands me better than any man I have known in my life, and two beautiful children who I would lay down my life for.

When I was growing up my parents drummed into us that family was everything. You stick together no matter what. They were right in one way. Families should do that. But not if the reason is to help bury dark and horrific secrets. My mum and dad used family bonds as a way of controlling their children, which was a terrible abuse of power. I believe they should be used to help support and enable all of us as we go through life.

I barely think of my dad now. A few months ago, I had the TV on in the background when I was sorting my hair, and recordings of his confession tapes came on. I was standing there, brushing my hair, and his voice came out of the speakers, clear as day. And the strangest thing was, I didn't recognise it. I knew it was him, but it just didn't sound like him to me any more. I wasn't transported back twenty years, as you might think I would be, at all. It was something from another world, a past life.

As for my mother, I do still think about her from time to time. I can't imagine how things will pan out for her as she lives her remaining years in custody. Although her final letter to me showed some self-awareness, I doubt that will turn into honesty and remorse. Along with lots of other people, I still ponder the question of her guilt. I'm convinced that she has not told the full truth and that is the very least the victims and their families deserve.

I would hate people to feel that such happiness as I've found means I don't care about the crimes my parents committed. Or their victims. I will never stop caring. Heather is never far from my thoughts. I know I carry what people call survivor's guilt – a feeling that I did something wrong by surviving when she didn't. But I continue to be aware of that unseen force which has looked after me and continues to help me through. Sometimes I find myself asking why. Why was I helped to survive? Why have I put so much effort into doing so? I know it must all be for a reason, but I can't always see what that is.

But then I think of my children. Of Amy, a young woman now, making her way in the world, with hopes and dreams of her own. Sometimes when we're out having lunch or looking round the shops, I stop and look at how beautiful she is. I'm so glad our relationship is so different – worlds apart – to what mine and Mum's was. Amy has come through so much with me and I want to continue to help her onward into whatever the future brings for her.

307

And Luke makes me laugh and smile every day, and I want to see what the future brings for him too. Once, when he was a toddler, we were in his bedroom and he told me he wanted to go downstairs to play but he was worried there might be monsters. He asked me to go down with him.

'Why do you want me with you?' I said.

'Monsters would never hurt me when you're with me, Mummy,' he said.

I know he feels safe and loved every day.

That alone feels reason enough.

References

1 Howard Sounes, *Fred and Rose* (London, 1995), page 286.
2 Stephen West and Mae West, *Inside 25 Cromwell Street* (London 1995), page 205.
3 This and quote on page 188 from Geoffrey Wansell, *An Evil Love* (London, 1996), page 71.
4 Letters from page 205 and here from Gordon Burn, *Happy Like Murderers* (London, 2011), page 199.
5 Anne Marie West with Virginia Hill, *Out of the Shadows* (London, 1995), page 70.

Acknowledgements

I would like to thank my sisters, especially Louise, who never sees how much she is truly loved and how blessed I feel to have her in my life.

To my worldly-wise daughter who is far more knowledgeable than her years. Many times I have caught myself smiling when we are together, I am that proud. And to my son – you are equally sensitive, kind and loving as you are energetic. I thank God for both of you.

My close friends who took the time to get to know me without prejudice or judgement.

To my husband – thanks for the laughs, you never let me take myself too seriously.

My deepest thanks to Victim Support. Over the years you have helped me practically and emotionally, having volunteered your time and support whenever I have needed it.

Many thanks to Amanda Harris and Neil McKay for all your hard work and dedication to the book. It was a long time in the making but we finally did it.

And to Heather. Unknowingly your tragic death brought about the end of many families' pain. I know what it feels like to not know where a loved one is and, although the outcome was not what they hoped or prayed for, they finally had the answers and could try to move on with their lives. You are forever loved.

ACKNOWLEDGEMENTS

If you have been affected by a crime and need support, you can contact Victim Support via the 'Contact us' page on their website: www.victimsuport.org.uk